THE EDUCATION
OF A GOLFER

BY SAM SNEAD
WITH AL STUMP

DRAWINGS BY BURT SILVERMAN

SIMON AND SCHUSTER

NEW YORK • • • 1962

PUBLISHED IN CANADA BY
THE MUSSON BOOK CO., LTD., TORONTO, ONTARIO

FIRST PRINTING

LIBRARY OF CONGRESS CATALOG CARD NUMBER: 62-9601
MANUFACTURED IN THE UNITED STATES OF AMERICA
PRINTED BY MURRAY PRINTING COMPANY, FORGE VILLAGE, MASS.

CONTENTS

1

PECKERWOOD KID: OFF THE TEE

DISCOVERED DOING NOTHING • THE DRIVE ALVA BRAD-
LEY DIDN'T BELIEVE • BACKWOODS BOYHOOD DAYS •
SMOTHERED DRIVES AND DUCK-HOOKS

A man who was a total stranger came up one night when I was cleaning mud off a ball back of the caddie house down home. He was swinging a shiny, black-headed driver with a chrome shaft of tempered steel that made my mouth water.

At the time there was about seventy cents and a whittling knife in my pocket. In winter and spring of 1936 I was so poor that money thought I was dead.

"Saw you play in the tournament today," the man said. "You don't drive a ball a country mile. You hit it two miles."

"Yes, sir," I said. Everybody was always telling me about the smokers I hit off the tee, but nobody did a damned thing about it.

For example, the job I was working at when this stranger walked up to me was to run errands, sweep up, clean clubs, replace divots, and help the caddie master at The Cascades Inn at Hot Springs, Virginia—for which the management paid off with a nice friendly handshake and a ham sandwich. I didn't draw a dime in cash. All I got from the first golf job I ever held was a free lunch and a spare-time chance to hustle a few guests into taking lessons. If they handed me two dollars for a lesson, The Cascades didn't mind if I kept it.

That particular night my mind wasn't on anything but the

trout that were jumping in the stream below the clubhouse, where sometimes I caught my dinner. But this man had a sort of smile in his eyes, along with clothes that said he was an important person, so I thought I'd better give him an honest answer.

"Well, I can hit hard," I said, "when I'm able to get the ball higher than my shoe tops. My trouble is hitting too many grass cutters. And, when the ball does come up, sometimes I'm wild as a hawk."

"Never mind that, boy," he said. "You've got a golf swing that's amazing. Where'd you learn it?"

"Nowhere much. In a hayfield over home," I said. "That's in Ashwood, up the road a ways."

The stranger said nothing, just studied me, and I began to fidget, remembering that it was dinnertime and I had a long hike home ahead of me. Each night I walked three miles from The Cascades to home, smelling my ma's cooking all the way.

"Well, now, don't be in a hurry, boy," the man said. "Which of these Virginia pros has been working with you?"

"Not any pro. I never had money for lessons or greens fees; just watched my brother, Homer, and practiced in the back pasture. Homer hits about the longest ball you ever did see. The rest of it mostly came natural for me."

The man couldn't seem to believe it. He said, "The longest balls I ever did see, and I've seen a few, were peppered by you today. When you drove over that 330-yard ninth hole and had to chip back, you did something I never saw Jones or Hagen do. How old are you, boy?"

"I'm twenty-three," I told him.

"They told me at the clubhouse that you've never been out of these hills, nor ever seen the big-timers play golf. Is that so?"

The hills he meant are the Back Creek Mountains of Virginia, which are part of the Appalachians, with the Blue Ridge to the east and the Alleghenies to the west, and where the valleys are so narrow that the dogs have to wag their tails up and down. I was a hill kid. They called us "peckerwoods," and I could run a coon or a fat bear up and down ridges until he was ready to drop and then shoot him for the table. At home we used a Chic Sale and went barefoot and rode horseback three miles into the nearest settlement to pick up the mail. Where I lived, near Bald Knob, the roads got littler and littler until they just ran up a tree. Big cities were something I'd just heard rumors about.

"It's true," I said. "I've been to Bluefield and Roanoke and over to Appomattox to see the courthouse, and that's about it."

The man looked at my golf bag, sitting nearby.

"Do you mind?" he said very politely.

What he saw was enough to curl your toes. My No. 1 driving wood had a cast-off head that had split and which I'd glued together and a sprung wood shaft which I'd tried to cover up with a nice glaze by treating it with pitch, then rubbing on shellac and linseed oil. It was part of a halfbreed set of nine sticks I'd bought for nine dollars from a fellow named Walt Williams in Hot Springs. Williams had held out for ten dollars for these culls, some wood-shafted and some steel and with nothing matching. But nine dollars was all I had, and he finally broke down. There was a sand wedge in there I wasn't ashamed of, though. I'd mail-ordered it from a Sears Roebuck catalog for three fifty.

"And you shot a 70 today on a tight, tough course and finished second by a shot in the tournament," said the stranger. He was more or less talking to himself as he fingered my clubs, remarking that the day's winner of The Cascades Open had been Billy Burke, the 1931 United States Open champion, and that Burke had been scrambling to beat me.

"My name," the man said, "is Mr. Fred Martin, from The Greenbrier Hotel at White Sulphur Springs, and how'd you like to go to work as a full-fledged professional for me?"

That threw me for a complete loss of words. "Are you joshing?" I asked. The Greenbrier, across the state line in West Virginia, was old and world-famous, one of the toniest places going. Presidents like Fillmore, Tyler, Van Buren, and Pierce and General Robert E. Lee had lived there, and the three Greenbrier courses drew people like the Astors, Biddles, Kennedys, and Vanderbilts. None of us peckerwoods ever expected to get even inside the gate, let alone out there with a club in our hands.

Mr. Martin, who had a powerful eye, looked at me hard and said, "Let's not waste time. I'm the manager of golf at The Greenbrier. One of my pros, Al McCoy, is leaving the club soon and a job is open. We'll pay you forty-five dollars a month and room and board. Anything you make teaching our guests is yours, and I can promise you it won't be penny ante. Do you want it or not?"

"Mr. Martin," I said, "I don't know how fast you move, but when you get back to your pro shop, the first sight you're going to see will be me."

All the clothes I owned could be packed in a shoe box, so the next morning, when the birds were just chirping, I was standing on The Greenbrier first tee, ready to tackle anything that was available. The other pros on the staff were big names in teaching and came fancy-dressed. My total wardrobe consisted of two white shirts, a sweater, and a pair of gray wool pants. My clubs were a joke. What with people like Lady and Sir Harry Oakes and the Du Ponts on the course, the head pro, Steve Gagan, figured I needed a little smoothing out before taking on any pupils, so he suggested I play around for a few days and get used to the layouts.

Even before this first big break of my life had lasted a week, I almost blew it by getting fired.

One of The Greenbrier guests who was treated the most respectfully was Mr. Alva Bradley, president of the Cleveland Indians Baseball Club and a director of the Chesapeake &

Ohio Railroad Company. The C. & O. owned The Green-brier. On top of that, Bradley had an awful grouch about his golf game. Because of a good-sized paunch, which he had to hit around, he attacked the ball from the outside in, instead of the inside out. He also loosened his left-hand grip at the top of the backswing. As a result, he had one of the worst slices of all time. No pro had been able to cure him, which caused Bradley to rant and roar whenever he shot another round in 90 or 100 strokes.

"Just keep far away from Bradley until you've got your feet on the ground," the other pros advised.

That I took care to do, until one morning on the fifth tee of The Greenbrier's "Old White" course, when I noticed that Bradley and his party were holing out on the green up ahead. The hole was 335 yards long. So I hauled off and tagged one and that little dog caught some breeze and just kept going. On the green I could see somebody jumping up and down.

Halfway down the fairway I met Bradley. He had come back looking for me and was as mad as a man can get. "How dare you drive from the fairway into an occupied green?" he shouted. I couldn't get a word in edgewise while he bawled me out. "Do you know what you did?"

"No, sir," I said. "But if you give me a minute to explain—"

"You hit me! Your goddam ball bounced and struck me right here as I was bent over to pick my ball from the cup!" Bradley was rubbing his hind end.

"Well, I'm danged sorry," I said, "but I don't think you know how it happened."

Bradley wouldn't listen to an explanation; he just asked me my name. I should have said I was Ebenezer J. Twiddle from Bar Harbor, Maine, but I was so rattled that I admitted to being the new Greenbrier pro, Sam Snead.

"We'll see about that!" bawled Bradley, charging toward the clubhouse. "I won't have fairway snipers on this course."

At the club he informed Mr. Freddie Martin that I had

no manners and ought to be sent back to the hills, and when I reached the clubhouse my goose seemed to be cooked. Martin didn't want to fire me, but his hands were tied.

"Holy smoke, Mr. Martin," I said, "that wasn't my *second* shot from the fairway that hit Mr. Bradley. It was my *tee shot.*"

Luckily, I had a witness—my caddie.

Freddie Martin and his entire staff were called on the carpet by L. R. Johnston, The Greenbrier managing director, and when Martin told how it'd happened, nobody wanted to believe it.

Bradley wanted me cut up like catfish bait. "That's a ridiculous alibi," he said. "It's impossible for anyone to drive that green. In the fifteen years I've played here it's never happened."

Johnston was wringing his hands and Martin spoke up.

"No, sir, it's true. Over at The Cascades course at Hot Springs, on a hard fairway with a following wind, Sam has knocked his drive onto the No. 1 green—410 yards—twice. He's just an unbelievably long hitter, Mr. Bradley—and it's my opinion that he should go out onto the big-league professional tour."

Bradley just snorted. So I stuck in my nose, saying, "If you'll play around with me, I'll try to prove I'm not telling a lie about this."

He agreed grudgingly, and out we went next morning.

Being desperate, I let out extra shaft and swung fit to rupture myself in six places. My drives must have averaged 290. On No. 5, where I'd hit Bradley in the butt, the carry was a good 300, and with a few bounces I did it again, reaching the green. He was left speechless but still wasn't sure that it wasn't some kind of fluke. On No. 16 he pointed to a bunker 270 yards away.

"Can you drive into that trap?" he demanded to know.

"No, sir. If I go to bunting the ball, it'll wreck my game."

Bradley made a funny noise in his throat.

So I put the tee shot 75 yards over the trap and into the frog hair around the green.

"*Jumping Judas!*" yelled Bradley. "Wait'll I tell Babe Ruth about this; he'll be down here to take lessons from you." Apologizing, he told me I was a ring-tailed wonder and ought to go far and hired me as his personal instructor for the rest of the Greenbrier season.

Working with Bradley taught me a good bit, since I was still experimenting with my own swing and had to reason things out as I went along.

He was typical of golfers over fifty years old. Right away I saw what other pros had seen—that he had a restricted left side that kept him from pivoting freely. He more or less froze his left side in order to get the driver around his stomach. Bradley took a short backswing, taking the club away on a gradually increasing outside path. After a three-quarter back-swing and weak turn, his left hand loosened and his right elbow swung out from his body like it hated his ribs. That made the clubhead come back on an outside-in angle or path—the cut-across. So he had this banana-ball slice that sometimes sailed over two fairways.

Bradley knew what was wrong—it'd cost him maybe $10,000 to find out—but a way for him to return the club squarely to the ball on the right back-and-down path—to hit around his belly—still hadn't been found.

Older men can't make as full a golf pivot as young players, but they can turn to a far greater degree than they suspect. First, they should loosen and relax their left side. Then they should use plenty of shoulder-turn action. Their hips may not be so supple, but they can still get those shoulders around and set themselves for a good cocking of the wrists.

"Let's get those shoulders free to move," I told Bradley.

Being a baseball man, Bradley was all ears when I put it to him like this: "Those fellows who play for your Cleveland

Indians keep their shoulders practically on the same level when they swing a bat. It's a flat swing. Now a golf swing's anything but flat: you want the right shoulder going up and the left shoulder coming down around under your chin on the backswing. On the downswing, it's just the opposite. Like a teeterboard."

We worked at this until Bradley's left shoulder was dipping in under his chin, with his left arm coming up between his neck and shoulder—what a pro calls "the slot"—and his right shoulder rising. In doing that, his hips took more turn than before, striking up some rhythm with his shoulders. His hands were allowed to bring the club back from the ball in a more nearly straight line, or in a line just inside the path of flight. A good part of his slice was prevented right there.

On his other problem, loosening fingers of the left hand at the top of his backswing, I asked Bradley, "Would any of your ballplayers change their grip while in the middle of throwing to a base? If they did, they'd heave the ball into the bleachers. When you relax or open any left-hand fingers, you drop or loop the club and throw it into another arc."

He stood behind me while I showed him how this happened.

The cure was to make sure Bradley's grip at the top was the same as it was at the bottom when he addressed the ball. I turned his left hand until not one and one-half but two and one-half knuckles were showing—which was about as strong as the grip I used. Looking down, I could see most of three knuckles in those days, and I didn't do any changing over the years.

With his wider shoulder turn, Bradley also was able to cock his wrists more strongly. Aside from losing his slice, the big bonus was that he added 40 to 50 yards to his tee shots. One helpful thing here was to make him feel the cadence of a swing. I'd always hummed a tune while driving balls in my folks' back pasture. Bradley said he felt silly humming "The

Merry Widow Waltz," but he did it. On the one-count he took the club back; on two he paused at the top of the arc; on the beat of three he started the club down—*hips leading the shoulders and arms*, not the other way around; on four he finished his swing.

But he didn't complain the first time he broke 90. Or when he got into the low 80s and stayed there. Bradley went out of his mind with joy.

"Here, buy yourself some new clubs," Bradley said, handing me $100. But I needed clothes and transportation even more than clubs, as I saw it, so I bought myself a tin-lizzie jalopy, a dark suit, and a sport jacket. On the hunch that Freddie Martin hadn't been crazy when he suggested I try my luck on the P.G.A. circuit, I wanted to test myself in some local tournaments. The nearest golf meet I knew about was scheduled 156 miles away at Huntington, West Virginia.

As it turned out, I missed the tournament, but when I got there somebody mentioned that the course record for the Guyon Country Club was 69, held by Denny Shute. In 1936 any round played in the 60s was something to crow about.

"Well, I'd just like to take a crack at that," I said.

A local crowd followed me around, just to laugh at the peckerwood kid who thought he could beat a man as great as Shute—who was P.G.A. national champion—and it made me a little raunchy. A thing that's helped me in golf was to learn that every knock is a boost.

So in the morning I shot a 67. In the P.M. I eased around in 66. The crowd stopped chuckling and one man even shoved an autograph book at me, the first I'd ever seen. I thought he wanted me to read it until he explained the idea of the thing.

My boss, Freddie Martin, had driven with me to Huntington, to see what I could do, and coming home I gave him a hell-bender of a ride around mountain curves. I just floored the gas pedal of my jalopy and let 'er rip. We did 80 mph on the straightaway and almost as much on the curves. I was singing and talking a blue streak, out of sheer happiness, and Freddie was hanging on with a death grip while he bounced about.

"Stop the car!" he yelled. "Let me out of here! I don't drive with nuts! What's the hurry, anyway?"

"If I get home before dark," I said, "I can still get in some practice time on the tee."

Martin groaned. I guess he realized then that his new boy would cause him some problems, being in such a rush to get ahead.

Back at The Greenbrier, after considering what had happened, he said, "I'm going to take another gamble on you. You're still a green pea at this game, but we're holding an exhibition match next week for the guests, featuring Lawson Little, Johnny Goodman, and Billy Burke. I'm pairing you with Goodman in a four-ball match against Little and Burke."

When that news got around, there was general feeling that I'd soon be the youngest has-been that ever was. Little and Goodman were past National Amateur champs; Burke was ex- U. S. Open champ. And until a few months earlier I'd been eating brush rabbit and squirrel soup in the backwoods.

Of the 650 guests at The Greenbrier, about 90 per cent showed up for the match, with every man and woman and child hoping I wouldn't disgrace the home club too much.

Little and Burke, two of the biggest hitters in the business, had the honor at the first tee. They put their balls way down the field. Goodman's shot was up with theirs, high and far over Howard's Creek, which lies below the "Old White" course first tee.

Bending over, I had to take both hands to tee up my ball. The ball looked all blurred as I stood over it. My nerves were hopping right out of my skin.

And then I stepped away and did something I'd been practicing. I just let my mind take a rest by not thinking of anything in particular. If I thought of anything, it wasn't the crowd or the match, but sort of a mixture of all the good drives I'd ever made. Some people call it concentration, but to me it's more the trick of not thinking at all, of letting the world go by. It's sort of like pleasant daydreaming about a wonderful place you've been or something happy you've done, but with no details dragged in. In that frame of mind, the ball isn't anything fearful; it's just a thing you're going to hit well.

This is something you can teach yourself to do, and I recommend it to all golfers who get the tee jitters.

I swung and, upon looking up, heard the crowd gasp and saw my ball rolling down there 25 or 30 yards past anything else that had been hit. A good 280-yarder.

My second shot stopped in tall grass edging the green. The "away" balls were shot onto the green—all lying there, with a par 4 for the 1-putters, a 5 for the 2-putters. Taking a sharp iron, I sighted on the pin and shot from 45 feet. She bounced on with a good roll. Then she went *clunk*—right in there for a birdie 3.

Little and Burke just sniffed. They'd seen local boys get lucky before.

But the upshot of the day sort of left them puzzled, because I scored a 68, Burke a 70, Little a 71, and Goodman a 73. Only three holes were won that day—with Goodman and me winning the match, 3 and 2—and the nobody in the crowd, Snead, had accounted for two of them. Freddie Martin was laughing up his sleeve at the expression on Little's face.

"Lawson can't understand it," he whispered to me at the last hole. "He outdrives everybody in golf, but you've had him breaking his back all day just to keep you in sight."

So they began to talk about me in Virginia and West Virginia, and I guess I did a little strutting. My jalopy had a push-button horn on it that went *kee-haw!*, and all the girls from Hot Springs to White Sulphur could hear me coming. I did some dating, took up dancing the Big Apple, and learned to blow a jazz trumpet. When I was up on a bandstand as a guest player, some folks said, "Look at Sam—blowing his own horn again."

Far as I could see, if I didn't, who would? There wasn't many of the boys born down in those mountains without money who ever got to see the outside world, and my hankering to travel and play golf was strong.

A little later, they held the closed pro championship of West Virginia, where in one round I carded a 9-under-par 61, which Bob Ripley printed in "Believe-it-or-Not" as an all-time U.S. record for eighteen tournament holes.

But, as the weeks went by, nothing happened. Freddie Martin had a proposition before The Greenbrier management to finance me on the big-time pro tour, but for a long time nothing came of it. I worked from dawn to dark on my game and read golf handbooks which told about famous competitions at places like Scioto, Winged Foot, Oakmont, and Interlachen, which I'd never seen and probably wouldn't until pigs laid eggs.

If I'd only realized it, I was lucky as a cat with ninety lives to have the gift of hitting tee shots straight and far—part of the time. One reason I didn't appreciate it enough was that it came so easy at first. At seventeen and eighteen years of age, a 325-yarder wasn't unusual for me, even though I weighed just 165 pounds. Later on I was educated to the fact that over a steady period of time nobody makes wood shots that don't push or pull or slice or hook or are skied or smothered—and it was then I stopped patting myself on the back and gradually began growing into a golfer and not just a golf-ball walloper.

"Slammin' Sam" Snead wasn't nearly the natural the sportswriters always have made him out to be. My long-artillery game needed plenty of fixing in the beginning. Listen and I'll tell you about it.

The first drive I have any recollection of making was hit outside the Ashwood, Virginia, Methodist Church one Sunday morning when I was around seven years old. My folks, Harry and Laura Snead, had a little cow-and-chicken farm in Ashwood, a few miles from Hot Springs. Ashwood wasn't much: some said the 400 people in the town didn't match the number of moonshiners up in the timber.

When the chores was finished, all of us Snead kids scattered for the hills. We were rounded up on Sunday the way they call hogs. My mother, who had a good, strong voice, would let out a war whoop that could be heard over the next mountain, and when we straggled in they scraped off the mud and wood ticks and put us into clean clothes for churchgoing.

My older brothers—Homer, Jesse, Lyle, and Pete—weren't quite as wild as me. One Sunday I sneaked away from Bible class and spent the morning fixing an old wooden clubhead I'd found to a buggy whip.

The organ was finishing off the sermon when I came down the road, swinging at rocks and dried-up horse turds. One of the rocks took off like a bullet, went through a church window, and sprayed the congregation with glass.

The preacher, whose name was Tompkins, was the first one out the door, but all he found was an empty road. I stayed in the woods until dark, then wouldn't admit a thing when they gave me the third degree. They never did prove it on me.

Years later, in 1949, I presented the Ashwood Methodist Church with a new electric pipe organ—just another sinner who came to repent.

My brother Homer was my hero, but he was twelve years older than me and without much time for us little kids. Homer was a star at every sport—football, swimming, boxing—and could rip a golf ball about as far as anyone I've ever seen. He'd let me shag balls for him in the pasture. Then he'd leave for his job—as an electrician—and his club would go with him. So I'd cut a swamp maple limb with a knot on the end, carve a rough clubface with a penknife, leaving some bark for a grip, and swing by the hour, imitating Homer's roundhouse wallop.

Barefoot, with that swamp stick, I could hit for twenty fence posts, about 125 yards. If the ball sliced, it fell into some mucky bottomland. By trying different grips and stances, I got so it would sail both far and fairly true.

The way I became a caddie was that a Negro kid named Franklin Jefferson Jones came along one day when I was seven and a half and said, "Sam, let's go swipe us some candy."

We went down to a crossroads store, waited until the old man who ran the place stepped out, and grabbed all the chocolate bars we could carry. Back in our hideout I tried to eat some but couldn't. I began to bawl. "That poor old man," I said. "We're gonna put this stuff back." So we had to hide in the brush by the store all that hot day until we got a chance to creep in and replace the candy, which by now had melted into a sticky mess.

Frankie thought I was out of my mind but suggested that we could earn candy money by packing clubs over at The Homestead Hotel links in Hot Springs. A set of clubs weighed nearly as much as my sixty-five pounds. Since my shoulders weren't wide enough to support a bag, I hung it around my neck and staggered along behind the golfers.

Eighteen holes of this was worth fifty cents to a caddie, but the trouble was that the track was too long for me: after eighteen, I fell down and couldn't get up. The hotel doctor came along and saw me stretched out in exhaustion. He said that if any more golfers let an unformed infant carry their clubs, he'd knock them so high that they'd starve to death coming down.

"Why, this baby can ruin his health," he said.

My folks didn't know about it, since I was always missing from home, anyway—to spear bullfrogs or chase coon—and so my caddying didn't end until winter came and a man hired me to pack for him in the snow. Being barefoot, after nine holes I couldn't feel a thing below my shins. "Mister," I said, "I think I'm froze." Dropping his bag, I started to run.

When I reached the caddie house and got next to a fire, they found that all ten toes were frostbit and in a few more minutes might have been permanently damaged. So then they took away my caddie badge for good.

That hurt, because I was a hurrying kid with ambition. Horsehair Brinkley and Piggie McGuffin, two pals of mine, had to run to keep up with me. I tried every which way to learn to play golf on a real course, but when I was ten and twelve years old there wasn't a chance. The Homestead and Cascades Hotel courses were for wealthy tourists only. Any time we peckerwoods sneaked onto the local "Goat Course," which was a nine-holer for hotel employees, a cop would holler, "Hey, you little bastards!"—and we'd have to scatter for the woods without even time to putt out.

Since that door was closed, I went back to pasture practice, got so I could knock a ball out 200 yards or more in my bare dogs using a swamp maple, and then made myself a little five-hole course by sinking tomato cans around the farmyard. The hazards were loose chickens, the pump, a hayrake, and the outhouse.

In order to judge where a long drive should go, you need some depth perception. Likewise on chips, pitches, and putts. I think mine came from playing horseshoes with an uncle of mine. Back of the barn we tossed ringers by the day and week. A long time later, while winning the Brazilian Open at São Paulo, I stunned a gallery by shooting three straight holes without taking a putt—chipping in from off the green each time from distances of 40, 25, and 100 feet. It all went back to those horseshoe matches.

Me and Horsehair and Piggie and my brother Pete couldn't wait until the frost was gone so we could stop wearing shoes. By the next winter my toenails were practically all torn off and my feet were tougher than boot leather. I could stomp a chestnut burr and not feel a thing.

Matter of fact, when I got older and wore shoes they didn't

feel normal. Right then golf began to get complicated for me. Instead of just swinging from the heels, I began thinking about what I was doing. Thinking instead of acting is the No. 1 golf disease.

If I could have played barefoot all these years, I believe my scores would have been lower. Footwork, which I'll discuss later, is the most overlooked factor in golf: when you're really dug into Mother Earth, you have a true feeling of balance—and I proved it to myself in 1942 at the Augusta Masters Championship. Taking off my shoes, I played two of the toughest holes barefoot and birdied both. Then (and I'll tell about this, too) Gene Sarazen and others raised hell because they claimed it wasn't dignified, and back on went the shoes.

Not to claim that this is any sort of secret, but any time I've had balance trouble I've kicked off my shoes and found myself hitting straight again.

If you lead a horse away from water, he'll find it somewhere else. Not having the opportunity to play much golf as a kid, when I got to high school other sports became my main interest and pasture pool faded out so far that I almost never came back to it.

At Valley High School, which had only 150 students, I turned out for everything—baseball, football, basketball, swimming, track, and tennis. As a halfback for the Hornets, my running was slippery enough to cause college scouts to take a look and make offers. Virginia Poly, Davis-Elkins College, and Virginia U. wanted to sign me, but several things happened that got in the way.

For one, I damned near got killed in football.

While we were a puny country school, the schedule often sent us against Class A high schools of 1,000 or more kids, and the slaughter was terrible to watch. We had three substitutes as our whole bench; the other schools had two dozen or more. Against Covington, I was the ballcarrier on a sweep around end, where a gang of tacklers piled in at once and buried me in a water puddle. By the time I was lifted out, I was half choked to death on mud and had to be carried away and pounded on the back until I was breathing again.

After making a diving catch of a pass for a touchdown against Victoria, the opposition laid for me and on the next play separated my rib muscles and knocked loose some teeth. In the huddle I spit blood and told my teammates, "Now, look, I've had enough. Let somebody else carry the ball."

Nobody else would. We'd either send Snead in to be butchered or else do the only thing left—throw a long, incomplete pass.

Finally, after cracking a bone in my hand, I turned to baseball and track, where I ran the 100-yard dash in ten seconds flat. For a while there, I had my mind set on becoming a professional pitcher—especially after a game with Eagle Rock when I struck out eighteen batters and had a no-hitter going in the ninth inning, when the hitter lifted a high fly to center field. Our outfielder crossed his legs, fell down, and the ball rolled into a cornfield behind him. While he was hunting for it amongst the corn stubble, the run scored that beat me 2-1.

Things like that helped me make up my mind to stick to a sport where you didn't depend on other people's efforts—but only on your own.

Which got me back to golf, where Valley High competed each year in a schoolboy tournament held at nearby Woodberry Forest Academy. The big feature was a long-driving contest, including the strongest swingers from west-central Virginia. Never in the tournament itself did I finish better than fourth, but in my sophomore and junior years I won the long-drive contest. In my senior year I didn't have a doubt that I had it in the bag. It stung my pride when I drove 301 yards and lost the title to a big boy named Toby Tobias, who whaled a ball 318 yards.

The reason was clear enough: Tobias used a full driver off the tee, while I had to use a brassie because of an inability to get the ball up into the air with a No. 1 wood. The more lofted brassie got it up, but at the sacrifice of distance.

At that time, in 1932, when I was nineteen years old, I was no part of a golf-swing analyst and couldn't understand what caused me to hit grass cutters. Sometimes I got a duck-hook effect, where the ball shot out low and took a left-hand dip downward into the rough. And sometimes I smothered the shot entirely, driving the ball into the ground just beyond the tee for no reason I could explain.

This is one of the most exasperating problems faced by many players when they take a driver into their hands. They don't want to tee off with a brassie or spoon or 4-wood, but they have no choice.

Somehow I saw that I had a powerful right hand and arm, from having pitched baseballs, footballs, and horseshoes, and that the trouble must be connected with that.

Over at the Homestead course, where I now was admitted to play once in a while, I told an old-time club member about my problem. He thought a moment and asked, "How would you describe your swing?"

"Why, all I know is that I trust it whole hog, except with a driver," I said. "I know you're supposed to think of a lot of different things when you swing, but a baseball pitcher doesn't pick his windup and delivery and follow-through to pieces, so neither do I. I'd rather depend on the feel of my hands. They let me feel the pull of the clubhead when I start my downswing, and after that I don't worry about the whys and hows."

I might have added that the only thing I thought about in swinging (and still do) was to keep the arc of my swing as wide as possible. I want that clubhead as far from my body as my arms will allow at every stage of the swing. My arms are like the spokes of a wheel, although not stiff or rigid. Keeping them out and away from my body gives the clubhead a uniform arc.

"Well, you're thinking along good lines there," the old-timer said, "so I'd look for the trouble in your grip."

Going off by myself, I took my stance. Then I lifted the driver without changing the angle of my hands and arms, pivoted, and studied the position of my hands at the top of my backswing. At first I couldn't see where I'd changed the position of the clubface at this point. I used the standard Vardon overlapping grip, which I'd seen sketched in magazines, with the club boxed inside the left fist and held by the fingers and palm of the right hand. After hitting some more drives that skimmed the ground and then duck-hooked at about 150 yards, I checked again. Then I saw that the clubface was tilted slightly forward at that stage of my windup where I was coiled to strike, which meant it would come into the ball at that same angle. I was looking at what pros call a "shut face"—which term I didn't know at the time.

What caused it? In addressing the ball, I hadn't tipped it forward or backward; I had soled the club at a right angle to the target. As I studied my left hand and wrist, it seemed to me that something was straining them at the top of the arc. When I started the club back to the ball, I could feel and almost see a slight "give" in the left wrist to the left side. "Maybe it's not in a natural position," I thought.

Experimenting, I found that both my hands were turned too far over to the right on the shaft. The right hand, especially, was too much under the grip. As soon as I began my downswing, the strained left wrist shifted to a more easy position, the right wrist rolled over it, and the sum total was that the clubface became somewhat closed or shut.

This was interesting stuff. My failure to get the ball up and the duck-hook were closely tied together, as some experiments proved.

If the face was closed only slightly, I got a hook. If it closed still more, the shot was smothered.

To correct this by opening the face didn't take the mind of

a genius. Replacing my hands, I made sure that a little less than three knuckles of my left hand showed when I looked down, whereas before I had exposed more than three knuckles. My right hand moved well over the club, rather than being placed to the side of it. As a good check point, my right thumb, which had been on top of the shaft, now was more between the top and left side. After I formed this habit, shots began to leave my driver with more elevation and with less hook.

Somehow I felt I should figure out such things for myself, and so I never took a golf lesson from anyone—not that they were being offered in those days.

In baseball I'd squeezed the bat hard enough to wring sawdust out of it, but I saw where the golf grip had to be less firm and not with an equal amount of pressure applied by the two hands. Up to then I'd gripped the club strongly and muscled the ball down the course. My arms were like two steel bands, my knuckles turning white from the pressure.

About six years later, when Gene Tunney came to me for lessons, and in the 1940s, when I taught Joe Louis the fundamentals, both of these powerful men tried to do the same thing, the reason being that they were used to bunching their fists tight within a boxing glove. They wanted to deliver a KO punch, and all they got was smothered hooks or wild slices. Both became experts—Louis reaching a 2-handicap—when they got the hang of what I learned by myself as a kid. The thing that made my swing smooth out was that I relaxed my hold at the address and balanced it. Golf is a two-handed game where the right hand always wants to take charge. To get balance, I took my right-hand grip with about half as much pressure as that of my left hand. That got the left hand, which is your control hand, back into the act.

At first I argued with myself about this, saying, *But if you relax the right hand, you'll lose power.*

A lot of practice proved where that was wrong. Though the

right hand wasn't tight on the club through the backswing and into the downswing, old Mother Nature took over then and gradually the grip became firmer until at contact with the ball I had a natural right-hand whip or lash that didn't waste an ounce of power. I couldn't see this happening as I came into the ball, but I could feel it, and I knew that it happened automatically, without any deliberate thought or action on my part.

Those were the two big fundamentals I had to get clear before I could hit a straight, long lick: blocking out the shut face at the top and arranging grip pressure so as not to shortchange the left hand.

The education was only beginning, for in the next few years my inclination was always to let the right side take over and other ways had to be figured to prevent wild hooking of shots from the tee and fairway. As it stood in 1933, when my high-school days ended, the problem at hand was not golf but how to feed my face and not depend any longer on my folks—who had troubles enough of their own during the depression.

About then a foxy-faced fellow from the Bald Knob country came to me and said, "Say, Sam, how about us fixing ourselves up a little mash-and-spring-water still back in the hills and cooking some lightning? We can sell the rotgut for ten and fifteen dollars a quart."

"What happened to the partner you used to have?" I asked.

"Oh, those louse-eaten revenue agents raided us and shot Billy through the hip. He's got such a bad limp now that when he gets out of jail he won't be any help to me."

"Well, you don't have to hang from a tree to be a nut," I told him, "and that's what I'd be if I got mixed up in your racket." But, even as I said it, I wondered how I'd make a living.

For twenty dollars a month I took a job jerking sodas at Doc Ridgeley's drugstore in Hot Springs, and after that I ran a short-order restaurant—frying eggs and hamburgers—which was owned by my mother's half-brother. Some of my high-school friends, who already had good-paying jobs, would drop in for a burger and kid about poor Sam, who had to slave over a hot griddle and probably never would do better. I lacked the money to play golf more than once a month, and then I had to borrow Doc Ridgeley's clubs.

You've seen these small-town star athletes who ran out of eligibility and don't marry a rich girl or land a job selling stocks and bonds and hang around the hometown pool hall and cigar store, wondering where the cheers went. That's the way I seemed to be headed.

Then one night a customer came into the restaurant. While I was cooking his dinner, he mentioned that he was a pal of Freddie Gleim, the professional at The Homestead, a big re-sort hotel in the neighborhood. "Put in a word for me," I said, "if he's got a job open."

It happened that Gleim did, and after an interview I was hired at twenty-five dollars a month as a flunky in the pro shop. The position lasted two weeks and two days. A lady who weighed about 180 and had never played golf came along and insisted that I give her a lesson, since Gleim and his assistant pro were booked up.

"I'm just a hired hand around here," I told her, "and Gleim wouldn't like it if I did any instructing."

The woman, who was wealthy, practically took me by the ear and marched me to the tee. "Never mind Gleim, whoever he is," she said snappily. "Just show me how to strike that nasty little ball so that I can play with my husband and I'll pay you well."

After spending three days with her, I was called into the office by the boss. I figured he'd fire me. Instead, he said that the woman had told The Homestead's general manager that Sam Snead was a nice young man who should have a club job of his own, and that therefore they were promoting me to another of their hotel properties—The Cascades—four miles down the road. There I'd be "apprentice pro" and general handyman.

"This is a great stroke of luck for you, Snead," said the boss.

"It sure is," I said, wondering about salary, which for some reason hadn't been mentioned.

It turned out that my paycheck each month at The Cascades came to $0.00—not a dime—and that my pay was supposed to come from teaching hotel guests to play, at two and three dollars a lesson. After a year of not many pupils, but with plenty of time to practice on a real course, I was thin as a razorback hog and had sharpened into a long hitter with a fair amount of ability at chipping and putting, while not having a prospect in sight for getting up in the world.

In the early part of 1935 the boss pulled me back to The Homestead, without any explanation, giving my job to a young pro named Nelson Long.

"What'd I do wrong?" I asked.

"Never mind," he said.

Some friends, who were on the inside of things, told me, "What you did, Sam, was to shoot too many rounds in the 60s. Whether you know it or not, people are starting to talk about you. The professionals who've been here for years are jealous, so they've decided to stick you in the back shop where you won't be noticed."

For months I repaired clubs and hardly saw daylight. Then came The Cascades Open of 1936, and nobody could stop me from entering it. After I'd finished third in it, collecting $358.66 —the most money I'd ever seen, but most of which I owed to creditors—along came the man I told about at the start of this chapter: Mr. Freddie Martin of The Greenbrier. By a stroke of luck, Martin had dropped by that day and saw me hit a few smokers.

The minute he walked up to me and started talking, my fortune was on its way to being made.

SAM SNEAD'S COMMENT:
A BEGINNER'S APPROACH TO PLAYING WOOD
SHOTS

The following summary of *how I learned to play golf the simple way* is intended to show that *feel* is more important than mechanical action. If I'd become tangled up in the mechanics of the swing when I first hit shots, chances are I'd have been only an average player.

My secret is that I learned by feeling my way along—and "feel" still is the biggest word in the world to me. If my grip or stance on the tee didn't feel right when I began playing, I asked myself, "Why not?" Then I studied on it until it did feel comfortable and right and the results were good.

As that system worked out, I don't remember ever having shot a 90 on a golf course, and mighty few 80s.

Golfers depend too much upon outside help and worrying over details and not enough upon their own senses. For example, having chopped plenty of wood as a boy, I knew you didn't jerk the ax back. And you didn't give deep thought to swinging it down. You only brought back the ax with as little effort as possible, took a half second or so to aim, and laid the blade on the block of wood where you wanted it. Hands, arms, and feet all worked by feel. I felt confident that I'd split the block from the time I spit on my hands because of long practice and no agonizing over *how* I'd do it. If I happened to miss, I took a breath, slowed up a little on the swing, and corrected the mistake—just by sensing what needed to be done.

Golf wasn't that simple, but by making mistakes, experimenting, and correcting by myself, rather than having others tell me what to do, I put together a game almost entirely by feel. I don't say most beginners shouldn't have pro lessons. But after they have the basic information, and trouble appears, they should practice, practice, practice, until their own brain and nerves have solved the problem. They'll be ten times as strong as the average player for it.

In the full swing from the tee, the main natural areas of feel for me have been these:

THE LEFT HAND

The thumb produced more sensation of "right" or "wrong" for me than any finger of this hand. Any time I let my thumb lie loosely on the side of the shaft, it lost its ability to send my mind a message. So I formed the habit of sticking the thumb firmly against the shaft so that a notch, or gap, could be seen between the thumb end and the first knuckle of the index finger. Since I have very supple hands, the notch was deep and balanced my left-hand grip.

The thumb balanced it because another pressure point was the little finger. To keep the clubshaft solidly boxed in my whole left hand during the entire swing, without any loosening or wavering, the little finger had to take a snug grip. When it did, I had a favorable feel from both sides of the shaft.

THE RIGHT HAND

This caused me plenty of trouble for a while. At first my hand was too far under the shaft, as explained earlier in this chapter, instead of riding well over on top of the left hand. As I swung, the right rolled over on the left, giving me a duck-hook. Feeling

Right hand too far
under shaft causes . . .

. . . it to roll over and
produce duck hook

was missing until I began holding the club in neither the fingers nor palm of this hand but in both. The combination gave me that good feeling of both strength and control.

The right forefinger is the one I've had to watch most. It controls your swing, with help from the thumb. I discovered this by noticing that the upper part of the forefinger, the part nearest the palm, gave me a sensation of delivering a strong punch on the downswing. The more I felt this, the more I suspected that the right forefinger is the payoff finger. As a matter of fact, it and the thumb produce the right-hand lash or whip that means distance off the tee.

COMBINED HAND PRESSURE

I was a "grabber" at first; then I relaxed to grip the stick with about the pressure you put on a billiard cue. When I could feel any tightening of the muscles in the forearms, I knew my hold was too tight. It also made sense to me that the left-hand pressure must be stronger than the right's, because you start taking the club back with the left and just steady the action with the right.

THE KNEES

Any time I started to scuff or smother shots I could bet that my knees were too tense. Tension builds up here as much as anywhere, but you can feel it and correct it. I just walked around a bit, flexing my knees, until they felt limber, then readdressed the ball with the knees bent a little bit and my tailbone extended. Locking the knees—especially the right knee on the backswing—is pure poison. Try it on the dance floor sometime and you'll find yourself dancing stiff-legged.

One of the key points of my swing is the straightening of the right leg as I take the club back. About halfway through the backswing my body shifts against my right foot and the leg loses all knee bend and becomes straight. But there's never any lock or feeling of overtension.

THE WRISTS

You can't oil your wrists, but they should send back the feeling that you have done so. In my beginning days I checked them for free movement by wiggling and waggling the club back and forth before and after stepping up to the ball. If they didn't move easily, I stepped away and started over again. Another wrist loosener is to lift the club from a soled position just by breaking your wrists straight up. That's the only way the wrists break or cock at all during the swing, and if you're tense at the start, it'll only get worse. Imagine the ball is just a dandelion tip you're going to clip and you'll unlock the wrist muscles.

The right wrist can cause the most trouble, by overpowering the left, so here I just let my right arm go a little limp and the wrist relaxed with it.

INSIDE OF RIGHT FOOT

They said I had perfect foot roll from the first time I swung in competition. If so, it was mostly due to pivoting on the inside edge of the feet, especially the inside of the right foot. When I set myself to swing, I dug in with my cleats on the inner edge—not just the toe—of the right foot. It gave the feeling of being well braced. Upon contacting the ball, that inside sole pushed against the resistance of the left foot and gave me an added kick, which added up to power and 300-yard drives.

THE LEFT HEEL

From watching all the stars of the 1930s drive the ball, I got the idea that as the backswing gets under way the settling down to a strong anchorage of the left heel was one of the most important details of long-shot making. It seemed to control the action of the rest of the leg and body movements. So then I made sure to feel that the heel was well planted. The only way to get the feel is to practice until the act is as automatic as blinking your eyes.

That sums up how I learned golf without lessons and by letting my senses guide me. By taking the natural way, I developed timing—which is coordinating all the actions into one continuous, easy, relaxed motion, like sorghum molasses pours from a jug. Later I'll tell about some more advanced lessons I had in tee and fairway play.

THE MOST VALUABLE LESSON I LEARNED

Earlier in this chapter, I told of "going into a sort of pleasant daydream" when I had the tee jitters against Burke, Little and Goodman. There is a real payoff idea behind this.

The practice swing of most ordinary players almost always carries most of the main ingredients. The fundamentals are there. But when they are in a match, the difference is terrific. The feet are no longer easily set. There is a cramped body turn. Hands and wrists are rigid. When this happened to me, I began thinking in terms of *performance*, not *results*. By this I mean I had no thought beyond the ball—of traps, ponds, rough, or out of bounds. All I did was to go back to my good practice swing, on which I could count, and then to think *with* my swing— not *ahead* of the swing. This takes will power, but it isn't so hard to let your mind relax and say to yourself, "Here goes my practice swing—and I don't care where the ball lights or lands. If I can't play like a good golfer in actual play, at least I can go back to my practice swing and let nature take its course."

Call on your will power to "let the rest of the world go by," and dust that thing with the form you have when nobody is watching—and watch your score go down. Climb inside your old, regular personality, not the one that wants to take you over when the pressure is on.

2

FIRST LOOK AT THE BIG BOYS:
DON'T QUIT ON THE HOLE

THE HERSHEY (PA.) OPEN OF 1936 • THE MIAMI AND
NASSAU OPENS OF 1937 • THE OAKLAND (CAL.) OPEN
OF 1937

The big law dog in the hills where I grew up
was Sheriff Charley Gumm. He was always re-elected because
nobody was idiot enough to want Gumm's job. One night he
had the top of his head blown off, and for a while there the
whole valley around Hot Springs looked ready to cut loose in
a shooting war—as had happened before.

Mostly it was the revenooers against the moonshiners, and
it was no joke. My father called a meeting of the Sneads.
Present were my brothers Lyle, Homer, Pete, and Jesse, plus
me, the youngest.

"Gumm was killed last night," my father said, "when he went
to take a gun away from old man Messer and one of Messer's
boys got to the trigger first. Now you boys want to walk careful. Sam, what have you been up to lately?"

"Running a trapline," I said. My homemade traps bagged
coon, fox, wildcat, and muskrat, and I could sell the pelts for
four bits to a dollar, which kept me in licorice and movie
money and financed bets down at the town pool hall.

"You're running too wild. Stay home. The boys are cooking corn up there and they'll shoot anybody full of holes who
comes near."

30

But it didn't stop me from trapping. Not to brag, but at fourteen and fifteen I was a good woodsman. Once I stalked a buck deer to within twelve feet and he didn't hear a thing until I dropped him with one shot through the head. Wild turkeys couldn't tell my gobble from their own. The moonshiners, though, used mules as lookouts—their big ears being able to detect anything coming sooner than any dog's—and I never could fool them. Every now and then I'd stumble onto a hideout still built into one of the hollows. Every second after that I was risking a bullet. Two or three hidden rifles were aimed at me, I knew, so I'd whistle sort of carelessly, shoot the animal I'd trapped, and mosey along, acting like I hadn't seen a thing.

One time, I remember, a tree limb that'd been cracked in a storm crashed behind me when I got halfway down the mountain and I ran out of my shoes all the way home.

Almost anybody could build a ten- or twenty-gallon-a-day still and brew mountain lightning, but our family stayed honest. We managed to get by without ever going hungry, even though my father, Harry, earned $125 a month maintaining the boilers at a local hotel and dirt-farmed on the side to make ends meet. In depression times that wasn't bad money. He was Dutch-German, born down in those Allegheny hills, and he wore a big, bushy mustache. Until he was in his sixties he was tough as a nut—captain of the hose-and-reel brigade of the Hot Springs Fire Department, which won the state championship for hooking up a hose over a 125-yard course in twenty seconds flat. He was a left-hander who never touched a golf club in his life.

My mother was Laura Dudley, from over in Rock Bridge County, Virginia. She was forty-seven years old when I was born.

The time seemed to creep by until I was grown and on my way to working under Freddie Martin at The Greenbrier Hotel, where golf became everything in the world to me. It was late summer of 1936, after I'd played in some local tournaments (which I'll tell about elsewhere in this book), that I saved up seventy-five dollars and had my first look at the outside world. The first train ride of my life was in a day coach, which landed me at the Pennsylvania Station in New York. After getting lost and wandering around, I made connections to Hershey, Pennsylvania, where I'd heard they were playing a $5,000 Open.

It was strictly big league, and that's what I most wanted to see—the famous stars in action in real competition. The last thought in my mind was to try and match any of them, even though I'd recently done well. All I wanted was a look at such champions as Walter Hagen and Craig Wood and Bobby Cruickshank in the flesh and to get a rough idea of what chance I might stand someday.

I had hay in my hair, all right, there at the first tee at Hershey. Four men in expensive outfits were about to start a practice round. I asked, "Is this where they're holding the tournament?"

Only one of the men didn't grin at my scuffed old bag and my cheap clubs, of which I had only eight. He was a short, soft-spoken man with kind eyes. He sized me up quickly and said, "It is, kid. Go change your shoes and you can play around with us."

The others showed that they didn't want any part of a rube, but this man waited for me—he was George Fazio, a fine pro and teacher, as it turned out—and before we teed off, he gave me a rundown on the first hole at Hershey.

"This is 345 yards. Just play straightaway and try to get on the green in 2."

My swing always had been big, with a full fifty-degree turn, and being scared of this crowd I sliced one a country mile into a chocolate factory off the right fairway. It was unplayable. My next drive was into the factory again. The third went into the water just in front of the tee. Three whacks and I still didn't have a playable ball. I wanted to turn and run away. One of the foursome let out a snort and said, "What the hell kind of a guy have we got here?"

"Yeah, who let him in?" said another. He and the others had played pro drives of some 260 yards down the middle.

Fazio only said, "Hit another, son."

It slowed me down, and this time I remembered, on my downswing, to let my left side and hips lead my arms into the ball—rather than rushing out of my pivot with a fast arm action—and to uncock my wrists smoothly.

Somebody hollered, "Where'd he go this time?" Fazio didn't say a word. He just stood there staring at me.

Then one of the other three yelled, "My God, he's on the green!" Even my new friend, Fazio, was shook up.

My ball lay something like 20 feet from the 345-yard flag and they couldn't believe it, just stood around the pill, looking first at it and then at me. At the time I was five feet ten and a half and weighed about 165 and my big wrists were concealed by the long-sleeved white shirt I wore. Once, on a 525-yard Greenbrier hole with a breeze behind me, I'd reached a bunker in front of the green. Any time I could relax I could be sure of giving the ball a real ride.

On the second hole at Hershey they almost always played a drive short of a creek far down the fairway. It was a hazard nobody had ever carried, though a lot had tried. Fazio didn't stop me when I went for the carry—and made it with some to spare. On the 600-yard third hole I was past the back edge of the green in 2, with nobody close to me.

"I'm a son of a bitch, it isn't true," one of the big-time stars with Fazio kept muttering.

Not counting the 3 tee shots I'd fouled off on No. 1, I shot a 67 for the round.

All sorts of things began to happen to me in a hurry after that, but the attention I got didn't stop me from remembering a lesson that's stayed with me right until today. I'd hit 3 hopeless shots on No. 1 and still played the hole in only 1 over par. The lesson was that no matter what happens—*never give up a hole.* Since Hershey, I've seen golfers galore who string together several bad beginning shots and in their disgust or embarrassment give the hole the Big Quit. They play it out to the cup any old lackadaisical way, because they're so sure they're looking an 8 or a 9 in the face. So they wind up with a 9. They can't see or refuse to see that there's always hope left. Most 90-and-up shooters are guilty of this. The sequence of shanks or slices or topped balls blinds them to the fact that the next swing might equalize everything and get them right back into the ball game.

Some time after Hershey, I saw Jimmy Demaret quit cold. I wish now I'd let him keep it up. We were coming down the stretch in the New Orleans Open with me leading the field, Demaret close behind. On the par-3 fifteenth Jim topped a little pooper from the tee. His recovery was into rough. Demaret was mad enough to chew his 7-iron to pieces, but he settled for taking a one-handed swipe at the ball. He double-bogeyed the hole.

"You can have the ——— money," he snarled.

"Now come on, Jim," I said, "let's not be foolish. If you bear down, you might finish birdie, birdie, birdie and still get a piece of the purse."

On the next hole he sank a birdie 12-foot putt, on the next he dropped a birdie 25-footer, and on the clubhouse hole he birdied in from 20 feet. Meanwhile, on the seventeenth, my ball moved as I was addressing a chip shot, costing me a penalty stroke.

The New Orleans $2,500 top prize which I had all locked up didn't go to me but was won by Demaret. By 1 stroke.

I'll be damned if he deserved it, however—which my old sidekick, Jim, will freely admit.

In tossing in your cards after a bad beginning you also undermine your whole game, because to quit between tee and green is more habit-forming than drinking a highball before breakfast.

To quit is to violate the percentages in your favor, and anyone who does it should attend a class on fundamentals. Close to 60 per cent of golf scoring is done from within 125 yards of the flag. If you've just shot an 85, for example, you took approximately 49 shots with your medium and short irons and putter. Even after muffing 2 or 3 wood shots, you still have a 60-40 chance of bailing out the hole with a 1- or 2-over-par score.

Even a novice doesn't find the 5-iron and 6-iron, which are the key clubs in the average player's bag, too difficult to master and use well. If you're also a fairly steady putter, to quit on any hole is stupid.

Yet when things go wrong 75 per cent of players stop trying and dog it the rest of the way. Some do it subconsciously—and of course they'll deny their guilt all day long.

My Hershey practice-round experience of 1936 just began to introduce me to the idea of turning bad shots into good ones. The word got around there that an unbelievable, long-hitting hillbilly was on the premises, and after the famous Henry Picard had watched me play he took me aside.

"In the tourney," he said, "you'll be paired with Craig Wood. I'll give you a tip. Wood represents the Dunlop Tire & Rubber Company, one of the big golf-ball makers. I think he's considering you for Dunlop."

I didn't know what Picard meant. "Considering me for what?" I said.

Picard kind of sighed at my ignorance. "I mean, he may sign you up as a Dunlop representative."

"My God," I said.

"Now, don't tell Wood I let you know this," went on Picard. "Just do all you can to impress him."

Picard knew it'd have to be by my golf; he couldn't help noticing that my pants were too long and my jacket was off a small-town rack.

Wood was one of the great siege guns of golf, a Ryder Cupper. After ten holes I'd held him about even without ever turning loose my driver, and then we came to No. 11, which was well over 300 yards and uphill, with a blind green. We drove, and when we reached the green, one ball lay just short of the near fringe and another lay on the back of the green. Wood naturally started around the trap to the farthest ball.

"Mr. Wood," said his caddie, "this is your ball here in front of the green."

Wood colored up a bit. He wasn't outdriven often, and never by a guy with no reputation. But then he took his first serious look at me. "Who's been teaching you?" he asked.

"I never had a lesson in my life, Mr. Wood," I replied honestly.

"What's the best you've ever shot?"

"At The Greenbrier on the No. 1 course I had a 61 not long ago. But I 3-putted the eighteenth hole."

Like Fazio had done, Wood just stared at me. I was beginning to feel like some kind of freak the way people were popping their eyeballs at me.

After the tournament, my first away from home, the scores showed that I'd finished fifth. Wood offered me $500 cash, two dozen balls a month, and a set of new clubs to sign with Dunlop and endorse their products. I was reaching for a pen before he stopped talking. My life savings at the time, if I hocked a few things, amounted to $300. With $800 I could risk going out on the P.G.A. circuit.

At the Miami Open that winter, when I finished a poor tenth and won $108, Picard was discouraging. "It's a cutthroat racket, this touring, and you'd better think twice. You'll have to place one-two-three every week to make even expenses. After all, you have almost no experience."

Wood saved the day when we got to the Nassau Open. My driver wouldn't behave and I won nothing. Wood said, "Go ahead, Sam. If you go broke, wire me and I'll send you transportation money home."

The boys were guessing that I might last two months before taking Wood up on his offer. Another bachelor and golf rookie, Johnny Bulla, came along just then. Bulla was a big, handsome brute, also poor, who had a '36 car with not much tread showing on the tires, and so the two of us headed for California and the P.G.A. winter tour. Bulla had real talent but was always moaning about his bad shooting, so I called him "Boo-Boo." Most of my $800 was gone by now and Bulla wasn't holding much, so we split all expenses down the middle and ate hamburgers at cheap motels, squeezing nickels until the buffalo groaned.

Heading for the Oakland, California, Open, we were approaching Fresno with Boo-Boo at the wheel when another driver crashed into us. We piled into a third car and everything but the top of Bulla's jalopy flew off. After climbing out of the wreckage, we ran for the trunk of the car, without bothering to check on possible broken bones.

"It's OK," I told Boo-Boo. "Nothing's broken." At least our golf clubs had come through without damage.

The repair bill on the jalopy was $140, which hit our bankroll so hard that we went on a chicken-salad sandwich and soup diet and lived in a fleabag hotel. One of us had to place high up in the money at Oakland or else we were finished. First money was $1,200. But when you dropped to fourth money, it was only $342.50, and tenth money was $80.

There wasn't much hope for us when we signed in at the Claremont Country Club, since all the ranking pros were there and had been scorching the course in practice. On the scoreboard they had spelled my name "Sneed."

"That's not right," I said. "It's S-n-e-a-d."

"Who's he?" the scorer asked.

After thirty-six of the seventy-two holes I was in the running with rounds of 69 and 65, but Bulla was far down and it was up to me to save the partnership. My gallery consisted of my caddie and one old man who kept hobbling after me, coughing and snapping his false teeth when I was putting. Even at that, I was glad to have him. My third-round score was 69, tying me for the fifty-four-hole lead with Johnny Revolta and Ralph Guldahl. It wasn't until the sixteenth hole of the last round, though, that anybody noticed Snead.

Then there was a hell of a noise. All at once about 3,000 people came running from hills and hollows and began fighting like madmen for gallery space around me. "What's going on here?" I said.

Bulla, who was choking and trying to catch his breath, explained that I had a chance to win. Boo-Boo was absolutely white in the face. I was so excited and confused in all that noise that I couldn't understand what he was yelling at me.

The sixteenth was what the pros call a barrel hole—that is, it had interlocking trees forming a canopy over the 380-yard fairway. I decided to play a straight-faced 1-iron down close to the ground to avoid that overhead forest. The shot was true, but as I was approaching my ball a crazy-eyed fan charged through the crowd, knocked down Orville White, the Chicago pro, almost upended Bulla, and began screaming in my ear, "Snead, all you've got to do to tie for first place is to par in!"

Information at a time like that freezes you clear to your marrow, and I proceeded to put my second ball right up in the treetops. It finally trickled through, dropping amongst a bunch of people, who stampeded and squashed it into the ground.

Bulla was ready to be carried away and I wasn't much better off.

What I didn't understand, of course, was that the story about an unknown hillbilly had spread and everybody in Oakland wanted to see me win or blow the $1,200.

Under the conditions, I could have given up on the hole without disgracing myself, but the lesson I'd had on the first tee at Hershey was still fresh in my mind. When things look the worst, a great saver of a shot may be just around the corner.

Digging in deep and swinging more flatfooted than usual and

with plenty of forearm muscle applied, I scraped the ball out, watched it climb and drop on the green. The crowd roared and I started breathing again. Two putts gave me a bogey 5, where it easily could have been 7 or 8 strokes.

"Now you've got to birdie the eighteenth!" they were shouting at me.

It was my parring of the tough par-3 seventeenth, though, that made all the difference, as I realized later when I mentally replayed the round. By sticking the spurs into myself and staying with it when the crowd and my nerves had me down and not letting up even a fraction, I actually won my first P.G.A. tournament. Feeling calmer, I walked down the course to study the situation.

With a mild sort of dogleg left, the par-5 No. 18 was faced with thick trees and a big ravine to the left. The right side was wide open.

"Jackson, for the Lord's sake, keep it up to the right!" Bulla begged me. My middle name, if you haven't heard, is Jackson—after a grandfather who knew Stonewall.

"I think you're wrong," I said. "I'll shave it left."

"What in the —— for?"

"Wait a minute and you'll see." I've always had a lot of gambler in me, even when my knees are knocking.

It was risking everything, but I placed it down the left side along the trees on the theory that even if it hooked too much on me I had some margin for error left and that I could gain a shorter, better angle to the green if it held the fairway. It held. An easy 2-wood short of the green, a pop-shot over a bunker, and a 4-foot putt gave me a finishing birdie.

After I'd torn loose from that mob, which wanted my pants, putter, and hat for a souvenir, I was running for cover when some photographers grabbed me. "Stand still for a picture," they demanded. "You've just won this thing."

"Get away from me!" I said, jerking free. "There's still some of the boys out on the course, so don't go counting my chickens."

"We're trying to tell you that you've *won* it! It's all over," they came back.

I fought them off with both hands and was hotfooting for Bulla's car when Freddie Corcoran, the P.G.A. tournament director, caught me. The Irishman was burned up. "What's the matter with you? The press is mad as hell the way you're behaving. Come on in the press tent and make a statement."

"I won't do it! Craig Wood and a lot of the boys are still out there. I haven't won anything yet."

It dawned on Corcoran that I was so green to tournament golf that I'd never heard of the communication system on courses, which already had established my 69-65-69-67—270 as two strokes better than the next best possible score, which was Guldahl's. He explained the facts of life. So I went in and told the press I was sorry.

Bulla was buying drinks for the crowd like he owned a saloon. We had a cool $1,200.

Corcoran wasted no time taking the hillbilly angle to me and playing it for all it was worth, and that has been considerable since 1937. Without any effort on my part, he wasn't left short of material at any time. Forty-eight hours later I ran across Henry Picard, who showed me my picture in the New York *Times.*

"How in the world did they ever get that?" I asked Henry. "I never been to New York in my life."

News services and wirephotos were Greek to me. The night before I'd sat up late writing my folks a letter, telling them I'd won. Otherwise I figured they'd never know it.

Somebody wrote that Ring Lardner had gone into the Ozarks and invented me. Some new golf terms had come into use about then, and one fellow upped to me and said, "Say, Sam, we'd like you to attend our clinic."

"I'm feeling fine," I told him. "Even if I was sick, I got my own personal doctor down home."

They asked me how I powdered the ball so far and I gave

them a natural answer. "I just try to do it the most simplest way I know how. I don't bother thinking about it; what I do is just take that club back nice and lazy and then I try to whop it right down on the barrelhead."

Later, in Chicago, Toney Penna and some golfers introduced me to my first nightclub, the *Chez Paree*. Toney told me at the last minute that the cover charge was ten dollars.

"What's that?" I asked.

"You pay ten dollars as a minimum charge. Drinks are extra."

"You mean I've got to pay ten whole dollars just to sit in that chair?" I said. "Why, I don't even drink."

While the others had champagne, I ordered as many soft drinks as I could handle, about a dozen bottles. I drank until the pop was coming out of my ears, and when I left I carried those refund bottles out of there with me.

My reputation for being so tight with money that I buried my winnings in tin cans in my backyard began about then, mostly due to my unwillingness to hang around clubhouse bars after tournaments and swap drink checks with the boys. One pro said, "Snead's so tight he'd spend his last dollar buying a pocketbook to put it in." They said I was a "loner"—and some of the P.G.A. athletes who liked to live it up after a show didn't care much for me. They didn't consider that I might be scared or homesick. Or that I didn't drink hard liquor and was a ten o'clock bedtime guy and an early riser, because of my raising in the hills. One time in Oakland, Freddie Corcoran arranged to meet twelve of the touring pros in the Leamington Hotel lobby at six-thirty A.M., after which they'd drive to the Lake Merritt Club for a publicity breakfast. Not one showed up; they were upstairs, sleeping off a hard night. But I was there, and had been waiting an hour for Corcoran, raring to go.

"What a publicity ham that Snead is," some said.

The writers named me "Slammin' Sam" and my career started with the Oakland Open, you could say. Three weeks later I won the Bing Crosby Open at Rancho Santa Fe in a cloudburst of rain. From there on I was hard to beat, finishing my first year on tour with $10,243 in winnings and third place in the P.G.A. standings and landing a place on the Ryder Cup team as a freshman. The headlines called me "an overnight miracle" and "Daniel Boone with a driver." With all that applause, I tried not to miss the important point. Most strong young kids—about 99 per cent—fade out of the P.G.A. circuit fast. One of the main reasons I stuck was the lesson of Hershey and Oakland, where I didn't quit on the key hole—learning right at the start to avoid the error which the pros call *thinking yourself out of action.*

Any time I've slipped up on this it has cost me a stiff penalty.

As an example, the year after Oakland, 1938, I noticed that in one tournament after another I was paired with Jimmy Thomson, who shared billing with me as the world's longest driver. It was easy to see why. Certain promoters of P.G.A. events were boosting their box-office take by advertising their show as a duel between Thomson and me. People flocked out to see us pretend like we didn't give a hoot about the ballyhoo, then twist ourselves into awful-looking knots and swing from the heels.

This was bad for my game, since overdriving—putting too much emphasis on power—had become a problem.

Protests got me nowhere. Thomson and I went on slugging the rubber off the ball. I was determined not to let Thomson outwallop me by 20 or 30 yards, and the Blond Bomber was making damned sure I didn't outdrive him by even 1 foot.

It threw me so far off that at Crosby's tournament, which I'd won in 1937, I collected just $5.55 on scores of 73-75-71-69—288. When we reached the Pasadena Open I was boiling mad. The draw for pairings at Pasadena placed me with another golfer— and then, in a last-second switch, they teamed me again with Thomson.

"Maybe I'll pull out of here," I threatened.

"You do," the local officials said, "and the P.G.A. will sock you with a fine and suspension."

The forty-one shots I took on the opening nine was about the last straw. We came to the twelfth hole, where I hit a quail-high hook under a tree. It wasn't such a tough recovery, but I knocked it out of bounds. All at once I couldn't see myself taking a 7 or 8 on the hole.

"I'm through," I said. Picking up, I headed for the clubhouse and by nightfall was on my way out of town. And then I really caught it in the headlines:

SNEAD IN TROUBLE—ANGERS OTHER PROS
and
FACING BLOWUP, SNEAD WALKS OUT

They roasted me all the way to Pinehurst, North Carolina, where I did it again—picked up and left—when facing a "lost" hole. One write-up of Pinehurst began. "They sneered when Snead strode off the glittering Pinehurst fairway last Friday, his card torn to shreds, and called him a breaker of the faith and a quitter. . . ."

I didn't see how it was so serious. Bob Jones had picked up in the British Open, Tommy Armour and Abe Mitchell did it in the U. S. Open, and Gene Sarazen walked off in the Masters. I found out how wrong I was, and when I learned how much people disliked a quitter I cured myself of the habit forever.

I had my reasons for picking up; all golfers do. Mine was that I believed the gallery hadn't paid to see bad golf from me, that by leaving I was doing all concerned a favor. "When I'm cold," I argued, "I'm not going to make a fool of myself."

That's false pride talking. It's a loser's way of thinking, not a winner's.

My thinking was the same as Arnold Palmer's when he broke into the P.G.A. tour in 1955. Arnie is a power hitter and a go-for-broke gambler like me who also had the impression that a few bad shots strung together ruin your round. After taking a 78 in the Cavalcade of Golf in '55, Arnie withdrew. In the Mayfair Inn Open he shot a first-round 72 and quit. At the Motor City Open in Detroit it was a 77—and goodbye Palmer.

What cured Arnie? As he'll tell you, the 1958 Azalea Open at Wilmington, North Carolina, had much to do with it. Dow Finsterwald and George Bayer were leading Palmer by 2 strokes into the final round. Finsterwald hit 2 perfect shots to reach the first green in 2. Palmer pushed his drive into the woods and then looped an iron wide of the green behind a big hump slanting downward to the hole 60 feet away from his ball. Arnie couldn't pitch over the bulge to the down-sloping green without badly overrunning the cup. He was in a real jam.

With only one thing left to do, Arnie tried a little roll and run, hitting his ball into the forepart of the hump so that it held the turf and ran up slowly and over and down. And the long shot came home: into the cup she rolled for a sensational birdie 3. He finished the round with a 68 and the next week, profiting from the lesson, won the Masters Tournament with many a fine recovery.

It brings to mind big Vic Ghezzi in the Los Angeles Open. Big Vic was sweating blood when he found his ball wedged in the fork of a tree limb behind the green. A fat woman standing there smirked and said, "Let's see you play this one, buster."

Vic gave her a look. Then he whacked away and the ball stayed stuck. "Ha-ha," said the woman. "I warned you."

Using the toe of his iron like a billiard cue, Vic poked it out. "Great golf shot," the woman gave it to him.

Vic was burning; he'd used up 4 shots on a par-5 hole. "Hold onto your ——, lady," he said.

Then he chipped 45 feet with his 8-iron right into the cup for his par.

He got in the last sneer as the fat woman stood there with her mouth open.

You'll never know what might have happened if you quit. Once in the Westchester Open I hit 3 straight drives so far out of bounds on the third hole that the Eagle Scouts couldn't have brought one of those balls back. But I kept plugging along. And I wound up being carried off the final green on the shoulders of the crowd when I won the tournament. In 1938 at Shawnee-

on-the-Delaware, Jimmy Hines had me the next thing to whipped
when we reached the fourteenth green, where I laid him a stymie.
In those days we played all stymies. Unable to bend a putt
around me, Hines used a niblick to chip over my ball. He pulled
off a beautiful shot—straight into the cup from three feet.

You couldn't guess the rest. Jimmy's ball grazed mine in
passing, started it rolling, and we both stood there dumfounded
when it followed his ball into the hole. That freak of chance
gave me the heart to come back and shoot 4 straight 3s to beat
Hines, 1 up.

When you land in water, you're most likely to quit on a hole
and take the penalty. At least, I found it that way in my early
golf schooling. After trying to move a ball from water without
luck, you develop a sort of complex. Rather than give up, I
studied the problem, and one day in the International Four-Ball
at Miami the chance came to either blow up on a hole or try
saving it. U. S. Open Champion Ralph Guldahl was paired with
me against Billy Burke and Craig Wood. The eighth hole is an
iron shot to a green guarded by a lagoon. Wood hit one stiff to
the pin for the other team while my ball splashed into the pond
25 or 30 yards from the flag. It was almost totally submerged in
water and thick, sticky mud.

"C'mon, Sam," called Guldahl, "pick it up."

With Wood only 3 feet from the cup, the odds were a
million to one that he'd win the hole with a birdie 2 to my 5 or
6, so they all laughed when I said, "No, sir, I'll go for it."

Water is hard to compress. It stops the clubhead up short,
offering terrific resistance, so I took my heaviest wedge, hit down
at a sharp angle with all my strength, and up came mud, water,
rocks, and the ball.

Sure, I was soaked, but the shock of the water was nothing
to my feeling when that little dog bounced up on the green, ran
toward the cup, and stopped, leaning against the flag. When the
stick was removed, in she fell.

That fantastic deuce stunned Wood. He missed his 3-footer
and I won the hole with a birdie to his 3.

Discouragement and disgust usually lead you to give up, but never overlook the matter of cockiness. Overconfidence that comes with a long lead on an opponent can cause you to "give up" in reverse. It happens every day in weekend play by ordinary golfers when a high-handicap man who's bearing down on every shot wipes out a low-handicap player who's so sure he'll win that he falls asleep. In the pro league, Bobby Cruickshank once had Al Watrous 7 down with nine holes to play and conceded an 8-foot putt. Watrous got busy and won the match.

It hurts me to think about the Ryder Cup matches of 1953 at Wentworth, Surrey, England, which paired me against Harry Weetman. A bushy-haired pro with just a fair reputation, Weetman didn't bother me because on this tight golf course he figured to make several mistakes on the pressure holes. After thirty of the thirty-six holes, this had come true and I had him 4 down and my record of never having lost a Ryder singles match was as safe as money in the bank. In my mind I was ordering a nice thick steak for dinner when we walked up to No. 31.

On No. 31 I rolled my drive toward the edge of the rough and it finished up in tail-high heather. I took a 6 to Weetman's 4.

On No. 32 Weetman outchipped me to win another.

On No. 33 I drove into the trees and took a 6, losing again.

On No. 34 I hit into a deep ditch and had to play backward between my legs for another losing 6.

On No. 35 Weetman's birdie 4 beat my 5.

We halved No. 36 to complete one of the worst flops of my life—Weetman winning, 1 up. He damned near couldn't believe it either.

A good rule is: never collect any trophies in your head until you have them in your hand.

After about 7,500 rounds of golf, I can think of only a few cases where a player was justified in tossing in his chips. One happened at The Greenbrier when I was giving a woman guest a few pointers before she teed off. She was the sedate type, Junior League, very prim and proper and self-conscious before a crowd of watchers.

"Take a few practice swings," I suggested.

After a few swings, I noticed something pink peeking out of the V neck of her blouse. Before I could do anything, she swung again and out popped one of her falsies. It bounced a few times, rolled around in pretty little circles, and stopped on the ground in front of us.

Everybody was staring and there was an awful silence and somebody had to say something to pass it off, so I took the honor. "That's OK," I told her. "Just leave it there and we'll tee up right off it."

She went sprinting and sobbing to the clubhouse, all lopsided, and I guess she blamed me for it, because she never came back for the lesson. In fact, I heard she gave up the game of golf.

SAM SNEAD'S COMMENT:
QUITTING ON THE HOLE

Think back to the number of times you've followed a sequence of poor shots with good ones; the number of times this has happened should surprise you. Now work to increase this pattern in your game. Eliminate "quits," develop a "staying" attitude, and your score will drop.

Be aware that missed tee shots are less critical than they seem; midirons, short irons, and the putter are your scoring weapons nearly 60 per cent of the time. Usually the percentage favors your chance to save a "lost" hole.

Imagine that par on a hole is one more stroke than the card shows; in this frame of mind, when you've landed your opening shot or shots in trouble, you'll be better able to stay in there and bail yourself out.

Don't fool yourself that you can form the "what-the-hell" attitude on some holes and play even average golf; the habit will wreck your game from stem to stern. Fight back against disaster, and the self-respect it brings is worth plenty in saved strokes thereafter.

Far more matches and tournaments are won by dogged

recoveries from trouble than by blowups when a golfer is in the lead.

Before folding on a hole, remember that more than one-fourth of the clubs in your bag were designed to help you escape trouble. The tools are there if you'll use them. Your pitching wedge, sand wedge, 8-iron, and 9-iron lead the list.

And don't "quit" because you're far ahead: play your hardest when you're sitting the prettiest—and stay that way.

It's a pleasure to relax or slough off a hole or two per round, but personally I can't afford it. Most of my wins have come from charging up from behind—by never quitting. Two examples:

After carding 73-75 opening rounds in the 1949 Masters, I was far back in the pack—then won on "closers" of 67-67. One bad hole would have killed me.

In the '52 All-American at Tam O'Shanter, a third-round 74 lost me the lead, put Tommy Bolt in front, and left me weeping in the rain. Man, that was a wet golf course. But then I played the final eighteen, hole by hole and bearing down every second, in 65, and took home George S. May's first money.

3

MORE TEE AND FAIRWAY TROUBLES

WHEN THEY TOLD US TO EAT DIVOTS • PICARD SAID:
"THIS CLUB MIGHT HELP YOU" • A BAREFOOT BRAWL
AT THE MASTERS: FOOTWORK • FLAT-OUT SWINGING
KEPT THOSE TIN CANS FILLED

Some of the things I didn't have to be taught as a rookie traveling pro were to keep close count of my nickels and dimes, stay away from whiskey, and never concede a putt. Where money is concerned, the saying I've always gone by is: "Put all your eggs in one basket, then watch the basket."

After a North Carolina tournament one year, the sponsors made a flowery talk about my winning it with a 12-under-par card, then wound up by presenting me with a giant trophy and a check for $2,000.

The crowd applauded and then I stood up and said, "It's a mighty pretty cup, and I thank you, but I can't accept this check. It isn't certified."

After a short pause, while the sponsors and gallery pulled themselves together, they made other arrangements on the purse end that were more suitable to me. They took that check downtown, had it certified, and we parted friends.

At least I felt friendly. After that, the sportswriters began to play me up as the money-hungriest pro who ever counted noses at an exhibition match to make sure the box-office payoff was correct, and some of the fans believed the story that I buried my winnings in tomato cans in my backyard because I didn't trust banks. That's OK with me, even if it isn't true.

49

One of the nicest bankers I ever dealt with once bet a set of automobile tires that he could beat me if I spotted him a stroke a hole and 2 shots on every par-5 hole.

After losing by a couple of strokes, the banker said, "Sam, it was a pleasure, and I'll have those four tires shipped to your home."

"Four?" I said. "Where I come from, a set of tires is *five*. I'd sure like to see that spare in there when those rubber dough-nuts arrive, if you don't mind."

The banker gulped, sputtered, and then shipped me five tires, along with a note saying I'd probably wind up owning the state of West Virginia. In my younger days I didn't see anything wrong with driving a hard bargain, and I don't now. When Boo-Boo Bulla and I were beating our way around the country-side in '36 and '37, we often were tapped out and didn't eat as well as the hoboes alongside the road. We could have starved to death for all any of the golf "lovers" and tournament spon-sors cared. Their attitude was that if circuit pros went broke— let 'em eat divots. Nobody invited us into the club for a free meal. Promoters put up skinflint purses of $2,500 and $3,000, for which 170 pros scrambled while their wives and kids were in need. Except for just a few winners, we got by on guts and a tight belt. Nobody thought it strange that Joe Louis earned $350,000 for one title fight against one man while Ralph Guldahl won just $1,000 for taking the '37 United States Open over a field of eighty of the world's finest shooters. Compared to Guldahl, Louis had a cinch.

The U. S. Open was a horrible example. It grossed $30,000 annually at the box office alone during the 1930s, yet it contin-ued to pay the winner only $1,000 until after World War II, when it went to $1,500. In 1938 it cost me $500 to travel to and play in the Open at Cherry Hills in Denver, where I won $60. The three big blue-ribbon shows of the late 30s were the National Open, the Western Open, and the Metropolitan Open, whose combined prize money was $11,500. A man sweeping all three—which would compare to a pitcher throwing three straight no-hit games—could collect the stupendous amount of $2,400. Except that after paying his way to and from the event, plus hotel, meals, caddie fees, and whatnot, he'd net about $1,000.

Those were the days when you could find an ex-pro in every poorhouse. In those days I'd stand over the boy at the gas station, making sure he wrung the last drop from the hose, and I washed my socks in three-dollar-a-day hotels.

I remember Ben Hogan standing outside the Claremont Country Club at Oakland, California, in 1938, beating his fists against a brick wall.

"What happened, boy?" we other young pros asked.

"I can't go another inch," groaned Ben. He was as close to tears as that tough little guy can get. "I'm finished. Some son of a bitch stole the tires off my car."

Not long before that, Ben had gone through a four-day seventy-two-hole tournament with nothing to eat but fifteen cents' worth of oranges—he was that poor—and then he came to Oakland in a junk-heap car with about $8 to his name. He couldn't afford a parking lot, so he left the heap in a vacant lot. When Ben returned, somebody had jacked it up and taken his tires.

"How bad can things get?" he asked me.

Some way or other Hogan lasted through the Oakland tournament, winning $380, which kept him alive. And with 99 per cent of the pros it was the same problem of hanging on by their thumbs and praying for a break. Byron Nelson and his wife, Louise, lived on next to nothing in those days, hocking whatever they owned so that Byron could buy clubs. None of us suspected that before long the country would go pro-golf-mad, that the cash awards in the P.G.A. would jump six times in size to $600,000 by 1946, to more than $1,100,000 in 1960, and head toward $2,000,000 in 1962.

Or that Hogan, Nelson, myself, and a few others would drive

golf scores from the 70s down into the 60s, which brought on the boom, and then would take the sponsors by the collar and say, "All right, boys, now pay us what we're worth."

Things were such then that a man had to be thrifty. All the pros cast about for a way to make an extra dollar. One of the schemes I came up with was to jump into the monkey-breeding business.

My monks came from Africa and were what they called "bush babies" down there—real cute, a male and a female. I could see them multiplying by the hundreds, figured I could sell them at fifty dollars per pair to zoos and pet stores, and get richer than I'd ever be in golf. First, though, they had to be smuggled through Customs in New York, in order to avoid the big import fee.

"You're playing with dynamite, Sam," said Boo-Boo Bulla. "They catch you, you'll go to the can for life."

"Well, it's just a risk I'll have to take."

At the airport unloading ramp, I put the monks inside my overcoat, and since it was warm in there they fell asleep after first giving me a good biting and chewing. I couldn't take any more of their teeth. So I half walked and half ran through Customs, and one of the officers stopped me.

"Nothing to declare," I said.

Just then the monks woke up and I quickly stuck my hand inside my coat and, when the monks began to twist and squirm, pretended to be scratching myself. The officer did a double take when I explained my moving overcoat by saying, "Fleas. Don't know where I picked them up traveling around, but they're all over me."

Before he could say anything, I was past him and he didn't whistle me back. By now I was perspiring hard and the bush babies were raking me with their claws and screeching, too. My coat was jumping; people were staring. The best thing I could think of was to head for a telephone booth. From a terminal redcap I got a small-goods box. Inside the booth I tried to transfer the monks from me to the box, but they broke loose and were all over the booth, one minute on top of my head, the next under my feet, and the three of us going round and round.

A crowd gathered to watch. A man can't look more foolish than when he's wrestling monkeys in a phone booth, and before it ended, people were hanging onto each other from laughing and I was bitten in twenty more places.

Once I had the monks boxed, there was still the problem of getting them down home to Virginia, where I planned to set up breeding operations; but first I was booked to play in the Masters Tournament at Augusta. After a train ride to Augusta, I smuggled the box past the desk clerk at the Hotel Richmond. After buying a five-foot-high birdcage, I set the bush babies up in style in my room, fed them mashed bananas, and then went out to play a practice round.

On returning that night, I found the room a wreck—curtains ripped down, pillow feathers flying, and the monks tearing around in circles. They'd picked the lock on their cage. The way they zipped around, there was no catching them, and when I did grab one, he sunk his teeth into me. After an hour of this, the hotel desk clerk phoned and rubbed salt into my wounds by saying, "If that party you're throwing in your room doesn't quiet down, we'll have to ask for your key."

About midnight Claude Hastings of the Wilson Sporting Goods Company walked in and found me standing on a chair, trying to pry a howling monk off the chandelier with a 9-iron.

"What the hell is this?" asked Claude. I explained, and he said, "Tomorrow you tee off in the biggest event of the year and look at you. No sleep. Your hands all bitten. Sam, what do you think this golf game is, anyway—a joke?"

"I'm gonna catch these little bastards and breed 'em if it takes all night!" I promised him.

With two other pros helping, we finally made it; then the

monks' noises kept me from sleeping, and next morning my score in the Masters was a fat 73. Each day the hotel desk was on my neck because of the noise. My room smelled terrible.

"That hillbilly," I heard a bellboy say to another, "doesn't know enough to ask for maid service." How could I let a maid in? She'd have found the monks.

Scoring 290, I finished seventh in the Masters, packed up my monks, and went home, where the first thing they did after being caged in my basement was to escape up the chimney. A woman down the valley had the wits scared out of her one night later when "a horrible hairy thing" peeked in her window. That was the last heard of them or of the Snead Monkey Farm.

Hastings was right: I had to take things more seriously. Earlier, this had been pointed out at the Los Angeles Open of 1937, where my driving became so hit or miss that I was embarrassed to stand out on Misery Hill, the practice tee, in front of the fans.

In the first place, although I was advertised as "The Slammer," driving wasn't the strongest part of my golf game by a long stretch. The pitching wedge was the club I used best. Next came my putting, then my long irons, and after that my ability to play from traps. Driving was the thing I did fifth best . . . and at times I spray-hooked balls all over the field.

Delivering the long ball is important, but if you can't place it safe from trouble on the fairway and in the best spot to open the green for your second shot, you can't call yourself a pro or even a good amateur.

From the experiments I've described earlier, I was sure that my grip wasn't causing the big right-to-left curve of my drives. The hook remained a mystery. Sometimes I was able to block out the hook by dropping my left elbow down a bit when coming through on the swing, but the results weren't consistent. Power swingers always have more trouble correcting driving faults than average players, since their turn is greater, their arc wider, and their clubhead speed faster.

As the hook grew worse, Boo-Boo Bulla decided it was time we rearranged our partnership. From the time we'd started touring together in the winter of 1936, we had an agreement to split our earnings, figuring that our combined "take" would keep us going longer than if we struck out strictly alone.

"We'd better call off our deal," said Boo-Boo. "You're not going to make any money with that hook and neither will I watching it."

I felt kind of hurt, but Bulla had every right to cancel the deal if his confidence in me was that low. Mine wasn't much better. And now we were in Los Angeles, which offered an unusually juicy pot—$8,000, with $2,500 to the winner. But if you didn't finish in the top eight, you collected $75, and from twelfth place on the payoff was $40 down to $25.

Just before the firing opened at the Griffith Park course in L.A., Henry Picard walked up and asked, "How are you hitting, Sam? I hear you are bending them halfway to Santa Monica."

"I'm so wild I've about decided to quit the tour and go on home."

Picard watched me whip out some drives and thought my feet might be the problem. He claimed I was spinning around while in the hitting zone onto my right toe, instead of moving more laterally into the ball on the inside of my right foot. Toning down foot action didn't help.

"Let's look at your driver," said Henry.

"I'll admit it doesn't feel right," I said, "but it worked for me in Virginia and in Florida and I don't like to change it."

"This stick is too whippy for you," said Henry. "Do you remember the photographer who tried to catch your swing at Hershey last fall?"

Thinking back, I remembered that Lambert Martin, one of the top cameramen of the New York *World-News*, had set up cameras aimed at catching all points of my swing. Martin "stopped" the action until we came to the point where my descending clubhead was 2 feet from the ball, and then all he got was a blur—even with the camera set at 1/1,250th of a second. Martin said it was the first time he'd been unable to stop a whole hitting sequence. Later they timed my clubhead speed at almost 150 mph.

"Your hands are too fast for such a light and swingy club," declared Henry. "I've got an Izett driver in my car that might be the answer for you."

The Izett felt like a dream the minute I took ahold of it. The first poke took my breath away. The ball traveled an easy 300 yards down the middle. I waved the caddie back further and further, and even when letting out full shaft, my driving improved about 35 per cent. "How much will you take for the club, Henry?" I asked.

The Izett was a true-tempered model, stiff-shafted, and a regular telephone pole in weight at more than fourteen-and-a-half ounces; the loft was a normal eight degrees and the length—forty-three inches—likewise. The shaft carried five ounces of the weight, and that was the great difference. George Izett, a top Philadelphia clubmaker, had built it.

"Try it in play, and if you like it, we'll make a deal," offered Picard.

Lighthorse Harry Cooper smashed par, the tournament record, and all opposition with a 69-70-69-66—274 to win the marbles at Los Angeles, but in my first West Coast showing the Izett enabled me to shoot 71-71-72-69—283, which was good for sixth place and $400. Bulla cost himself $200 by canceling our deal, for with a 299 score he finished out of the money. One week later, with the hook under fair control, I won the Oakland Open, then the Crosby Invitational, as mentioned in the last chapter. Rain washed out all but one round of the Crosby, so that over five rounds in the two competitions my scores read 69-65-69-67-68.

I'd have paid Picard any part of the purses I'd won—$400 at

L.A., $1,200 at Oakland, and $762.50 in the Crosby—for that driver. And Henry had every reason to stick me for plenty, having finished a few shots behind me in the latter two events.

"That'll cost you just five-fifty," said Picard, "which is what I paid for the club."

That act of generosity by the Hershey Hurricane could never be repaid, because that No. 1 wood was the single greatest discovery I ever made in golf and put me on the road to happy times. It proved that with the full coil of my body and the strong forward thrust of the right foot which went with my wrist snap at impact with the ball I naturally accelerated the club faster than I could control any ordinary driver. The increased drag of a heavier, stiffer shaft and clubhead compensated for my speed. It harnessed me to just the right degree.

The popular story that I slept with the Picard driver and never let any man swing it is only half true: only the last half of that statement is a fact. It's also a fact that until two years ago, twenty-three years later, I was still pulling it from the bag—at least, what was left of it. Most of my major titles have been won with that big blaster: three P.G.A. championships; the British, Argentine, and Brazilian Opens; three Canadian Opens; the All-Americans; the Tam O'Shanter "World"; the Nassau and Panama Opens; the Tournament of Champions—along with three Masters Tournament titles and a string of Ryder Cup wins.

At the close of 1961, my lifetime record stood at 110 tournaments won and about $400,000 collected, which they say is the world record, and I'd estimate that I used the Picard driver while accumulating three-fourths of those totals.

Once, in San Francisco, when my back was turned, a local pro drove off the tee with the club. I all but blasted him off the course when I found it out. That's how I felt about that stick.

When it broke, I fixed it and never turned to another wood.

At Sequoiah, California, years ago, the head flew off, sailed down the fairway, and I let out a howl like a hurt wolf and ran all the way after it while the gallery roared. At St. Paul the club broke off at the binding close to the head and I didn't hit a satisfactory shot until it was repaired. That five-fifty stick was good for maybe a million drives in every kind of weather, even though as the years went by the club face became eaten out toward the toe and the experts claimed it was finished.

"That'll be the day," I told them. New inlays were inserted and it behaved as well as ever. This went on until the inserts composed almost a new face. But, no matter what happened, I never thought of the club as changed. Unlike any club I've ever owned, it gave me a feeling of confidence just to pick it up.

The exact Wilson Company duplicate of the original which I use today gives results, but in the 1959 Greensboro Open, when I was sniping the ball deep right because of getting my hands too flat, or laid over, at the top of the backswing and then rushing the downswing, I brought the Picard out of retirement. And I played seventy holes without missing a fairway.

Hooking has returned to bother me more than once since 1937, but generally the Picard wood saved me the trouble of changing my whole style in order to counteract the hook. It proved one key point in golf to me: find the driving tool that's best suited to your size, reach, and swing; then stay with it.

After that, the lessons that took me from the crude stage and smoothed me out came thick and fast.

Returning to the Masters Tournament—this time without monkeys to slow me up—I was chatting with Bill Boni of Associated Press and other sportswriters when Freddie Corcoran came along. The Cork was always giving me fatherly advice and promoting Sam Snead with the press, until finally—when I had built up enough reputation—he took over management of my bookings and advertising testimonials.

"You scribes don't know how versatile Sam is," bragged Corcoran. "Why, he could throw away his spiked shoes and beat this field in his bare feet."

"Yeah?" said Boni. The other writers snickered, too.

"Go ahead, Sam," urged Corcoran. "Show 'em how you used to murder par in your bare dogs down home in the hills."

Somehow it didn't seem quite the wise thing to do at a dignified affair like Bob Jones' Masters, but the newspapermen acted like I was afraid of falling on my face, so out we went to the first tee, where I kicked off shoes and socks, rolled up my slacks, and squirmed my toes around in the soft grass. I said, "This sure feels great. Just like the old days. Maybe they ought to outlaw shoes in golf so that people can really get the feel of it."

By now I'd drawn quite a crowd. The next day a couple of shoe manufacturers who signed up golfers for endorsements passed the word that I ought to be shot.

Teeing off on the par-4, 400-yard first hole, I belted one out of sight. My 7-iron second went 120 yards, stopping 3 feet from the flag. "I'm telling you the truth," I said. "I feel better when I'm standing up to the ball in bare feet. Those thick-soled shoes keep you too far off the ground. I haven't been as close to hole in two shots as this in the last three years."

The putt was a plunker all the way. It cruised right in there for a birdie 3.

Everybody cheered and I birdied another hole and went on to card a round of 68 on a course where 72 or 73 was a respectable score any day.

But when I came in, Gene Sarazen, the Square Squire from Connecticut who'd won every title in golf and won it again, was waiting on the club steps—and Sarazen and other Masters old-timers were boiling.

"Whose corn-plaster stunt was this?" hollered Sarazen. "What are you trying to play around here, Snead—Huckleberry Finn? What we need these days are real 'masters' and not barefoot hillbillies. Can you imagine Walter Hagen or Henry Cotton playing barefoot on this course?"

"Listen, Sarazen," came back Corcoran, "Snead can stand on his record. I'll match him barefoot against you for any amount of money."

That sent the Squire right up on his tiptoes. "*His* record! Why, I've won all the big tournaments, including this one, which he hasn't, and I won them wearing shoes—not kilts or cowboy chaps or a Boy Scout uniform. Let Snead win something with shoes on before he tries grandstand stunts!"

He was so right about one part of it—Sarazen had a pair of U. S. Opens, a Masters, three P.G.A.'s, and the British Open to his credit, while at the time my tally was zero in these events— that I stood there red in the face, trying to pretend my feet weren't naked. "Heck, Gene," I broke in, "I only wanted to see how good the grass felt."

"*Mr.* Gene Sarazen to you!" he snapped, giving me a look like a flash of lightning through a gooseberry patch.

Such a hullabaloo followed that my name got to be known just about everywhere. The papers quoted Mayor Angelo Rossi of San Francisco as saying, "If I could break 100 by doing it, I'd throw away my shoes tomorrow." Bill Corum wrote in the New York *Journal*: "Wild Man Walter Hagen not play barefoot? Hagen would play in a bathing suit if the mood struck him. Sarazen would, too, if he thought it'd help win. Gene should be the last to squawk—all golfers remember his weird proposal to enlarge the cups to eight inches."

Some critics sided with Sarazen. They wondered if I was even housebroken. But the California Golf Writers Association made me an honorary member—"for putting the game back on its feet."

From then on, Sarazen needled me in print whenever possible, once remarking that if it wasn't for golf, I'd be back shining shoes in Hot Springs, Virginia.

Jimmy Demaret answered that one. "Heck," he told the newspapers, "if it wasn't for golf, Sarazen would be back on a banana boat between Naples and Sicily."

While this debate went on, the barefoot experiment caused me to think more and more about the part the feet play in the full golf swing. The hands are important because they're the only part of the body attached to the club. But the feet are still more important, being your only connection with the ground. Swinging within myself was one of the most difficult acts I had to discipline myself to do. Like most other golfers, I often fought a losing battle with the urge to overpower my tee and fairway shots, and most of my overswinging started in my upper body, in the arms, shoulders, and back muscles. When that happened, I was no longer a "wheel," with my head the solid hub around which the arms operated as spokes. My feet were unable to stay firmly planted, my sense of balance was lost, and I fell out of my swinging groove. Wildness had to result.

The difference between swinging hard and overswinging was a big one for me. At 100 per cent of power, hitches appeared in the transference of weight from left to right and back again. The only time I dared hit flat out—with everything I had—came on the unusual occasions when I felt perfectly balanced and my timing was exact. Experimenting again with shoes off, I found that I naturally cut down until I was using just the right medium of swing, or about 85 or 90 per cent of full power, without thinking twice about it. The reason was that a man won't overswing if he doesn't have spikes gripping the turf for him. Barefoot, your nerves are exposed to the ground. You're able to "feel" balance, to judge how big a turn and windup is possible without disturbing the leverage of your body. You get that shade of restraint that counts.

Replacing the shoes, I found that now I was swinging no harder than when barefoot—not trying for more than I could handle. Yet I had a good arm and body flow at close to maximum effort.

Naturally, this experiment wasn't done in public. My Masters experience was enough to last a lifetime.

Watching the best players, I decided that footwork is the basis of hand action—rather than the other way around—and that the pivot called the shot all the way; it was the key to everything I did on the tee. Experts talked about swinging the clubhead, but they put the cart before the horse. Although a good pivot includes hip, leg, and shoulder movement, it must start and finish with the feet. When the pros I played against lost their driving touch, in 98 per cent of the cases the fault traced to the one place they didn't consider—their feet. Even a veteran pro takes them for granted after a while.

We were in Florida, for instance, and Toney Penna, a tough, experienced star player, suddenly went wild and began scoring in the middle 70's. He couldn't understand it; neither could his friends. Since we were competing for purses, I didn't tell Toney what I'd noticed. Not until he said one day, "Come on, Sam, everybody else has had a crack at me. What am I doing wrong?"

"You've always had a beautiful swing and a nice follow-through and you still do have," I said. "Your trouble's in your pivot."

Penna wouldn't believe it. He was positive the fault was hidden somewhere in his grip, or at the top of the arc, or in the wrist-whip he took going through the ball.

"Sure, it might look that way, but try this: just get away from your hands and arms and hips and try taking the club back with your feet."

"How the hell can I do that?" snorted Penna.

"I mean just direct your mind to making your feet control everything, from the backswing to the finish. Make yourself feel you're hitting with your feet directing things. Forget everything else."

Penna concentrated so hard that he broke out in a sweat; then he saw it—or, rather, felt it. His feet had been working one way, his swing another. Penna's particular trouble was that he was shifting his weight from the left foot to the right a bit early, causing him to move off the ball in a slight sway. Once he coordinated everything, Toney shot a 67 round and began winning money again.

"I never thought the feet meant so much," he admitted.

This was one of the hottest tips I picked up, purely by observation: that the greatest players failed to check on foot faults that
could creep in. I saw dozens of them overreaching without sus-
pecting it. This is the common fault of raising the left heel too
high at the widest point of the pivot, disturbing your balance.
Harry Cooper, one of the cleanest, straightest hitters of all time,
made sure that his heel didn't leave the ground more than an
inch when he was poised to strike. Coming through, Cooper
always hit against a very solid left side because his heel was
trapped, ready to snap exactly back in the position from which
it had been only slightly lifted. The sooner that heel gets back
to earth on the downswing, the better the right side can move
into the stroke.

After Bob Jones made the first of his Hollywood films, he
didn't believe what he saw on the screen. He was coming up on
his toes in the hitting zone. Bob had to scrap the film and
remake it.

Course strategy and tactics, I found, depend on an honest
knowledge of what you are able and not able to do. In the
National Open of 1937, where I finished second by a couple
of strokes (and more on this performance later), one tee shot
set the pattern for my way of attacking a golf layout in future
years. While I was playing with Johnny Goodman, the situation
began building up on the second hole at Oakland Hills in
Michigan.

On No. 2, a 512-yarder, 2 big wallops put me hole high just
off the green. Then I duffed the third shot, almost whiffed
entirely on the fourth and took a 6 on the hole. On the 447-yard
fourth I staggered all the way—missing my drive, missing my
second shot, half missing the third and fourth, and only salvag-
ing a par 5 by holing a 30-foot putt. Now I was 2 over par.

"In four holes I've missed six shots," I moaned to Goodman.
"I ought to walk off this field right now."

"Hang on, Sam," said Johnny.

At that point—of the first U. S. Open of my life—the gallery was betting I wouldn't break 80 and Grantland Rice, who was in the gallery, later wrote that he didn't see a chance for me to break 75.

Pretty soon we came to a 220-yard par 3 with about 15 yards of green to aim for and traps galore and a wind blowing left to right. The other pros had been hitting a conservative 4-wood here. The gallery let out a gasp when I reached for the 2-iron. It was a gamble, but I'd found that against the wind, by keeping the ball low, a 2-iron often will outweigh a No. 4 wood.

I'd seen others play into a left-to-right wind by driving to the left, with the idea of letting the wind swing the ball back to the middle of the fairway. Far as I could see, it only aggravated the condition. My idea was to play for a slight draw—aiming down the right side and bringing the ball back left as a controlled hook. (In the comment portion of this chapter, I'll explain the advantages of the draw shot.)

My long iron stayed low because I used no tee and kept my hands well ahead of the clubhead right through the impact, which with backspin stopped the ball 25 feet from the pin. I holed out for a birdie 2.

The second shot on the next hole called for another long iron to an elevated green, with traps beyond the pin, and this time the ball finished in position for an easy birdie putt. But the 2-iron drive on the previous holes was the one that got me started and settled me down for a comeback score of 35 on the front nine after my bad start. My back nine score was 34, for a 69 total that tied the competitive course record and left Grant Rice very puzzled.

"You looked like a fighter who'd been all but knocked out in the opening holes," said Rice, "and then everything changed. You go after a golf course like you hated it."

"I was playing safe at the start," I replied, "and for me that's the worst mistake of all."

Rice listened and took many notes as I explained how a 225-

yard drive down the middle into a nice, easy lie wasn't good enough for me. I powdered them hard and into possible trouble because the percentage was with me. "I'd rather play a wedge second shot out of rough than a 5-iron from the fairway if I gain 40 or 50 yards by doing it. Lots of pros will get 2 under par after a few early holes, then protect their score by being cautious. I believe in building on any lead I get, early or late. If you play safe, you make bogeys because you start to steer the ball and wind up pushing or cutting or pulling it.

"Many times I've played safe off the tee with a 3- or 4-wood and regretted not using the full driver. On par-4 and -5 holes I'm always looking for the birdies and the way to get them is to turn on the extra power and keep it on. Then I may have not a wood shot to the green for a second shot but an iron shot that gives me more control and accurate placement."

"Whether you believe it or not," replied Rice, "you're going directly against the book. Golf is a position game, a matter of picking your spots for the gambling shot. You'll also wear your-self out with this sort of wham-bam game. You must pace your-self. But I can see you're a stubborn young dog and will go your own way."

That I did, despite horrified sounds from those who watched me take what they called the broadest, freest sweep ever seen. To me, playing terrain had to come second to reducing distance from tee to pin with the opening shot. At times my method kicked back and let weaker golfers beat me out of purses. But the duels I entered into with Ben Hogan, later on, were all the proof anyone would need that the controlled tee shot never will offset the distance drive. After World War II, Hogan, whose low hooking was driving him wild, developed a fade, or trained slice, which was valuable in getting the ball up and stopping it smartly where he wanted it on hard fairways such as you find in the P.G.A. and U. S. Open championships. At the 1949 Masters Tournament, Hogan was fading them in practice while playing with Henry Picard. The day before, on the par-5 No. 13 and No. 15 holes, Picard had seen me reach the green in 2 strokes, hitting hard and straightaway.

"Ben, you'll have trouble beating Sam, because you're giving away too much distance," warned Picard. "He'll be on in two against your three on the par fives, and over four rounds you can't spot him that much."

Hogan disagreed. And he finished down a ways while I won my first Masters with 8 birdies, 7 pars, 3 bogeys, and a 67 score in the closing round—chiefly by risking trouble on dogleg corners by flying my drives over the trees and gambling that I could carry mid-fairway traps.

From then on, when playing against me, Hogan usually drove straightaway or with a little draw to the ball. I always thought that Ben was a greater golfer on days when he let himself go off the tee with a draw at the tail end.

Along that same line of thinking, in the 1947 U. S. Open at St. Louis when my driver was misbehaving, I left it in the locker and used a brassie, or 2-wood. It worked well enough for one round of 72 and three rounds of 70, forcing a play-off with Lew (The Chin) Worsham, a long hitter. Normally, I'd outdrive Chin. But my brassie, with its extra loft and whippiness, played tricks all day, sending the ball high into the wind and to the right when the course contours were all to the left, landing it in rough or off line on the sixth, tenth, eleventh, thirteenth, fifteenth, and seventeenth holes. Worsham consistently outdrove me. And in a neck-and-neck finish he won the Open by 69 shots to my 70.

In Hollywood, where in recent years I've performed in a "Celebrity Golf" television series, it sticks out like a sore thumb that most of the star athletes amongst the movie stars are afraid to crank up and hit hard. They're big, strong boys who seem to be overconscious of their size and lack zip going through the ball. Randolph Scott could add 20 to 30 yards to his drives if he'd put his long body and weight into swinging. Big Fred Mac-

Murray has a nice backswing, not much punch. A man as huge as Johnny Weissmuller should knock them into the next canyon, but Tarzan has only a three-quarter backswing, defeating his own purpose.

"If you had a nice, full backswing," I told him, "you'd pick up another 50 yards. Think what that would mean. When a man can play a 7-iron for his second shot instead of a 4-iron, it makes a heck of a difference."

"I'd rather keep the ball in play," argued Johnny.

"Well, you'll lose in the long run," I said. "There's ninety ways to get out of the rough after a long drive, but no way at all to pick up those yards you've lost by hitting them soft."

It's also a great lift, from the mental standpoint, to open a match by forcing the other man to swing from behind you after the opening shot. In my earliest days as an unknown player I hooked up with Leonard Dodson, who was rated a boomer from Boomerville on the tee. On the first hole Dodson's drive was well short of mine.

"What happened?" he said, surprised.

"I hit a rock and it bounced on down," I said.

Next hole, the same thing happened. Dodson couldn't understand it, and I said, "I hit a rock."

On No. 3 he was 40 yards short again, and when I gave him the same answer, he ran up, grabbed my arm, and yelled, "Listen, it seems to me you're hitting *a hell of a lot of rocks today!*" He thought maybe I was kicking my ball ahead; when he learned the truth, Dodson sagged a bit and I beat him easily.

From the fairway, one of the most helpful wood-shot lessons of my youth was to put some caution into my pretty much wide-open game. The fairway wood is one of the toughest of all shots. When tempted to use a brassie or spoon from a lie that wasn't favorable, I ruled against myself and sacrificed distance by using a 4-wood or an iron. Very few average players and not many pros have the power and hand action to consistently get the ball up from a sunken lie with a brassie or 3-wood. Offhand, I'd say

Jimmy Demaret and Lawson Little have been the only surefire shotmakers in this category. In any cuppy position, a driving iron, 2-iron, or 4-wood was my selection . . . even at the cost of 10 or 15 yards.

Once I had a few driving secrets planted in my head, the boys on the tour noticed that, after being on the shy side, I was becoming more outspoken. A favorite joke of some of the other pros was that I was early-to-bed and didn't smoke or drink. I saw more than a few pros floating around barrooms at night, trying to kiss the bartender good night because they couldn't tell him from their girl friends, and I wanted no part of that. There was one famous pro who could put an interlocking grip on a bottle that nobody could break and who was irritated that I wouldn't be a party boy. He kept insisting that I join him in whooping it up. Naturally, he wanted to see me fried, so that next day I'd see spiders and snakes where my ball ought to be. He grabbed me at a hotel elevator one night when I was heading for bed.

"No, thanks," I said.

"You know what we call you?" he sneered. "You're so tight you squeak. You're old curfew-legs; all your joints close at ten o'clock."

For a second I thought of popping him on the chin, but then I reached in my pocket and pulled out all the cash I had —$500.

"Tell you what," I said. "I'll just lay you this amount that in the tournament tomorrow my score will beat yours."

"I couldn't be bothered," he muttered.

"I'll even spot you one stroke," I said, speaking so that his pals nearby could hear every word. "Those last six whiskey sours you had are worth that, easy."

"Ahhh, the hell with you," he said, hanging his head and shuffling away. Having been called, and been found wanting in guts, this dude never bothered me again.

And then I played in the North-South Open at Pinehurst,

North Carolina, and discovered that too much cocky talk can boomerang and that I wasn't as smart on the tee as I believed. By averaging 69 shots per round for fifty-four holes, I got rid of hard competition from Hogan, Nelson, Lloyd Mangrum, and Little. Sleeping on a lead isn't easy, but the last night at Pinehurst the boys could hear me snoring. No one was closer to me than that big old Carolina boy, Clayton Heafner, when the two of us reached the short seventeenth hole of the final round. With two holes to play, Heafner was 2 down. That made me feel pretty sure and sassy.

Heafner didn't even blink when my tee shot hit and rolled to 10 feet of the cup. Being sure I'd jolted him, I decided to shake him up some more.

"All right, Heafner," I said, good and loud, "let's see you match *that* one."

His eyes narrowed to slits and, without saying a word, he clipped one that split the green, bounded up, hit the cup, and stopped within an inch of going in. It was me who let out a "Yipe!" By just that tiny margin he missed wiping out my 2-stroke lead. His shot gave me such a shock that I missed my putt by a mile.

Now only 1 up, I had to scramble to win the North and South on the last hole.

The rule with me after that was never to stir up the animals. A shut face on the tee hurts you. A shut mouth is worth money.

SAM SNEAD'S COMMENT:
ADVANCED TEE AND FAIRWAY PLAY

I believe in giving the ball some sweet talk on the tee. Driving is about 75 per cent mental, and if your state of mind is out of kilter, ten thousand lessons and a team of mules won't help you. The idea is to have an even, automatic swing, the kind you don't have to think about. If your swing varies considerably from day to day, you'll try to even things up by thinking, and at that point you're more juggler than golfer. To remind yourself of six or seven things you "must do" will mess you up. So I take a firm grip on myself and hold my thinking to never more than one idea when I address the ball.

There's at least two ways to make the mind behave:

TALK TO THE BALL

"This isn't going to hurt a bit," I tell the ball under my breath. "Sambo is just going to give you a nice little ride." Or I might say, "Hello, dimples, I see you're sitting up fat and ready; let's us have some fun." Under heavy pressure, I've told a ball, "Let's win this hole for Jackie." (Jackie is my teen-age son.) By acting as if the ball's human, I distract myself—leaving no time for thoughts of this and that. Sometimes the ball looks back at me and seems to say, "OK, Sam, but treat me gentle." That's a ball that's friendly, the kind that will go for you.

You've seen baseball pitchers rub a new ball, then toss it back to the umpire. They're looking for the friendly kind of ball that throws strikes. Get chummy with your golf ball if you want pars and birdies.

GIVE YOURSELF A SINGLE "KEY"

The power of suggestion (that you'll fail) also can be beaten if you form one mental picture of what you want to do, forget the rest. Johnny Farrell thought only of his feet: of getting a smooth pivot started. Arnold Palmer thinks only of hitting along the line he's picked to the hole, drawing the line with his eye. Byron Nelson tried to see the clubhead flatten out at impact. My own keys depend upon how I'm going.

If I'm hooking, my only thought is to lock my left shoulder along the line to the flag. When I'm not hooking, my key is swinging within myself, at about 85 per cent power.

TEE AND FAIRWAY CLUBS

The man who can't feel his woods is worse off than a tomcat on a log. Finding the driver and fairway clubs that suit you isn't easy. The average golfer doesn't know what kind of a driver he should use—and neither did I in 1937, until Henry Picard straightened me out. Many people mistakenly order the same clubs I swing, and that's a mistake. The shaft of my driver is OK for some others, but the head is too heavy for most. The Sam Snead model, fitted to the size, age, and style of the player, is what they should buy. Furthermore, I see many fast, hard swingers who use a limber-shafted driver, which sounds good when they whip it but which gives them little control. Then there's the man who swings very easy and lackadaisical and just tries to fan the ball out who uses a big old stiff shaft that gives him no help. The first man needs a fourteen-ounce or more stick with little shaft flex; the other wants a very flexible shaft to give him more head speed.

Handmade clubs aren't worth the extra cost. Pro shop clubs of reputable make when fitted to you will do the job. Skimp by buying cheap clubs and you'll never learn the game. Remember that clubhead weight should be in proportion to the flex of the shaft: a stiff, heavy shaft needs more weight in the head or it'll lack feel of the head during the swing. The lighter, more flexible the shaft, the less weight needed in the clubhead.

The theory that a short man should use a short driver and the tall man a long club is just the opposite of the fact of the matter. Bobby Cruickshank, only five feet three inches tall, used a forty-four-inch shaft. Medium-sized Chick Evans swung a fifty-inch driver (my own is forty-three inches and I'm five feet eleven inches and have weighed 180 to 190 during my prime).

As men reach middle age, their nerves multiply and they get more anxious. Instead of thinking more clearly, as you'd expect veterans to do, they make more errors. So they begin to play beneath themselves. To counter this, they need more distance off the tee, and this can be accomplished by using longer wooden clubs and irons. These shouldn't be treated as such, with allowance for their length in swinging, but just as any other club. Practice will make you familiar with them.

At my present age (fifty on May 27, 1962), my turn isn't quite as full as it once was: some of the elasticity of the body muscles has slipped. Now I use a 1½-wood off the tee. This is a regulation deep-faced driver, but with added loft to the face. It gives me that little added help. It's safer than the tricky driver. I find the brassie too shallow-faced on the tee and recommend the 1½-wood to my own pupils, especially those troubled with getting the ball up.

BALANCE

Once, when I played with President Ike Eisenhower at White Sulphur Springs, he remarked that his restricted backswing was causing him to lose sleep. "They keep telling me to turn, turn," said Ike, "if I want more distance off the tee."

I said nothing, and when we finished, Ike asked, "What do you think?"

"Stick your butt out more, Mr. President," I said.

Some of Ike's bodyguards were shocked, but he only blinked.

"I thought it *was* out," he said.

Well, it wasn't—not enough, anyway. The big hitting muscles are located in the back of the legs, shoulders, and in the middle back, and that's one reason your weight shouldn't be forward on the balls of your feet or toes but back through the heels. When these muscles are in full play, your rear end sticks out. Another reason is that the force of the downswing may pull the body forward, throwing the clubhead into a shank or scuff position. Ike wasn't settled back enough where he could dig in with good balance. His turn was on the short side, but some of the reason for that showed up when I spoke to his doctor. I mentioned that Ike wore glasses with small lenses, so that to keep his eyes on the ball he was forced to reduce his turn. Shifting his weight back a little and wearing larger lenses helped Ike later—or so I was told.

Stepping, rocking, and swaying all are caused by an off-balance stance. Hoagy Carmichael played "Celebrity Golf" with me, and I said, "You're taking a left step forward at the address; then on your forward press you're stepping back with the right foot." Hoagy said he wasn't. At a running of the TV film he was proved wrong. It astonished him, for he thought balance was one problem he'd licked. He was an example of a golfer who can't believe what you're telling him because he doesn't feel like he's doing a specific thing wrong. You must prove it to him.

Footwork, balance, is everything to me because of my life-long theory (and Ben Hogan agreed) that the more you minimize hand, wrist, and arm action, the better. I believe the body pivot launched by the feet is the *big* factor. Many golfers get too much wrist leverage into their shots, where I have as little as possible. If your pivot is good, a gradual speeding up of the clubhead as it nears the hitting area will follow without any forehand wham or rushing of the shot with the arms.

If the head and body stay behind the ball and the hips don't move in there too far and waste power before contact, you are set up to knock the cover off it. One of the ways I get distance is in the way my knees bend into position on the downswing.

And the knees can't put you into a power-hitting position unless the feet are working for you.

1) It's automatic with me that, in taking my stance, slightly more weight is placed on the right foot than the left and I feel an easy sort of looseness from the bottom of the foot clear up to my hip socket. I'm relaxed with no chance of a hip lock.

2) I'm in a slightly closed stance—about ten degrees on tee shots; the closed stance gives me more traction than any other.

THE HEAD

I used to watch Walter Hagen and Bob Jones tilt their heads an inch or so to the right before starting the backswing, and I saw why. They knew there had to be a small rotation of the head on the turn and wanted to be sure they were in a favorable fixed position before getting the clubhead under way. The old idea of gluing the eyes on the ball has caused much trouble, because if you freeze your head in one spot, the neck is tensed and shoulder turn is hampered. Even after turning the chin slightly, Hagen and Jones gave the head some freedom. My head rotates right a bit on the take-away from an original position slightly behind the ball. But it does no bobbing. Almost as important, on the follow-through my head does no turning until the club is three-fourths through the swing.

SHOULDER TURN

Byron Nelson, when I first saw him, shanked a lot, or hooked. He found he was bringing the club back too close to his body. I've seen other pros who were "all arms" on the backswing. I've been guilty of picking up the club with my hands and forearms, too.

If your feet roll your weight to the right side easily, your hips turn, and your shoulders will follow. Don't ever separate the action of hands-arms and shoulders. It's easy to do without realizing it: one pro often has to be told by another that he's dividing what should be a combined movement. Hands and shoulders must work together, but the shoulders take the lead.

Any time my backswing is off, I know it needs slowing down. "Draw the bead easy, boy," I tell myself, "or there won't be turkey dinner tonight." If the shoulders don't rush, my arms usually take the hint.

If I worked hard on anything as a youngster, it was to coil far back and carry my hands very high on top so as to get all the benefit of a long reach—but then to wait on the ball. Just knowing that a small wait was coming slowed me down all through the back turn.

AT THE TOP

With me, the most common cause of turning loose the club at the top of the back arc was taking too tight a grip at the start. When I got up there too tight, I was apt to relax, because I couldn't maintain such pressure all the way through. When a person takes a nice light grip, with the left hand the firmer—just strong enough so that the fingers don't part—he's able to maintain equal pressure at the top. When you weaken grip up there, all the troubles start: you regrab coming down and the shot is lost.

DOWNSWING AND THE SMASH

This is the part I like best. The left hip, with the right immediately joining it, leads me into the downswing. I want the force which begins building at my feet and then is generated by the whole body to pass through my arms and hands to the ball. So as soon as the unwinding begins, I go into a forward thrust—a drive into the ball—off my right leg. With my right elbow riding toward the right hip, the arm on this side is relaxed until I'm well into the downswing. The left side is taut, guiding the club and dominating things until both hands are below belt level.

During this, my right knee turns in toward the direction I'm hitting, and this action is very important. As the knee comes in fast, it helps release all the hitting muscles of the right side—especially giving me strong hip thrust forward.

At impact, my right heel is coming off the ground and the inside sole is pushing against the resistance of the left leg, which has straightened and braces my thrust, or weight shift. The right foot, digging in, gives me that bit of extra power that means yards of carry. The force thrown against the left foot may cause it to roll over, but with the heel dug in firmly it takes the pressure.

Notice I'm *digging in*—drawing all the help from the ground that I can—all the way down and through the ball. That's one

more reason why feet make a swing more than any other part
of the body.

I get maximum clubhead speed at impact the usual way:
by uncocking the wrists as late as possible and turning loose
right-hand power. But there's a bit more to it than that. At
contact I want both left and right sides of my body fully extended, as well as my arms. Extended, they give me full power
both at the ball and during the next split second—when the ball
is flattened against the clubface and rides with it. The longer
and stronger you can weld clubface and ball together, the
farther it'll travel.

If my left-side muscles don't feel "used up" in a flat-out
swing—if my left arm isn't straight all the way through—then
I'm wasting power. The right side I don't worry about; it hits
hell out of the ball naturally.

TEE AND FAIRWAY TACTICS I USE

In a big match with Arnold Palmer at Providence, Rhode
Island, in 1960, it was a seesaw battle to the fifteenth hole,
where I was 1 up. Right there a pair of fairway shots decided
the match.

The hole is 510 yards, 5 par, with a slightly elevated green
trapped right, left, and rearward. The doorway to the green
wouldn't accommodate two skinny men abreast.

Our second shots were long 3-irons. It looked to me like
only a close-to-perfect shot would reach that green, and you
don't get that kind more than once out of three tries. Also,
since Palmer trailed, I figured he might gamble. With a 3-iron
it's easy to push the shot right—and this hole sprouted heavy
rough and trees to the right. That gave me three reasons just to
lay it up there to the doorway, short, which I did. Palmer went
for the flag and flew right, leaving himself an impossible angle
to the green. In the end, that settled the match in my favor,
67 shots to Palmer's 68.

On tight fairways, 40 or 50 yards wide, you don't shoot down
them; you work them. Hitting straightaway, you have only half
a fairway, 20 or 25 yards, as a margin of error between you and

the trouble that's usually waiting both right and left. If the worst trouble is right, I'll aim down the safer left side, fading the ball back toward the center. If the trouble is left, the draw is the thing. Either way, you've left yourself the full width of the fairway for working the ball.

The draw shot has won big for me, since it fits my natural tendency to hook and is a great weapon on sharp right-to-left dogleg holes and into the wind. A ball purposely drawn from right to left will hold its line until late in flight and bores into the wind, while a fade may go yards off course and lacks distance. Drawing, I also swing easier—and relaxing is everything.

A single draw in the rich Goodall Round Robin at Wykagyl Country Club helped me to the winner's portion of a $15,000 pot. The fourteenth hole doglegs left sharp enough to break your back. I put sidespin on the ball by first closing my stance— right foot withdrawn—a good four inches. I aimed down the right-hand fairway. Ball position was just inside the left heel. By withdrawing the rear, or right side, I made room for an exaggerated inside-out club arc. My front, or left side, was in the way, making it all the more sure my arms would have to go inside it. My grip was changed so that my left hand was in a stronger position toward the right side of the shaft, with the thumb and forefinger wrinkles aimed inside the right shoulder. Last of all, I "ironed out" the follow-through, with the left arm kept firm and unbroken as long as possible.

The shot followed the contours of the hole perfectly, setting up a chip and birdie putt that won the prize.

If all that isn't enough to steer the average golfer away from experimenting with intentional draws or fades or other manufactured shots, I'll say this:

Don't try them. Hit hard and with no tricks, until you are master of the ball.

TURNING ON THE STEAM

As long as a man doesn't take a death grip and lurch off balance, it's not bad practice for him to haul back and swing with most of what he has. Soft swingers don't prosper as much as hard swingers. For one thing, when you prepare to hit with steam, your muscles tune themselves to the coming effort. The golfer who tries holding back goes into too slow and mushy a backswing; then when he realizes that he's in no position to give the ball a ride, he rewinds and begins hitting before he's ready. If he's intent on hitting hard from the word go, that's all he thinks about. All those hot flashes that come with cushioning the blow are removed.

Even better than that, you don't get weak at the knees but go on the offensive. Getting tough is the only attitude that can save the fellow who can swing smoothly in his backyard but chokes up when the ball is teed and money is up.

Many a golf course and many a big gambler would have eaten me up if I hadn't eaten them first by having a mean frame of mind.

4

KEEPING THE SHIRT ON:

GOLFER, CURE THYSELF

HOT TIMES IN HOT SPRINGS • HOW TO STAY COOL-MAD
WHEN HEXED • BUILDING A THICK SKIN IN THE U.S.
OPEN • SPECTACLES I'VE MADE OF MYSELF • WHAT A
TEMPER CAN COST YOU

What with my sashays into the woods as a kid to hunt and trap when I should have been at school, there were some people around Ashwood and Hot Springs who said Sam Snead would grow up to be so ignorant that he couldn't drive nails into the snow. Playing hooky wasn't the worst of it. Walter Hodnut, the school principal, finally threw up both hands and came banging on my folks' door.

"I haven't seen Sam for a week," he said. "Where is he this time?"

"Soon as we get ahold of him," the family said, "we'll rope and tie him and send him back."

"Well, first turn the hose on him," said Hodnut. "The last time he came to class, he hid the rear end of a dead skunk behind the radiator. We're still fumigating."

Some of the skunks I caught were big bastards, weighing up to ten pounds, and using a knife to de-scent them so that they could be sold as pets wasn't the sort of work to make me popular. I put the smelliest part of one woods pussy back of the school radiator partly as a joke and partly because Hodnut and the teachers were beginning to get on my nerves. They claimed

79

they were lucky to have me come in and sit down at a desk once in a while. Or, on second thought, unlucky.

Books didn't strike me as interesting. I thought of myself as Weasel-Eye, the Dead-Shot, and the best thing in life was to go swinging through the umbrella trees on a fifty-foot wild vine, with an eye out for game. One time I was stalking grouse with my brother Jesse. I owned an old twin-barreled shotgun with a hammer action I'd filed down to blast off at the slightest touch. The saying around home was, "When Sam goes out with that gun, let him go alone. That way only one person gets killed."

Well, I almost did it. Crossing an ice pond, I skidded, sat down hard, and the scatter-gun went *ker-boom!*—scorching the hide and hair on one side of my head. If the tilt of that piece had been an inch more my way, there'd have been a burial.

The upshot of my trouble with Hodnut came during an out-door basketball game at school, where we seventh graders chose up sides and played on a cinder court. Hodnut was the referee. Every time I'd try to shoot, the other guys would grab my pants or shirt or trip me, and I spent more time skidding through the cinders on my face than on my feet. Finally, I lost my head, wound up, and socked the kid guarding me, knocking him chin over hind end.

"Get upstairs to my office!" hollered Hodnut. "You'll be punished for this."

"Why don't you referee the game right?" I came back.

"Don't you talk back to me!" said Hodnut.

"The hell I won't!" I said.

Hodnut, having all the weight advantage over a fourteen-year-old, collared me, and then the fur began to fly. Both of us wound up the fight with most of our buttons ripped off, our shirts in ribbons, and covered with welts. It was a draw, I guess, which left Hodnut only one choice.

I was expelled from school. My family raised hell with Hodnut for jumping me, but I was out in the cold, ineligible for sports (which hurt most) and faced with either apologizing and behaving in school or becoming just another woods tramp. For two weeks I thought about it. When I told Hodnut I was sorry, he made me study right through noon-hour recess until I'd caught up with my classwork.

After that I reformed enough to get fairly good grades and graduate into Valley High School, where I wasn't the worst student around.

Letting your temper take you over, I saw, was a mistake. At Valley High, my coach and teacher, Harold Bell, one of the finest men I ever knew and who now is superintendent of schools at Harrisonburg, Virginia, told me, "I've known men who could get mad enough to fight a rattlesnake and give it two bites to start, but they lost more battles than they won. When you give in to anger, you lose control. A man who stays *cool-mad* will beat you every time."

In golf, the trick of developing just the right mixture of heat and coolness in competition was one of the most difficult I had to learn. The game turns lots of pros and everyday players into club-throwing maniacs. There's hardly a locker-room door left in the country without dents in it, and the number of clubs thrown or smashed gets bigger all the time. The number of first-rate amateurs and promising young pros who've let their dander rise up and ruin their game is more than you can count. On the face of it, the calm, quiet player should have all the advantage.

This is so far from true that I'll make the statement that any golfer who misses a shot and starts whistling is one of the easiest guys in the world to beat.

You've got to have that fire, that thing in you that sometimes makes it absolutely necessary to relieve your feelings—the thing which made Eben (Ed) Byers and Jesse Sweetser two of the world's greatest amateur champs prior to Bob Jones's time. Byers, Sweetser, and Jones all filled the air with clubs. Bad shots drove them wild. Chick Evans was another who got red-necked, and in modern times Byron Nelson could pretzel a club or beat a bush to death with the best. When Doc Cary Middlecoff first joined the Grapefruit Circuit of the pros, he was described in a newspaper as "cheerful and placid of temperament"—until the Atlanta Open when Doc 3-putted and slung his club half a mile and howled like a hurt wolf. Tommy Bolt has become famous for his rages. I've gone through all this and been as guilty as the next man, so that I've formed some strong convictions on the subject.

Show me the fellow who walks along calmly after topping a drive or missing a kick-in putt, showing the world he's under perfect control, yet burning up inside, and I'll show you one who's going to lose. This boy is a fake. His nervous system won't take what he's handing it. If you bottle up anger entirely, it poisons your control centers.

But if you go all the way in the other direction, the practice of kicking tee markers, abusing shrubbery, and wrecking equipment can become such a habit that it also spoils your muscular reflexes. Mad golfers keep their blood boiling and agitated all the time for a reason. Deep down, they look forward to tearing their hair. Without knowing it, they get to hoping they'll butcher a shot. We're all show-offs at heart, and guys who break up locker rooms enjoy every minute of it.

Doctors and mind experts go around explaining that it's perfectly OK to explode on the course because it releases your built-up tensions. They don't tell you, though, how you can rave like a wild beast and break 90.

Good golfing temperament falls in between taking it with a grin or shrug and throwing a fit. I believe you should blow up, at times, if it helps, but only if you can still keep your wits about you. I couldn't beat any pro if I didn't get my temper outbreak over with fast, then start thinking out the next shot. It's like opening a steam valve for a moment, then shutting it. An old-timer in Scotland once said to me, "Make your game as stormproof as you can," by which he meant that when everything went wrong, I should be capable of producing my best shots, regardless of my frame of mind.

Which is about as easy, if you don't work at it, as scratching your ear with your elbow.

The first lesson I remember getting along this line came in 1935 when I was still an apprentice pro in Hot Springs, teaching fat ladies to swing around their girdles, and entered my first money tournament, the Virginia State Open at the old Dominion Course at Newport News. I drove there from "Hot" in an old jalopy that'd cost me eighty dollars, all duded up in an ice-cream-colored sweater, fawnskin pants, and two-toned shoes. Even the village idiot had more of a reputation than me, so it wasn't until the last round that anyone realized that I just might bust through with an upset win. Maybe two dozen people gathered around—the first gallery of my life that I could call my own.

Down near the green of the eighteenth hole I could see the figure of one man.

It was a par-4, the closing hole, and if I birdied it, first place could be mine. I wanted that state championship so bad I was panting.

My second shot, after a big drive, had to be a spoon bounced up onto the carpet, because the greens were too hard to hold a No. 1- or No. 2-wood approach. Coming down right on line, the ball looked like it might bounce in there for an eagle 2. Just then all the joy ran out of me. The man I'd seen took it into his head to dash across the fairway, and the ball, hitting his foot, ricocheted to the left side and back of a trap, stopping in trampled rough.

Everything went red. "I'll kill that S.O.B.!" I shouted. "Where is he?"

"Simmer down," the older players with me said. They had shots to play, too, and didn't appreciate my tantrum.

"Show me where he went," I went on, waving the spoon.

I couldn't turn loose of the idea of murdering the fan—who'd wisely kept right on running—even when I stood over the ball, and so, instead of one of those nice, neat nip-out recoveries, the club bit in too shallow and merely nudged it into a bunker filled with big, dry clinkers.

At some point in every outburst of anger, if it lasts long enough, you throw yourself into reverse gear. You get mad at everything rather than just the original cause. The clinkers set me to cussing again, and the explosion shot out was short, after which I went entirely to pieces and 3-putted. A possible 2 on the hole and a probable 3 became a 6, which dropped me to a fourth-place finish in the tournament, worth $150.

A week later I was still too hot about it to eat or sleep, and then a little voice whispered to me: *Even after that fool fan kicked your ball, 2 sensible shots could have given you a 4. Why didn't you get it?*

Duke Ridgley, who wrote the "Diamond Dust" sports column in the Huntington, West Virginia, *Herald-Dispatch* and who was the first newspaperman ever to mention me—he called me "Swingin' Sam" in 1936 and never went for that "Slammer" stuff of the other writers—did a piece not long afterward that showed how I was getting along in the disposition department and how folks down home saw me, generally:

"Sam's the damndest combination of naïve kid, hillbilly, shy but cocky competitor, money-grabber, cool pressure shooter and teeth-gnasher it has ever been my privilege to meet and know. Some days nothing flusters him. But when he lets his top blow, even the he-bears run for the hills."

By May of 1937, the golf writers were talking up a "black hoodoo" and an "unshakable jinx" that had followed me for months and which they feared would leave me so mad at the world that it'd ruin my game for life.

It started a year earlier when I showed up at Richmond, Virginia, anxious to qualify for my first National P.G.A. Championship.

"Is your golf affiliation in Virginia or West Virginia?" the people in charge wanted to know.

"Well, I'm Virginia-born," I said, "but I just moved across the line from Hot Springs last March 1 to work at The Greenbrier, so I guess it's West Virginia now."

"Then you can't qualify here. You're supposed to be teeing off right now in Pittsburgh, which is your proper P.G.A. district."

"Jumping Judas, why didn't somebody say so? Don't you ever send out notices?" I said.

They were sorry—but I was in the wrong pew. With no chance to reach Pittsburgh in time, all I could do was straggle on home.

By the early spring of 1937 I was snakebit all over. After a decent second-place showing in the Houston, Texas, Open, I lit out for the Thomasville, Georgia, Open, driving two days and nights almost nonstop, skipping sleep and arriving dead on my feet one morning at a sign that said "Thomasville—10 miles." A colored kid by the road looked surprised when I asked him how everything was in Georgia.

"Can't tell you that," he said, "but things is fine here in Thomasville. Best dang town in Alabama."

"Alabama!" I yelled. "How'd I get here?"

Some way or other, misreading a road map, I'd landed in the wrong Thomasville. When I turned around and finally reached the right Thomasville, I was so punchy that no good shots came from my clubs. Dick Metz and Ed Dudley tied for first place with 284s, with me far down the list at 292.

A few weeks later, at the North and South Open at Pinehurst, North Carolina, a 32-36—68 first round left me a single shot off the pace of Horton Smith and Densmore Shute. The second day, playing with Gene Sarazen and Paul Runyan, my threesome found itself without an official scorer at the first tee. Being eager to have people like me, I volunteered for the job.

My round of 74 was good for third place at the halfway mark.

Just as we finished the eighteenth, a boy came running up to collect the scorecards I'd kept for the three of us.

"Wait, I haven't checked them over," I said. He practically grabbed the cards, and when we had showered and dressed, a bunch of committeemen with long, sour faces called me on the carpet. "There's a mistake in your score," they said.

"I had a 74 and that's what my card shows," I replied.

"Yes, the total is correct, but on the eighteenth you marked down a 4 for yourself instead of a 5."

"Well, I sure didn't mean to, and if the total is correct, what's the difference?"

They let me know in a hurry. Not being wise to all the technicalities at the age of twenty-four, I didn't realize what a crime I'd committed and was flabbergasted when they disqualified me. All the other pros except two signed and circulated a petition asking for my reinstatement. Sam Parks and Horton Smith said, "No, Snead will have to pay his pound of flesh, just as Paul Runyan did when he signed an incorrect score in the 1933 National Open. Why should he get a break when Runny didn't?"

The vast majority of players were on my side, because it was such a slim technicality, and I was sore enough to make a fight out of it, but then it struck me that a fellow needed unanimous support in a dispute of this kind. Being the new boy on the tour who was taking money away from the veterans, I'd never get Smith's or Parks's name on that petition. It took some hard swallowing, but I packed up and left town—after pinning a note to the scoreboard:

"I leave Pinehurst a wiser golf pro . . ."

From then on, I never teed off anywhere until I saw that an official scorekeeper was on hand.

In the Miami Biltmore Open in Florida, my opening round put me with the leaders, and then an infected left hand, which

I'd injured by rapping it against a tree, became so sore that I shot myself into a tenth-place finish.

Next came the Tournament of Gardens on the old Wappoo course at Charleston, South Carolina, where it looked again like I'd shake the jinx. A gale blew players off their feet, and by punching the ball low I led the field with a first-round 67, lost the lead to Henry Picard the next day, then recaptured first place with a 70. The sportswriters said I was playing golf like a wildcat with its tail on fire and couldn't miss winning. Every golfer dreads the bad luck of suddenly losing the feel of his clubs. It happens, sometimes, for no known reason. In the final round, I felt like I had two right hands on a left-handed club —of not being able to even swing the stick, let alone control it. In that kind of miserable shape, I took a 76, which let the "Hershey Hurricane"—Picard—sweep past me to win the $1,250 first prize. Jimmy Thomson also passed me, for second place. My third-place purse came to $550. The $700 difference between first and third money might not seem much today, when $30,000 tournaments are common, but in 1937 it was a power of money to me.

As the bad breaks kept piling up, I threw clubs and swore at people I didn't even know and snarled at my own relatives and then began to feel sorry for myself. When you start crying on your own shoulder, you're in trouble.

Right after that, the second week in May, I caught a train to the important Metropolitan Open at the Forest Hills Field Club, my first showing in the New York area, where about two dozen sportswriters cornered me to fire questions that made me dizzy.

"How do you think you'll do? Will the jinx get you again?" was the big one.

Whistling in the dark, I said, "No, sir, I'm ready to lick that jinx. I feel 100 per cent, and I'll tell you boys something— I think I'll win this one."

They made headlines from my pop-off—"HEXED HILLBILLY PREDICTS WIN OVER BLUE-RIBBON FIELD"—and I'd put myself on the spot for fair before a big-league crowd.

On a narrow course with traps everywhere, I hooked into the rough on the first hole, recovered to within 20 feet of the hole, and the birdie putt was in the bucket. On the 473-yard, par-5 fifth, a drive and spade mashie left me 12 feet away, and the eagle putt that fell made them roar. My drive said howdy-do to the green of the 290-yard twelfth hole; on the par-5 fourteenth I chipped stiff for a birdie; on the eighteenth, despite an approach that sailed over a plateau green, I recovered for a par—to check in with an opening round of 33-35—68. That tied me for the lead with Jimmy Hines.

The New York press grabbed me, wanted to know what I thought of the Forest Hills course and my chances.

"Why, it's a pretty easy little layout," I told them. "There's only two par-5s on it, and I don't see why I shouldn't take it apart from here on in."

Henry Picard, who'd earlier shot a practice round of 71 to my 67 and a 70 to my 68 in the opening round, was standing nearby, and without thinking how it sounded I turned to him and asked, "How come you say you can't break 70 on this course, Henry?"

There was a long, chilly silence. Picard was one of the most famous players going. As one writer said next morning under the headline "ROOKIE SNEAD MAKES PICARD'S FACE TURN RED," I'd stuck both feet into my mouth. "Here is Snead, a raw newcomer fresh out of the Virginia hills," he wrote, "not only beating champion Picard's best scores in the Met, but then asking him how come he can't smash par. The Hershey Hurricane's face turned crimson at the question and he stalked off, uttering nary a word."

Reading that, I felt low-down, since Henry had been nothing but kind to me from my first break-in days. Sometimes asking

an honest question is the worst thing you can do. After that I
began to guard my tongue.

That night it began to rain. When I splashed out onto a
soggy course in the morning, I couldn't seem to make an off-
line shot—turning in seven 1-putt greens, bogeying only one
hole, playing the front nine in 33, and holing a long putt on
the short sixteenth for a birdie deuce. On the seventeenth, a
35-foot chip dropped in. My 65 score was a new competitive
record for Forest Hills. With a total of 133, I was 6 shots up
on the next man, Picard. For the first time in months I felt
unjinxed.

And then at noon the rain became a cloudburst and players
began to complain to Max Kaesche, the Metropolitan Golf
Association chairman, that the course was unplayable. Willie
Macfarlane came in drenched to the skin and was asked how
fast he had played through the storm. "At about four knots in
a head sea," answered Willie. Others picked up and walked
off the course. In the locker room, a shouting crowd gathered
around Kaesche. Some who'd scored poorly wanted the whole
second round thrown out and a fresh start made when the rain
stopped. Others who had low scores demanded that the com-
pleted rounds stand.

Lots of the boys were near mutiny and some of them—Wiffy
Cox, Vic Ghezzi, Charley Lacey, and others—did walk out.

"You will lose more than anyone if Kaesche washes out the
round," I was told by other pros. "You've got this tournament
all but clinched. If that 65 isn't allowed to stand, you should
tell the Met Association to kiss your fanny and leave."

While we waited for the decision, it was plain that this was
a tournament about to blow sky-high. I walked around in
circles, telling myself to keep calm.

Then Kaesche announced, "All rounds played today hereby
are canceled. They must be replayed tomorrow."

The jinx still had me by the neck. Missing the P.G.A. qualify-

ing in Pittsburgh . . . landing in the wrong Thomasville . . .
disqualified at Pinehurst . . . injured in Florida . . . loss of club
feel at Charleston . . . and now this. When Kaesche approached
me in the clubhouse, to see whether or not I'd join the walkout
that was taking shape in a big way, every eye in the house was
on us.

"It's a lousy break and I'm sorry," Kaesche said. "What
about it, Sam?"

Angry wasn't the word to describe me, but I mumbled, "I'm
staying to the finish. You did what you thought best, I guess."

With that, other contenders who had far less to lose than me
decided to stick around and the tournament was saved. The
headlines which had pictured me as a pop-off changed. "Snead's
gesture today," wrote Arch Murray in the New York *Post,* "was
overgenerous. It will be remembered for sportsmanship far
longer than any 65s he will unleash. The kid has arrived as a
real pro."

The popularity wasn't hard to take, but it was small comfort
when Jimmy Hines and Henry Picard got hot the next two days
to beat me out for the Met title. My replayed second round was
in 70 strokes. If my 65 had stood, I'd have won. As it was,
Hines finished at 279, Picard at 280, me at 283.

By not quitting at Forest Hills, I showed at least a start on
developing a golf temperament that could win for me. It was
only a start, because this series of bad breaks was just the beginning of terrible times.

Keep in mind that in mid-1937 I was being written up as the
most natural club swinger who ever had come along, a phenom
and surefire world-beater, and given the sort of praise that both
puts you on the spot and is bound to go to a kid's head. To be
beaten hurt twice as much as if I'd been able to break in
gradually, like everybody else from Hagen to Jones to Hogan to
Palmer. After my defeat in the Met Open, Jack Doyle's Broadway handbook listed me—a first-time starter in the event—at the
favorite odds of 8-1 in the National Open scheduled for Oak-

land Hills at Birmingham, Michigan. Tony Manero, the defending champ, was 15-1. Picard, Harry Cooper, Sarazen, Revolta, and other established aces were 10-1 and 12-1. The odds were ridiculous. No rookie ever had been favored in the Open. The pressure grew until I twisted all night like a worm in hot ashes and couldn't sleep.

After I stole the Open's qualifying round with a 71-65—136 and tied for the first-day lead with a 69, the odds shrunk even more, the gallery began following me, and I could feel the cold eye the other pros were giving me, since I had just seven major tournaments behind me at this point, including only two wins, in the Oakland Open and Crosby Invitational.

"Oh, Snead has ability, I'll grant you," one hotshot pro told the press, "but he'll fade fast when he's been around long enough to learn what the tournament grind feels like. Up to now he's been getting by on a helluva swing, luck, and a backwoods accent."

That burned me up. From what I'd seen of the top shooters, I had no reason to be scared of any of them. And I'd been matching shots with them since the previous December, for eight straight months, had lost 20 pounds and some hair, and still was second-highest money winner on the tour in June.

At Oakland Hills, a 73 and a 70 on top of the opening 69 left me tied for second going into the last eighteen holes, and in the stretch I took my jinx by the neck and strangled it—or so everybody there thought. On the eighteenth I hit as good a wood shot as I'll ever hit. From a close lie, my spoon carried 235 yards with so much backspin it jerked six feet toward the cup, stopping eight feet away. Teasing in the putt for an eagle 3, I drew a roar from the gallery such as you've never heard. My 283 total was the second-lowest Open score on record, which covered more than forty years, and nobody looked able to beat it.

About 5,000 fans fought to get into the locker room with me, where sports-goods people, sponsors, advertising tycoons, and others latched on, offering all kinds of contracts.

"Laddie," said Tommy Armour, "you've just won yourself a championship worth more than a seat on the Stock Exchange."

Ted Husing and the radio boys pushed mikes in my face and everybody toasted the smiling winner. In a few minutes I was due to collect money for endorsing everything from corn plasters to flea powder.

Then Ralph Guldahl, who'd been dragging his tail out on the course, went wild and came in with a terrific record-breaking score of 281. All at once it got real lonesome where I was standing. You could have shot off an elephant gun in my corner of the room and not winged a single sportswriter. As runner-up, I was nothing.

If ever I wished I was a drinking man, it was then. In high school I'd promised my coach, Harold Bell, that I wouldn't touch hard liquor, so the only relief was to get a gun and fishing rod and head for the mountaintops back home. That's the best remedy for anyone who is ready to smash his clubs and take up liquor and strange women.

Living with your disappointments builds up a thick skin after a while. Today, when I meet a player who tears his hair because he's lost a ten-dollar Nassau, it isn't easy to sympathize, considering the hard times I've been through. In the 1960s it's easy for writers to say that Sam Snead has had golf success, but how many remember what it was like twenty-five years ago when everything I touched went wrong? It was during this time that I developed what any golfer worth his salt must have— the ability to take it. Mad and discouraged as I was most of the time, I played pretty fair golf.

Just before the Open, there cropped up what looked like a plot by the veterans to block me from a position on the Ryder Cup team going to England late in June. President George Jacobus of the P.G.A. already had named eight of the Ryder members, with only two players yet to be chosen. When my name was mentioned, the digs became rough.

"Snead has many years ahead of him to make it," Paul

Runyan said. "Anyway, he's been in and out, and the older players are far more reliable."

Somebody else brought up a day I'd had at Fred Waring's course, Shawnee-on-the-Delaware. With a chance to win, I bogeyed the last five holes in a row to finish sixth.

Another pro said, "Sam can't even add. Look at his arithmetic at Pinehurst, when they disqualified him for a wrong score."

Others said if I couldn't find Pittsburgh or Thomasville, Georgia, how the hell could I find England?

Not willing to take such raps, I replied, "It looks to me like they'd want to send over their better players, young or old, instead of picking men just because they're nice fellows and play a pretty good game *now and then*."

After a lot of kidney punches and other low blows, the Ryder Cup committee named me to the squad. The way my luck was going, maybe you can guess one of the first things that happened in England.

On one of the early holes, forgetting to take one of the most common precautions, I hit a fairway wood after glancing at the ball. "Beg your pardon," said my opponent, "but you've just played my ball."

The loss-of-hole penalty tempted me to throw my brassie, but I held back when I remembered what temper can do to you. Hanging on, I won my Ryder singles match, 5 and 4.

Some of the U.S. players, who later became fine friends of mine, gave me the hey-rube treatment on the boat ride to England. One of them went around imitating my way of talking:

"Why, this heah golf is easy as pie. All yuh gotta do is whip out a drive, then take an arn (iron) and hit it on that flat li'l hill up thar (green) and then give it two more whops and you gets yo'self a pah."

When I fell seasick, the boys said the cure was to eat celery stalks and hard rolls and no other food and then do two hours of dancing every night in the ship's ballroom.

I tried it, groggy as I was, barely able to roll out of my bunk and pull on my pants, and damned if it didn't work. When that gag failed, they introduced me to one of the passengers as "Sam Snead, who's been a prizefighter down in Virginia and would like to challenge you."

"That right?" asked the man.

I admitted that at one time I'd done a little ringwork in the hometown.

He thumped my chest. "I'll try to work you in, pally," he said.

The big laugh, of course, came when I found the man was Tommy Farr, the British Empire champion, who was about to fight Joe Louis for the world title.

One way or another I stuck out that first year, and then another, becoming toughened to the fact that you never do shake hard luck and that without some built-in poise to meet it, you're finished. And also learning that a blowup is good for you, as long as it ends quickly and doesn't continue. Ordinary bad-tempered players could cut their scores by many shots if they realized this.

Each man's boiling point differs, and different types of aggravations touch us off. Bob Rosburg, a current star, can't stand a partner who dawdles around the course, examining every shot. Poor chipping made Byron Nelson blow up. Dutch Harrison couldn't stand a crackling popcorn bag in a fan's hand. Whirring movie cameras could make Ben Hogan swear out loud—and me, too, until I formed the habit of just dropping my club to the grass and staring holes through the movie fan: this is much easier on your nerves and game than calling him a low-grade, illegitimate S.O.B. On the green, I always have to remind myself to keep my head no matter what happens.

What drove this home was a round at St. Andrews, Scotland, where the fifth and fourteenth greens coincide into one huge rolling carpet. My approach wound up on the wrong green, leaving a 160-foot putt. The lag was 40 feet short.

"Dirty ———!" I swore, whacking my putter against the sole of my shoe and then swinging it again. This time it was such a wallop that I bashed in the cap of my alligator-hide shoe. The pain as that toe began to swell made me want to bust out crying. I could barely see, for the tears in my eyes, but wouldn't admit it to the gallery and forced myself not to limp.

At the next hole, the agony got so bad that I had to sit down, remove my shoe, and poke out the cap with the shaft of my club. While I blew on my toe, about 10,000 people stood around snickering.

Ten days later my toenail fell off, and I couldn't play at all until a new one grew on.

Other times I've paid through the nose for having the physical sort of blowup where you try to hurt yourself as punishment for a missed shot.

In the last round of the Augusta Masters, after a short putt rimmed out, I leaned on the putter, almost to the breaking point. A few holes later, on No. 16, I angrily bent the putter again. This time it was weakened enough to snap off at midshaft. An official tapped my shoulder. "Under the rules, you cannot replace that club."

From then on I had to putt with my driver, and on No. 17 and No. 18 I found myself putting for birdies and missed both. The money difference between making and missing them was the difference between $2,500 and the $700 I collected.

The lesson you never want to forget is that you can't stay mad in golf without it hurting you.

In the case above I got off easy; in another blowup, when the shaft of my putter snapped, the sharp end punctured my palm and put me out of action for a while.

In private matches I threw dozens of clubs before cooling off on this after meeting a caddie in Philadelphia who carries a silver plate in his skull from a club thrown by a mad golfer. Another kid who once carried clubs for the pros was killed when struck by an iron hurled by a country-club member. This member was exonerated, after an investigation, then threw another stick and was kicked out of his club for life.

In tournaments, I go by Mark Twain's advice, which was to count four when angry and when very angry to swear. Once in a while I'll step into the woods, out of sight, and beat the leaves off a bush. There's no club-throwing, though, nor abusing of officials, opponents, or the gallery. My practical side tells me that by blaming others, or your sticks, you show yourself to be a damned fool to people who might be valuable friends. A few years ago, the head of a sporting-goods firm asked me about a certain pro who was always picking up, wrecking clubs, and blasting officials.

"This boy has so much talent," he said, "that I'm thinking of paying him $50,000 to sign with us. What's your recommendation?"

"I don't have one. Do what you like," I replied.

In the next few weeks, the player created scenes in two tournaments, and when I saw the manufacturer again, he said, "I've dropped so-and-so from consideration. I wouldn't have him at any price."

SAM SNEAD'S COMMENT:
A FEW CLUES TO KEEPING CALM

What can a man do to curb his temper?

If you're talking about a young golfer, I'd say that Jack Burke, Sr., the late, great Texas pro and teacher, and Claude Harmon, the former Masters champion, had the proper slant. Burke's son, Jack, Jr., was eighteen years old when he appeared in a junior tournament in Houston, where he blew a payoff putt. Jack hauled off and banged his ball a mile off the green. Just then, his old man stepped from the gallery and, with fire shooting from both eyes, read the kid off in front of the spectators. "If you can't play without losing your head," he wound up, "give up the game."

Since then I've seen Jack, Jr., in spots where he'd love to bury his club in some noisy fan's skull. He has a tough disposition, having taught bayonet fighting and judo to combat Marines during World War II. But he walks away from blow-ups far more than he gives in to them. Jack keeps a lot of time and space between his moments of anger. With a temperament like that, he's won both the Masters and P.G.A. championships.

Claude Harmon's son is another fine player who once had temper trouble. "I just locked his clubs in the trunk of my car for a month," Claude tells me, "and from then on he took a grip on himself."

Youngsters around a course imitate their bad-acting elders. They think club-throwing is the thing to do, having seen so much of it from the start. Professional fathers catch the kid early and knock it out of him, where many fathers just go on setting a terrible example.

For the older man who snarls like a tiger if somebody just jingles the change in his pocket, there are two facts I learned the hard way:

The minute you blow, a charge seems to go through your opponent and he begins to play better golf; you've shown him a weakness and practically asked him to take advantage of it.

And, by blowing, you bleed off your own energy from the job of making shots. Getting sore and staying that way is hard work.

I have a saying about my own game—"all the wheels ran off the track." What that really means is that whenever I took an 80, as I once did in the Masters after leading the 1951 field into the final round, my temper got out of hand. I fought myself out of the money. It cost me a drop from first place to tenth at Augusta, 11 strokes off the pace I'd set for fifty-four holes.

Any time a wild spell is coming on, I try to switch my thoughts to something else. Doug Ford showed me how well this works when we were battling it out in the '54 Miami Open, a tournament I'd won five times previously. During the second

round a kid of about eight in a baseball cap began to tag after
Ford, asking to see his clubs and jabbering away. Between holes,
the kid never got off his back. I thought Ford would throw him
to the marshals on one bounce. A pro needs that absolute
concentration.

Instead, Ford talked to the kid and laughed with him all
around the course. Meanwhile, he fired a 67 and a 70 at me.
The kid was still sticking like a burr to Ford the next day when
he holed out an 80-yard wedge for an eagle 3 to beat me
in the Open.

"What is this?" I asked Ford later.

"If I couldn't get mad at that pesky kid," answered Ford,
"I couldn't get mad at *anything.*"

Another thing: at all times you should definitely know what
you're doing on the links, which isn't possible with your eyes
bulging out. There are many rules in golf, and the angry player
costs himself an edge here. In the 1958 Masters last round,
Arnie Palmer's iron shot on the par-3 twelfth hole was imbedded
in spongy ground off the green. The rains had brought a local
ruling that a buried ball could be dropped without penalty.
Just to pin it down, Palmer checked with an official, who said,
"No—you have to play it as it lies."

In Palmer's place, I'd have wanted to explode. Palmer *knew*
the man was wrong, and yet, there he stood, shaking his head
and shutting the door in Arnie's face. You could see Palmer
struggling with himself. Then he said, "You're wrong, but I'll
play it where it lies." He needed 4 shots to get down from
the mud.

And then, very cool, Palmer went back to where his ball
had been buried, dropped a provisional ball, chipped up, and
was down in par 3. "I'll want a ruling on this," he warned the
officials.

He got it three holes later—in his favor.

Palmer won the Masters by 1 shot—284 to Fred Hawkins'
and Doug Ford's 285s.

I don't say Palmer wasn't plenty riled. It was the fact that
he stayed *cool-mad* that won him $11,250.

Not so long ago I was playing around with Vic Ghezzi, the

old scrambler and automatic-machine tycoon, and with whom I've blown many a fuse. When I missed a shot, I twisted myself

into a full-body turn in order to throw my club for a new Snead distance record.

"Save it, Sam," said Vic. "You set a record long ago you'll never top."

"When was that?" I asked.

"In the Western Open at Canterbury, the time you disqualified yourself."

Then it all came back from fifteen years before—how Vic and I had teed off and after I'd gone sixteen holes in 3 under par he'd asked me, "Do you have all your clubs with you?"

Looking into my bag, I said, "Yep—all sixteen of them."

"Well, it's a long hike to the clubhouse and you might as well start walking in now," said Vic. "They put a new limit on clubs the other day. It's fourteen now. Or didn't you hear?"

Before leaving to be disqualified, I got down to the legal limit. Some of these days, I'll bet, one of those extra clubs will be picked up by the satellite-tracking stations.

5

OUT OF A PRESSURE COOKER—TWICE:
READING YOUR OPPONENT

VERSUS JIM TURNESA—THE 1942 P.G.A. CHAMPIONSHIP •
VERSUS BEN HOGAN—THE 1954 MASTERS PLAY-OFF

One of the Hite boys, the tough one, was scheduled to fight me in the semiwindup at the Odd Fellows Hall on a night in 1936. I'd have just as soon passed it up, but there was no way out. My buddies around town who were betting on Hite would have called me a yellowbelly if I'd dodged the match.

Everybody knew about Hite, how he was the terror of the CCC camps in Virginia and was hooking some good middleweights through the gym walls. "You've done dumber things," said my older brother Homer, "but this beats all. This boy's a pro. He'll wallop you worse than the old man did when you ran away."

I hadn't actually run away that time, when I was nine or ten years old—although I was all set for it and determined. One day I wrapped my clothes and some scraps of meat and bread in a bundle and hid it behind a buckeye tree back of the house, planning to retrieve it after dark. Then I figured to head out across the Blue Ridge Mountains and have a hell of a time becoming a hobo.

It was just my luck that a turkey gobbler wandered down from the hills and set up a hullabaloo near that tree. When my mother went to shoot him for the family pot, she found my bundle. My dad, Harry, cut a whip from the woods which was about as long as a cow.

"So you think you're too good to live here?" he said. My hind end and legs were sore for days after. I gave up the hobo idea.

For the big fight the posters around Hot Springs read:

> LOWELL (HURRICANE) HITE
> *168 Pounds*
> (Virginia CCC Champion)
> Vs.
> SAM SNEAD
> *165 Pounds*
> (Hot Springs Contender)

Calling me a contender was a joke. All I was contending for was a chance to do something that would pay me day wages with a golf game that folks told me wasn't bad for a kid. My stomach took a flip when I thought of Hite, who was hard as cement from working on road gangs, while I was just a beginning golfer with a job in the pro shop at The Cascades Hotel. The Cascades job, as I've said earlier, was all work and no pay—I didn't draw a dime of salary for acting as the pro and giving lessons, just my lunches. At twenty-two and -three I didn't have two ten-dollar bills to rub together—nor any idea that my golf future could turn into much. I figured that they'd taken James J. Braddock out of a breadline to win the world's heavyweight championship, so what could I lose by trying to be a fighter?

Never having been in a ring or licked anyone, I had to grind out some roadwork, and so I started running the three miles between home and the golf course. The second day I popped several charley horses and could hardly walk.

When they led me out for ring instructions, Hurricane Hite smiled at me through the smoke. He was grinning that easy sort of way. All muscle and ready to eat me up.

"Hit him with your 5-iron, Sam!" somebody yelled. "It's your only chance."

Some way or other, right off the bat in the first round, I threw a left and crossed a right that had Hite going—knocked him back on his heels and stunned him. But I didn't know what it was all about. Not realizing that I could punch that hard, I didn't see that he was groggy. I just stood there waiting for him to sock me back—stood there and let him recover when I had a chance to end it on the spot. Hite'd been all goofy-eyed, but he bobbed and snorted and fooled me into thinking he was OK.

"I guess I did wrong," I told my second, Louis Polane, between rounds.

"You ain't just whistlin' 'Dixie,' " he said sadly.

The next round, Hite was one mad pro. He let go a right that looked like a wagonload of hay coming, only I couldn't duck and it landed right on my chin. Rockets went off and birds were whistling and Hite tore into me, biff-bat, biff-bat, until I was a mass of welts and ready for the knockout. Just then I got an undeserved break.

All those blows to the head had the strange effect of clearing me up for a few seconds. I swung a lucky left hand that caught him by surprise and folded him up. His tongue flopped out and again I had him ready to put away. Only now it was too late.

In taking a beating I'd covered up with my arms and Hite had pounded all the strength out. He started running away from me. The best I could do was stagger around after him with my arms hanging limply at my sides and pray for the bell before he discovered I was finished.

At the end, they gave me the decision. But the crowd didn't toss more than coffee money into the ring. They knew I'd flubbed my chance back in the first round and that if it hadn't been for my fool's-luck punch, Hite'd torn my head off.

Later on I remembered this direct lesson and learned—by mistakes and by studying such smart veterans as Harry Cooper,

Henry Picard, and Gene Sarazen—that in golf you're most liable to win when you neither overrate nor underrate an opponent but are able to look through him and diagnose what he's thinking and feeling. You need to know just how strong or weak he is at a given moment. He may hide his emotions real well but still give away a little something under stress. How much pressure can he take before it catches him? Maybe he's ready for the KO but is running a bluff. There's nothing that will ease your own worry and panic in a tough spot more than spotting some tip-off or other that your opponent has been taken by the shakes.

At times I've been frightened by brave-looking golfers. If only I'd known it, all the time they were trembling like a bride standing at the bedpost.

This "reading" of the other shooters you meet works in all forms of golf—from weekend play for a dollar bet to P.G.A. touring, where one shot may be worth $50,000. The first time Bobby Locke came to this country from South Africa, old Baggy-Pants was putting for a barrel of money in the Tam O'Shanter at Chicago. He glanced over at the other guy. This man had been hard as nails all day.

But all at once a white streak about a quarter-inch wide had appeared down the side of the man's face.

"Don't you know, I realized I had him beat," Locke told us later. "All my shots were easy after that." Old Baggy-Pants won the tournament to the surprise of everybody.

Out in California there's a 10-handicapper I know who has all but a few of the players at his home club fooled. Naturally, they keep it to themselves. When this fellow is looking cool but is ready to fold up, he begins to scratch his backside and squirm around. As soon as he scratches and squirms, they suggest a "press" bet and clean up.

It's a nervous habit, a mannerism, he can't control. Which is all that those who collect steady bets from him need to know.

There are bigger things to know about golf than the other man's weakness, but a little study of the opposition is important because the game comes down to one thing. Mostly it's a matter of resisting and minimizing pressure. That "squeeze" you feel comes from everywhere, from places you might overlook. The Chinese, you know, say that a wise man never expects more of himself than he can reasonably deliver. That names one of the biggest pressure points in golf. I'd say the main mental hazards are these:

1) Blaming yourself after a shot which actually was a pretty fair effort, considering your physical equipment and handiness with the clubs.

2) Knotting up inside over what happened on the last-previous hole played when you have a fresh problem at hand.

3) Identifying a shot you're about to make with a similar shot of a week or a month earlier when you shanked one twenty yards.

4) Intimidation of yourself: when the club champion or any good player tees up against them, lots of golfers ask, "What chance have I got?"—and blow their game right there.

5) Giving in to fear: when the ball seems to wiggle its ears and stick out its tongue at you, daring you to move it, pressure has grabbed you all the way, brother.

That's only a beginning; I haven't mentioned galleries, bunkers, opponents who needle you, shots with money riding on them, 4-foot putts, and a hundred other forms of the heebie-jeebies. But the point is, you can relieve your own fear and tension if you keep your eyes open. It surprises me that so few men who have X-ray eyes in their business dealings bother to study their golf opposition even a little bit. You can tell me that they're too bound up with their own troubles on the course to see the advantage, but I ask you right back—could they make $30,000 or so a year if they stayed wrapped up in themselves?

Hurricane Hite suckered me in the ring when I failed to see how much I'd hurt him. In golf I learned to look beyond my own little fish fry.

The match that drove this home the hardest happened after I'd quit teaching to become a touring pro—at a time when I was under fire from the newspapers for winning everything but the major championships. It was May of 1942 and I was in Washington to see a man about enlisting in the U.S. Navy.

"Welcome aboard, Snead," this officer said, after I'd passed the physical. "Sign right here and we'll ship the body." He was a very jovial and friendly man.

"Well, now, hold on," I said. "I don't want to jump into any uniform *this minute*. The Pro Golfers Association meet is next week and I want to play there first."

"Oh, we'll let you off for that."

"Yeah, and maybe you won't."

"Certainly we will. Just sign here."

Something made me suspicious. I hung back. This officer was shoving papers at me, and it was a tight spot, and then he asked, "What's it worth to you, this golf thing?"

"About $3,000 if I win and a $2,000 bonus from my equipment company, plus endorsements and stuff."

His eyes got big. I guess he didn't know who I was, either— the Great Also-Ran of golf. I'd been runner-up in the U.S. Open at Oakland Hills in '37 when my 283 score was overcome by Ralph Guldahl's last-round 69. I'd been runner-up in the '39 Masters when Guldahl hung another one on me, runner-up in the '38 P.G.A. at Shawnee to Paul Runyan, runner-up to Byron Nelson in the '40 P.G.A. at Hershey. After five years as a circuit pro, I'd won close to thirty Opens, from San Diego to Miami, but not one national title. The papers called me a choke artist, a cheese champ, a "mystery," and a "hex-haunted hillbilly." One syndicated writer claimed I was the Shoeless Joe Jackson of the links—Jackson never being quite able to edge Ty Cobb for the batting title.

A hell of a comparison that was, even though it's true that I broke into golf in bare feet and in the back country, where our plumbing was a two-holer outdoors. Jackson had just Cobb and three or four others to worry about. When I was a young pro, I had Ed Dudley, Craig Wood, Vic Ghezzi, Horton Smith, Johnny Revolta, Jimmy Thomson, Lighthorse Harry Cooper, Dick Metz, Wild Bill Mehlhorn, Paul Runyan, Lawson Little, Ky Laffoon, Henry Picard, Denny Shute, Byron Nelson, Ben Hogan, Wiffy Cox, Ray and Lloyd Mangrum, Tony Manero, Jimmy Demaret, Jug McSpaden, and Guldahl, among others, to crack up against—maybe the greatest field ever assembled.

Anyway, I was the glorified bum who lost the big ones. In the Navy recruiting office I played my hunch and told the man I'd see him a little later. This was my last chance to try and even up with the experts before I didn't know how many years would pass.

Up at Seaview Country Club at Atlantic City, it looked like Army maneuvers were being conducted. Over 7,000 GIs from Fort Dix had swarmed the course to see their buddy, Corporal Jim Turnesa, win the P.G.A. I came through my preliminary matches with Sam Byrd, Willie Goggin, Ed Dudley, and Jimmy Demaret, and then it was Turnesa and me in the finals.

"This crowd isn't exactly pulling for you, Sam," said Ed Dudley, the P.G.A. president, as we teed up.

"Pull? I'll settle for less pushing. They almost knocked me down twice."

"They don't know you're going into the Navy," said Dudley. "You know how it is; they hate the man out of uniform."

"Well, don't tell 'em a thing. There isn't a sailor in sight."

I never felt anything like that crowd. Oh, how they wanted my blood. In order, Turnesa had eliminated Dutch Harrison, Jug McSpaden, Hogan, and Nelson—a terrific feat—which made him all the more popular.

We hit our opening drives and I had a quick moment to size up Turnesa.

He was an olive-skinned little guy not inclined to give anything away about himself. He played his ball, said little, and dared you to match him. At all times Turnesa was a perfect gentleman. You couldn't even get a little mad on at him to pep yourself up. I knew he was also a fine front-runner; let him build a lead and it might be Katy-bar-the-door.

My best chance was to jump in front, if possible, and see how he stood the pressure from behind. Sometimes a big gallery that's 100 per cent for you can hurt you more than help.

But few things work out the way you hope. On the eighth hole he went 1 up when my 4-foot putt lipped the cup and he holed a birdie 15-footer. On No. 13 he dropped a 35-footer, and on No. 16 he exploded from a bunker and ran down a 20-footer for another birdie. He was recovering like a fool and putting better. The soldier gallery wasn't handicapping him, either.

Twice on the back nine he hit well into the woods. When we got down there, his ball had been kicked out into the clear.

"Sam," said Ed Dudley apologetically, "we can't do anything about this."

"I know it, Ed. Did I say anything?" My blood was boiling, though.

The ball-kicking stunt wasn't finished, but nobody could stop it. The marshals weren't about to challenge Fort Dix.

After twenty-three holes of the thirty-six-hole final, I was 3 down and it looked to be all over, the way Turnesa was chipping and putting and the Army was using its boots and the crowd psychology was working on me.

The twenty-fourth, a heavily-trapped par 4, was where Turnesa made one of his first slips: he hooked both his drive and brassie second into the rough. After a long straight drive of about 290 yards, I paid some hard attention to the green, which had a narrow neck and then flared out fairly level. Out of bounds was to the left, with trees and scrub fringing the putting area on the right side. I wanted the ball to go one way—from left to right. The shot called for a delicate fade. To pull off a controlled slice, or fade, which I recommend only expert golfers attempt, I made two adjustments.

My left foot was drawn back into a more open stance than

usual—about 4 inches back of what would have been a square stance. I also shifted my grip a bit so that my thumbs rested more on top of the shaft than on the sides. The V's formed by the thumb and forefinger of each hand pointed more toward my chin than toward my right shoulder, as they normally would.

Result was that the clubface was opened a few degrees at impact and put sidespin on the ball when it cut across on an outside-in path. With both hands atop the shaft, you reduce whip of the club through a "dead" action of the hands and the clubhead comes into the ball a bit late, causing less application of power and making the ball die to the right.

This fade came off just right, the ball starting toward the out-of-bounds and bending back to stop alongside the green. An 8-iron pitch left me a preferred uphill putt of 12 feet, which I dropped. Turnesa's 2 hooks cost him a 5 on the hole to my 4, and I still had a chance. By the twenty-seventh hole, I was studying Turnesa closely. Now I was only 1 down, thanks to some accurate approaches.

What I needed for my own morale was some sign that my comeback had shaken or weakened him or at least had him breathing hard. When you've been an also-ran for five years, you need help. But he didn't show me a thing. Not a muscle in his face moved. He seemed as independent of the pressure I was feeling as a hog on skates.

The pressure got hotter when the gallery began to squawl and yell when I was putting. Ed Dudley stepped out to quiet them down.

"Hold it, Sam," he said. "This is terrible."

"No, let 'em rant and rave, Ed," I said. "I'd rather have the steady noise than to have it stop all at once—and then start again."

"All right," said Ed reluctantly. He saw my point. You can't win with a prejudiced gallery. They'd shut up, if Dudley demanded it, but soon as I got used to a dead silence they'd explode on me again.

On No. 27, another par 4, I was fighting my nerves and lucky to be just off the green in 2 and then to chip within 6 feet and drop the putt. Corporal Turnesa chipped 3 feet short and barely missed his putt. Which evened the match.

Now that I was a real threat, it got lonesomer than ever out there. You'd have thought I was a German or a Jap. But in the next few minutes I won the P.G.A. championship simply by keeping my eyes open.

As Turnesa stepped up to drive on No. 28, his face still didn't change. To look at him, you'd have thought he didn't have a worry. And then I saw something.

It was the way he waggled his club. The waggle is supposed to be a tension-breaker which loosens up the wrists and also gives you the feel of the clubhead. Until then, Turnesa had always taken two waggles before swinging—which I'd mentally noted.

But this time he took four or more distinct waggles, none of them smooth or confident. It was a good sign that he was hurt inside. Then he gave away something else there on the twenty-eighth tee. After taking those extra waggles, he went into a forward press which had suddenly changed. The forward press is the golf equal of the brief pumping motion of a pro football passer's forearm before he throws or a baseball pitcher's forward dip before he rears back to let fly. It's a slight downward-forward press of the hands which gives the backswing a smooth start.

Turnesa's press was jerky and overdone. That made it a sure thing.

My heart took a jump and my spirits shot up a mile. *I've got him,* I told myself. *He's on the ropes.*

I'll bet that not one other person in the crowd noticed those two little tip-off changes in his preparation to drive. To prove what they meant, Turnesa pulled his tee shot into the woods, hit a tree with his recovery, and stayed stuck in the woods. It cost him a 5 on the hole. After that, he landed another drive in the brush and 3-putted on the No. 30 hole. He had cracked, and one big reason for it was that after I knew the truth about him, my own tension disappeared and I began shooting my best offensive golf. Let's go back just a bit to get the whole point here.

Turnesa's pulled drive into the woods on No. 28 could have been a slight misjudgment indicating nothing special. But I knew better and *knew it in time* to get the lift to start cashing in on it.

On the short thirty-fifth, I was so loose and full of confidence that my 7-iron second shot was a chip from about 60 feet right into the money hole. It was one of the two dozen or so best tournament shots I've ever hit.

That did it: my birdie 2 on the thirty-fifth ended the match and won me my first major championship—after something like fifteen tries in the National Open, P.G.A., and Masters—by a score of 3 and 1.

"Sam, you really came scrambling back," said Turnesa when they handed me the cup. He looked at me kind of funny.

Naturally, I didn't tell a soul what had helped me do it. Maybe I'd meet Turnesa again in a big match.

To round things out, next day I was able to thumb my nose at those Army hecklers. I was P.G.A. champ on Sunday, and on Monday I enlisted as a Navy seaman and was off to Norfolk for training.

"I'm kind of curious," I said to a brass hat. "If I'd signed the final enlistment papers last week, would you have let me off for the tournament?"

He was all Navy, that man. "Negative, Snead," he said.

That's another lesson learned. Never sign anything when the other man has the gun.

A shot analysis of the closing part of the duel with Turnesa points up the importance of "reading" an opponent who's going strong and seems unbeatable.

On the first nine of the final round of eighteen, I opened with a par, a big bogey 6, and over the next five holes could gain only one hole back from Turnesa. After discovering that he was shaking and sighing inside, I came down to the finish like this:

$$\text{SNEAD:} \quad 444 \quad 344 \quad 44^2$$
$$\text{TURNESA:} \quad 554 \quad 444 \quad 443$$

Of the four holes from twenty-seven through thirty, I won three and was able to turn the tables about as fast as it's possible in match-play golf. In the newspapers you'll read about such matches: "So-and-so made a sensational comeback after facing sure defeat, suddenly finding his touch while his opponent abruptly floundered. . . . "

There's often a reason that isn't written about. Confidence wins for you. Confidence can come from observation. In golf, observation is the ability to pick out the unusual.

Jim Turnesa was under great control, a regular sphinx all day. But he still showed me a little something.

After the war, a Johannesburg financier and golf bug named Norbert Erleigh and Jack Harris, the New York promoter, offered me $10,000 to tour South Africa in a series of matches with Bobby Locke. It averaged out at about eight-fifty for every time I swung a club. For an exhibition purse I've seldom done better. The Locke tour and all the other winnings that have come my way over twenty-five years might not have happened if it hadn't been for Freddie Martin, the man who gave me my first boost.

Freddie, the chunky little pepper pot, now retired, manager of golf at The Greenbrier Hotel at White Sulphur Springs, West Virginia, in 1936, who rescued me from my nonpaying job at The Cascades, wasn't interested in my prizefighting for sure. Freddie saw me play just once and thought I had something special. My new boss went back to the time of Harry Vardon and Jerry Travers; he had more golf brains in his left little finger than I had in my whole head.

But Freddie didn't tamper with my grip or stance or swing,

which came natural. He did pull up a stool in the back room of the pro shop and hold class on such things as poise, tactics, and psychology in general.

"Matches," he said, "can be lost when you're not even holding a stick. By one little slip between shots."

I didn't get him.

"I notice you don't smoke, Sam."

"No, I promised my high-school coach, Mr. Bell, I wouldn't. Don't drink, either. I figure I might not be able to handle red-eye, so why take a chance?"

"About the smoking," said Freddie, "there's a better reason than your promise for staying away from it. About twenty years ago, there was a skinny kid up in Massachusetts. His daddy was a laborer. The kid couldn't afford clubs. He swiped some old gutta-percha Vardon Flier balls from the country club and went out in the woods and cut a stick with a knot on the end."

"I did that, too," I said. "My first club was a swamp maple I cut and used to knock acorns. Later, I hid in the woods off the fairway and hooked a ball now and then when somebody hit one in there."

"Short on money at home, Sam?"

"We didn't have a lot. I caddied barefoot when I was seven and eight to save shoe leather. Once when the snow was on the ground my feet got frostbit and then started to freeze. Another few minutes and I'd have lost my toes. I had to drop the man's clubs and run for the nearest stove."

"Probably good for you," remarked Freddie. "Bob Jones excepted, rich boys don't make important golfers. Now, I look to see you reach the big time some day soon. You've got every shot you need and the power of a mule. But you must concentrate on the little details; lack of that has destroyed many a wonderful prospect."

My boss lit his pipe and continued his yarn.

"Well, this kid up in Brookline built himself a three-hole

course in a weedy old cow lot. He practiced until his arms ached. Up at five-thirty, hitting shots until dark."

"I did that, too," I said. "I sunk tomato cans all around the farmyard and banged at them all day."

"And like you, too," went on Freddie, "he didn't smoke. But one of his opponents wasn't so careful. In 1913 the kid was a better than fair amateur, but he certainly didn't belong in a play-off for the United States Open championship against the one and only Harry Vardon and Ted Ray of England—which is where he landed. Sam, the whole country went crazy at what this kid had done. It put golf on page one."

Now I knew who he meant—Francis Ouimet.

"I know that Ouimet won," I broke in.

Freddie scowled. "Don't interrupt. You don't know *why*. Few people do. Maybe you'll be one of them if you sit and listen."

Said Freddie: "Vardon and Ray were certain to trim this young punk, but Ouimet matched their 38s on the first nine and held a 1-stroke lead when they reached No. 13. Vardon still had plenty of time to come on and win. He was debonair as a crown prince and patronizing to the kid, who of course was a bundle of nerves at having come this far. But, after the fifteenth, Ouimet still hadn't broken. Right there Vardon made his fatal mistake.

"You know, Sam, man is still a primitive being. Let someone betray a weakness and instinctively he's ready for the kill.

"Harry Vardon *never* smoked on a golf course. He knew what a tip-off it can be. After the fifteenth hole, though, he jerked a smoke from his pocket and lit up—and his hands were shaking so that the flame blew out twice.

"Ouimet saw that. And I shouldn't have to tell you what it did for his courage. It went up like the price of bum whiskey. He birdied No. 17 after Vardon hooked into a dogleg bunker, took a three to Vardon's five, and won the National Open."

The story made me tingle. "What other signs should I look for?" I asked Freddie.

"Watch their eyes. Fright shows up there first in enlargement of the pupils. Notice their pace. If they play a deliberate game and then start charging after the ball, they're losing control.

"Doctors will tell you that panic causes an adrenalin charge to hit the system, which they call blanching. If a man gets white around the lips or his complexion fades, it's a sure sign. With others, the neck cords tighten and stand out."

Before long, in local tournaments, I noticed how right Freddie was. If my opponent normally smoked a cigarette every four or five holes, I watched for any change in his habit. If he went to using a cigarette per hole, and then two per hole, puffing short and fast, I knew he was on the run. When I saw him chain-smoking, I went after him hammer and tongs.

Like Freddie said, it brought out the killer in me. Soon as I saw my man was hurt, I started stomping him with my best golf.

Such giveaway signs don't work with everyone you play by far. Some players twitch their muscles and light up smokes all over the place and it means nothing. It's when a mannerism or steady habit changes abruptly that you know. Amongst the pros, Lloyd Mangrum always had a cigarette in his face. He'd even putt for big money with his eyes squinted up against the curling smoke, and Mangrum was one of the great putters. I thought maybe I had a tip on Gary Player, the current South African star, when his mouth dropped open the first time I saw him. But Player does that naturally. He's like Ralph Guldahl, who used to cuss himself in a low tone. Those aren't giveaways, they're established practice—part of the man. You want to look for the thing that isn't customary.

Ben Hogan gave away less about himself than anyone I ever met. Jimmy Demaret played dozens of matches against him and told me he heard Hogan speak only two words.

"Of course, he said them on every green," said Jimmy.

"What'd he say?" I asked.

" 'You're away.' "

Keeping Freddie Martin's lectures in mind and profiting by

them over the years, I arrived in 1954 at the Masters Tournament in Augusta to find Hogan (as usual) the favorite. Up to then, Hogan hadn't lost a major tournament since sweeping the 1953 U.S. and British Opens and the Masters. My own game had been far off: I'd been shooting 70, 71, 72.

After seventy-two holes, Hogan and I were tied with 289 scores; and with a play-off coming up, the usual whispers started going around. For years, there was a story believed by many golfers—and it still is—that Hogan had my number. Not only Hogan, but Byron Nelson. The rumor was helped along by Gene Sarazen when he wrote this in a book about me:

". . . when Snead has won, he's felt a confidence in himself he always lacked when Hogan was on the course, and before Hogan, Nelson. Snead always seemed to be worried about what Ben or Byron was up to. He was almost fatalistically resigned to the fact that whatever he did, they would somehow edge him out."

All I know is that it's true that Hogan and Nelson won plenty of tournaments which I didn't, but any time Hogan and I met in a head-to-head play-off, I won. We met three times over the years when we were rivals. The score reads: Snead 3, Hogan 0. Anyway, at Augusta, my business associate, Gary Nixon, decided to test the strength of the belief that Hogan had my goat. He came to town with some cash money to bet on me.

"I can't find even one taker," Gary told me the night before the match. "Some like Hogan, but they won't put the money where their mouth is."

"That's OK," I said. "The way Hogan's been going, it might be a blessing."

On the first tee, Hogan said, "Good luck."

I said, "Good luck, Ben."

Then he froze. He went to work to take me apart, concentrating as he always did like there was nothing in this world but his ball and those eighteen holes.

After nine holes we were all square, with 35s, but on No. 10 I chipped a 65-footer into the cup from back of the green to go

1 stroke ahead. Hogan evened the match on No. 12. We came
to the thirteenth, a shortish par 5 of 470 yards but one of the
trickiest hellholes you'll ever see. A creek wanders all the way
along No. 13, there's a sharp dogleg left with thick trees border-
ing it, the creek cuts directly across in front of the green, and
the green sits on a plateau with more ripples in it than a snake.

The big gamble is—play safely to the dogleg turn and place
your second shot short of the creek or cut the corner and gamble
on clearing the water with your follow-up shot. Hogan played it
safe. I drove one past the trees so far that Gary Nixon, standing
down the course, lost the ball and thought I'd missed it entirely.
My 3-iron second cleared the creek, split the middle of the green,
and I holed for a birdie. Hogan played a cautious 4-iron short
of the water for a par. That gave me a 1-stroke lead.

"Want a drink, Ben?" I said at No. 14. There's a fountain
there, just off the tee.

He just blinked at me. If Hogan thought I was trying to dis-
turb him further, he was having no part of it. Anyway, I took
time out for a long, refreshing drink.

We each parred No. 14 and birdied No. 15, and it was all up
for grabs as we came to No. 16.

I'll always believe that this is where Freddie Martin's schooling of years earlier—to always watch for the little signs—gave me
my biggest payoff. The match was one of the most publicized
that ever was played. All those people watching hadn't seen
either Hogan or me show a sign of pressure.

I was watching every move of Hogan's when we each reached
the green of this 190-yard hole with our tee shots. Just for a
second, I thought I noticed a little hesitation in his movements.
He had about an 18-foot putt, me a 25-footer. Hogan didn't
like the looks of his putt. Seeing that, I decided to "charge" the
cup—play it boldly and add pressure, if possible. The green was
slow from rain, so when I got over the ball I reminded myself to
hit it a little harder and firmer than usual. The ball took a
pretty run up there and stopped maybe 10 to 12 inches above

the cup. Hogan now had to putt about as well or risk going 2 strokes behind.

Watching the time he took, I was surprised to see him hit much too soon. Watching his putter blade, I saw that his backswing wasn't more than 5 or 6 inches when he had to knock the ball 18 feet. Watching *where* he hit, I saw the blade strike too far back of the ball.

Correct position on putting blade

Correct backswing for long putt

When your backswing is too short, what actually happens is that you contact the ball before you're ready. There's no smoothness to the shot; it's neither a definite tap nor a stroke.

Hogan's ball stopped a good 5 feet short and made the crowd gasp. Ben never had duffed a putt so many ways since I'd known him. It was such a change from the usual that it made my skin prickle. His next putt could prove what I was thinking.

Putting straight uphill, he pushed the ball with another jerky backswing. It stayed out by an inch. Hogan didn't react, but he didn't have to.

That's when I knew I had him. Iceman Hogan was feeling the strain all the way and more than me. I dropped my 1-footer for a 2-stroke lead and walked to No. 17 with that million-dollar feeling—no doubt about anything.

It was lucky my confidence was running so high, because my tee shot on No. 17 stopped in a dangerous lie. Somebody had taken a divot, but it hadn't grown back, leaving a hard pancake of concave turf—and nested down in there was my ball. I couldn't put my club down in the address position because the pancake might move. In fact, the ball was balanced so tippy that any air current could shift it.

When you've got one like that, you can only play it like a trap shot. I swung my 6-iron up sharply, came down with fast wrist action, and cut through to take pancake, ball and all. There was no telling what'd happen—the ball might shoot out sideways, sail, or maybe hang and dribble 20 yards—but, knowing that Hogan's nerves were worse off than mine, I plowed it out of there with very little concern. It carried 120 yards to land 40 feet from the flag.

We each parred No. 17. On No. 18 my relaxed feeling came in handy again when I was bunkered to the right of the green. It was trouble, the kind that could cost the match, but my mind was at ease. You can't name me a greater advantage in golf than that.

Even though Hogan still had a chance to catch up, I pitched from the trap like there was nothing at stake and stopped 4 feet away. I didn't even have to try for the putt—just nudged it up to the lip and tapped it in to win the Masters championship by a margin of 1 stroke. To make it sweeter, I'd protected my record of never having lost to Ben Hogan in a play-off.

Next day a man who bets like Nick the Greek on golf games walked up to Gary Nixon, who'd found no takers against me earlier.

"If I'd seen you before the match," he said, "I'd have covered everything you wanted to lay on Snead."

"XX!!##!XX!" said Nixon.

Personally, I made a little speech to the newspaper boys,

which included some who'd agreed with Sarazen about Hogan having my number. "The sun doesn't shine on the same dog all the time," I reminded them.

But I didn't bother to educate them on what had happened on hole No. 16. In fact, until right now I've kept it to myself.

SAM SNEAD'S COMMENT:
READING AN OPPONENT

Whenever that Masters play-off is reviewed, somebody claims that I had "luck" going for me to beat Hogan. They like to quote these statistics:

Times reached green in regulation figures: *Hogan 18, Snead 14.*

Holes shot in par: *Hogan 15, Snead 10.*

Bogeys: *Hogan 1, Snead 3.*

These figures favored Hogan, but my five birdies to his three and fewer putts taken (33 to 36) balanced out one of the closest matches I ever played. The fact that I shot a 70 to Hogan's 71 comes down to the No. 16 hole, where alertness and ability to recognize my opponent's mental state proved the all-important factor. Had any sign of the putting "yips" shown up in me, I'm sure Hogan would have spotted it long before the gallery experts and his own game would have received a shot in the arm. Another thing: anyone can 3-putt from 18 feet, as Hogan did on No. 16, and still be in strong mental shape. I've been guilty of triple-putting, or worse, without feeling the shakes. The real clue here was the *way* he putted: hesitation, then hitting too soon, an overshort backswing and poor placement of blade on ball. Added up, they exposed the Iceman's true state of mind.

One lesson here is that "charge"-type putting, going boldly for the cup from a distance, further unsettles a golfer who's revealed himself. Once they weaken, you should pour it on.

And generally speaking:

Diagnosis of another player should begin by studying his set patterns of behavior. Does he normally play deliberately, moderately fast, or fast? Is his preparation for a shot grooved? Does he talk a lot or say little? How does he step up to the tee; how many waggles does he take? Does he usually sweat when exercising at golf? Is he a smoker with fixed habits? Does he shrug it off when a pressure shot just misses? When he's relaxed, what are his mannerisms? Any sudden change in any of these is worth your attention.

Some day it might even win you a hell of a bet. The least it'll do is improve your own score.

WHEN OVERSTUDY OF AN OPPONENT IS DANGEROUS

On the other hand, I have made the mistake of paying too much attention to an opponent—learning that the "dope" you pick up during a tournament is about as reliable as backyard gossip.

Once, in the Reading Open, I came to the final three holes with the tournament cinched. Or so I believed. At least ten people came up at the fifteenth hole to say, "Doc Middlecoff finished at three over par, so you've got this thing won, easy."

My letdown was immediate. Middlecoff, the only man in a spot to beat me, had been worrying me. I should have stayed worried, and played as hard as I knew how the rest of the way.

On the fifteenth, sixteenth and seventeenth holes, I played cautiously, just protecting my "lead." Then, coming to No. 18, I heard a yell go up and an official walked back to tell me, "Middlecoff just finished in three under par. You've got to birdie this last hole to tie him."

It was too late—I rimmed out an 8-foot putt on No. 18 and lost by one shot.

After that, I never let anyone in any gallery tell me how an opponent was doing. I listened only to one trusted friend, who tipped me during the last few holes on who was in with what score and exactly what I had to beat. Letting strangers "read" your opponents' scores is bush stuff. A pro needs his own intelligence department.

6

WHEN THE MIND LEAVES THE BODY:

PUTTING

LONG LAGS IN THE BRITISH OPEN • ROLLING THEM IN THREE WAYS • "YIPPING" PUTTS IN AFRICA • THREE YEARS OF PUTTING PARALYSIS • A MAGIC BLADE AND A COMEBACK

Before I went to Scotland for the British Open of 1946, I'd never met anybody with a "sir" or "lord" in front of his name. So I still wonder how the London newspapers expected me to know it was a duke sitting across the aisle on the train to Edinburgh and the North.

Because of the duke, things got a little hot for me in British golfing society.

Down home in the woods, I wasn't short of ancestors and relatives myself. Mostly we were proud of Aunt Maggie Mathews, who gave birth to twenty children, including stillborns, and my great-uncle John. Big John Snead stood seven feet six, weighed 365, and died of fever in the Civil War after killing a few companies of Union soldiers with his bare hands.

We might have been plain people, but we were unusual. One of my great-grandmothers lived to be 106 years old and could still outshuck anybody in a cornfield when she was past 90. But no Snead ever ate tea and crumpets or got a look at royalty, except me—and in my case it was just a long-distance glimpse of King George VI when he'd galleried the 1937 British Open, which was my first trip out of the U.S.A.

In 1937 as a kid contender I'd finished tenth with an even 300 shots at Carnoustie, Scotland, in the Open. In 1946 I was primed to do better. But then along came the duke, and then a whole mess of more trouble.

Along with Lawson Little, I rode a gully-jumper train up from London. We passed places with names like Kirkintiloch and the Firth of Forth and then we slowed down past some acreage that was so raggedy and beat-up that I was surprised to see what looked like a fairway amongst the weeds. Down home we wouldn't plant cow beets on land like that.

"Say, that looks like an old, abandoned golf course," I said to a man across the aisle, tapping his knee. "What did they call it?"

You'd have thought I stabbed him. "My good sir!" he snorted. "*That* is the Royal and Ancient Club of St. Andrews, founded in 1754! And it is not now, nor ever will be, abandoned!"

"Holy smoke," I said, "I'm sorry." But how could I tell that I was looking at the most famous links in the world, the course that Bob Jones said he respected most? Until you play it, St. Andrews looks like the sort of real estate you couldn't give away.

He was so insulted, this Duke Something-or-Other, that the British papers made a fuss about my remark and from then on I was dodging reporters who had the knife out for me. The only place over there that's holier than St. Andrews is Westminster Abbey. I began to think the whole trip was a mistake. In fact, I'd tried to avoid entering the British Open in the first place.

A few weeks earlier in New York, I'd met with L. B. Icely, the president of Wilson Sporting Goods Company. I used and endorsed Wilson equipment and drew top royalties for it, and Icely had a say-so about where and when I played. Icely listened to my arguments against going, then said, "No, Sam, we want you to enter. It's time you won a big title overseas. The prestige will be terrific."

What did I want with prestige? The British Open paid the winner $600 in American money. A man would have to be two hundred years old at that rate to retire from golf.

But Icely was firm about it.

"Have you seen me putt lately?" I argued. "It's awful. On the greens my mind just seems to leave my body."

"In this Open at St. Andrews the greens are double size. Big as a barnyard," said Icely. "They'll help you get your touch back."

I complained that a center-shafted putter, such as I used then, was illegal in English championships and that I hated to switch to a blade putter.

"Mr. Walter Hagen," came back Icely, "has done fairly well with a blade. He won the British Open twice at Sandwich, and also at Hoylake and Muirfield. I suggest you talk to Walter."

Hagen had the answer for my miserable putting when I saw him. "Just start hitting the ball above the equator," he advised.

"Goodbye, Walter," I said.

Hagen was no help. In advising me to hit the ball slightly above the center line, he was looking for end-over-end rotation, or overspin. But I'd long ago learned that too much overspin hurt me more than it helped. When the ball contacted the hole, whether on the right or left lip, it had a better chance of dropping without heavy top spin. I'd often discussed this with Ben Hogan. As Ben argued, "Given a lot of top spin, the ball retains too much energy at a point where you want it to die and often worms its way right out of the cup." Using Hagen's method, I'd seen many a ball go half in and flip out. And I'd topped far too many putts, also.

Whatever was wrecking my putting in 1946, it wasn't because I failed to try and catch the fat of the ball with a square action and apply a medium amount of overspin.

Once Icely had put down his foot, I went to England. And the jinx was on me all the way. Leaving New York, our Constellation sprang an engine fire on take-off and we stopped on the runway with smoke pouring into the cabin. All of us in there came popping out like ants. In London, which was still in bad shape from the war, you couldn't get a good meal or a hotel room. People were sleeping in the street. Carrying my golf bag, I knocked on the door of a private home in Kensington Road and asked to rent a room overnight.

"I'll be leaving in the morning. I'm going to St. Andrews."

"So I see," the owner said. "Having fun while the rest of us are on rations."

"Fun, hell," I said. "You should see me putt, mister." He slammed the door in my face.

At another house, a guy who looked like Boris Karloff with a monocle rented me a room for one hour for seven dollars. After one hour of sleep, I was kicked out and someone else got my bed. I slept in a depot and then caught the Edinburgh train. On the train, I began to get a light-headed, dizzy feeling. I thought it was from all the beans and porridge I'd eaten—there being no other food available. But an Englishwoman explained it. "You've been drinking a lot of our tea, haven't you?" she asked. "Well, it's quite strong these days, and undoubtedly you are suffering from a tea jag, which bothers most strangers. It's quite similar to being inebriated. Don't worry, in time it will pass."

Now I knew I'd putt myself out of the Open in the first eighteen holes.

Next came Duke Whoozis, and the insult I gave the Royal and Ancient course, without meaning to. After my remark that it was a pretty run-down old weed patch, the London *Times* gave me a good jab:

"Snead, a rural American type, undoubtedly would think the Leaning Tower of Pisa a structure about to totter and crash at his feet."

After that came caddie troubles. The way most golfers tell it, St. Andrews caddies are the world's best and can read the grass right down to the roots from Burn Hole, which is No. 1 on the Old Course, to Home Hole. Mine were a bunch of bums. I had four caddies in four days. One of them whistled between his teeth when I putted. After letting him go, I drew a fellow in sailor pants who couldn't judge distances or carry. On one hole he slipped me the 3-iron and said, "That's the ticket, mate." The shot left me 30 yards short of the green. The next hole he clubbed me with a 5-iron. This time I refused his advice, took a

7-iron, and even then landed over the green in a bunker. "Mate, you're sunk," I said, and gave him back to the caddie master. Then came "Scotty," guaranteed to be St. Andrews' best.

Scotty went to jail for drunkenness the night before the Open started, leaving me to figure the course for myself.

The gigantic double greens were a break for me. One of them measured almost two acres in size. I knew that nobody in the field, including the great Henry Cotton, Bobby Locke, Johnny Bulla, Dai Rees, and Lawson Little, would get close enough very often to hole out with one putt, which would help equalize my poor work around the pin. I thought that if I could beat them from tee to green, I had a chance to finish in the money. As it turned out, I never was longer off the tee. On No. 10, 312 yards, I drove the green three times in four rounds; on No. 12, 314 yards, I drove the green two out of four.

But it was the heavy-blade putter I was using that put me in a three-way tie for first place with a total of 215 strokes when the third round ended. I couldn't believe what was happening.

Later on I saw that a habit of mine on long putts had paid off. From 25 feet or more distance, I've never believed in going for the cup. On long-approach putts, any time you aim to make them you'll either overcharge by 10 or 15 feet or fall far short and wind up 3-putting, the reason being that from 25 to 75 feet no one can make a 4¼-inch cup his target with accuracy. From far out, I pick a line and adjust speed *to* the general area of the hole. Closer up, I go directly *at* it. I want my lag putts to die within easy second-shot distance of the cup.

There's another percentage involved here. A putt traveling fast enough to overrun by 2 or 3 feet must hit the cup almost dead center to go in, whereas a putt stroked up to the cup and no farther may fall in even if it's an inch or more off line from center.

A cup has a front and rear door and two side doors—four entrances. By not charging too hard, you take advantage of all of them.

Walter Travis, who was such an uncanny putt master that the British barred his center-shafted Schenectady mallet from their country for forty-odd years, didn't agree with that theory. He took dead aim every time. Billy Caspar, one of the best putters today, does agree. Doc Cary Middlecoff thinks he can hole every long putt and goes for broke. Lloyd Mangrum, one of the half dozen best on the greens I've seen, tried to drop 90-footers but advised average golfers to aim for a 2-foot circle around the pin. There's little agreement on this, but after the British Open I never questioned this part of the game again.

In the final round, a St. Andrews Bay gale made every putt a guess. It was so bad that balls jiggled and oscillated when you addressed them. Flory Von Donck, the Belgian, had a downhill 20-footer with the windstorm behind him. Von Donck turned his back to the cup, putted uphill away from the target, and then, as the ball rolled back down the hill, a sudden gust swooped it 15 feet past the hole. Others who tried to drop approach putts in that wind wound up chewing on their mufflers when their long rollers were blown every which way.

All I wanted was to be reasonably close and to lag for the safest possible position on my second putt. With the green sloping toward me (in any kind of weather) I'd rather be 3 feet short than over. It's 2-1 easier to make a 36-incher from an uphill lie than from a downhill or sidehill lie. Putting uphill, you take a firm, natural grip. Downhill, because of the extra momentum you'll get, you loosen the grip, and without realizing it you can get sloppy. On the No. 10 hole, from 20 feet away, I eased up to within 18 inches and dropped it for a birdie. On No. 12, from 30 feet, I did the same thing. With the 40-mph wind behind me, I stroked extra easy on those slick, dried-out greens. Against a crosswind, I allowed for a big break, up to 6 feet on long putts.

On No. 14, Hell's Bunker, a Scotsman stuck his whiskers in my face and said, "You can shoot sixes from here on in, laddie, and win."

I checked this with Richards Vidmer, the New York *Times* reporter, who carried a walkie-talkie radio.

"No, six a hole isn't safe," said Vidmer. "But you can take it with fives. Cotton, Rees, and Von Nida have blown themselves out of it. But Bulla and Locke are still close."

With that news, I gambled a bit on an 8-footer at Hell's Bunker and got it for another birdie. At the par-4 sixteenth, some genius had placed the pin on a little shelf at the rear green guarded by a steep incline. My 30-footer climbed the grade, then rolled part way back to me. Next time I putted stiff to the flag, but the result was 3 putts, 5 strokes, and a bogey.

On the Road Hole, No. 17, the gale took my pretty 9-iron pitch, right on the flag, and swooped it 25 feet away. Again just lagging up, I was paid off for being cautious. The wind provided an extra few turns and in she fell—my longest putt of the tournament.

"He could use his bloomin' puttah on every shot and win!" somebody in the crowd shouted. That was music to my ears. Back home they'd been saying that I couldn't roll a marble into a manhole with both hands.

The Road Hole won the Open. All I had to do was play out No. 18 in 7 shots—and I took 4—to finish ahead of Locke and Bulla. I'd been half drunk on tea, and had gone without sleep and a good caddie, but my 290 score beat all four of Walter Hagen's best totals in this tournament, two of the three winning scores of Bob Jones, and the best by Tommy Armour, Jock Hutchison, and Denny Shute when they took home the cup.

The purse of $600 was such a joke that I decided then and there not to defend the title. My traveling expenses alone were over $1,000, and nobody but me picked up that tab. On top of that, all my hitting muscles "froze" in the icy wind at St. Andrews. For days I ached in every joint.

Then there was my caddie friend, "Scotty," who got himself sprung from jail and begged me to give him the winning ball. "Maun," he promised, tearfully, "I'll treasure it all my days."

That ball was worth some cash, and Scotty proved it. An hour later he sold it for fifty quid. So he made more off the Open than I did.

For years afterward, British and American writers panned me for passing up the British Open, but like I've always said—as far as I'm concerned, any time you leave the U.S.A., you're just camping out.

For a while in '46, I thought my putting touch was back. It's easy to kid yourself about a thing like that, even though it's a well-known fact that putting is my biggest weakness. From a distance, I believe I can read contour and grass grain with any pro alive. But little putts of 8 feet and less that stayed out have cost me $200,000 or more, led me into a thousand experiments, cost me two or three National Open titles, and left me so ashamed that once I almost quit golf. I'm known as the "King of the Yippers." Far more commentators have hinted that I'm gutless under pressure than have said that now and then I roll a tough one in.

Maybe others can learn from my mistakes. I know I did. In the 1961 Las Vegas Tournament of Champions, which I won with a score of 68-67-69-69—273, my last stroke was a 52-footer from just off the green. The grain of the green and slope was strong to the right. Allowing for a 5-foot break, I nursed the ball in. Comedian Jerry Lewis, who got 10-1 odds from people around the green, and was betting with both hands, won $900 on that shot.

But also in 1959-60 I signed for a series of seven head-to-head matches with Arnold Palmer, the top money winner of recent years. Some people felt downright sorry for "old Sam" against the young fellow.

The result was four Snead wins, two Palmer wins, and one tie, and I guess it showed I'll be around awhile yet. But the score could have been 5-2 for me if I hadn't pulled the oldest boner in the putting book. On the fifth hole of our match at Boca

Raton, Florida, Palmer pitched to 4 feet of the pin in 4 shots, while I was 3 feet away in 3.

I'll just pick up an easy stroke or two here, I told myself.

Palmer has such skinny hips that I wonder how his pants stay up. When he tees off, his slacks drop about four inches below his umbilicus, which is a word Jimmy Demaret taught me to spell.

"Hit him in the umbilicus, Sam!" Demaret hollered at me one night in a café when a heckler was pestering me.

"Where?" I said, turning around.

Demaret pointed to his middle, and while he was explaining it, the drunken heckler almost crowned me with an ash tray. That's a word I won't forget—umbilicus.

But, above his thin waist, Palmer is all muscle and power and he isn't the gentle type with a putter. He's like Byron Nelson: he charges boldly at the hole. He makes a lot of 1-putt "hard-way 4s" that way, but it's my feeling he could use more caution. Anyway, at Boca Raton he canned his 4-footer. Then I lined up my 36-inch chippy, tapped it carefully, and missed by 4 inches.

This is where the mind leaves the body more than any other time in golf. Hardly looking as I disgustedly jabbed the 4-incher "into" the cup, my putter struck the ground. It rebounded and topped the ball 2 inches. Instead of a birdie 4, I took a bogey 6 to tie the match. It stayed that way to the end. A one-second slip cost me the win.

You'd think that after walking more than the distance around the earth on golf courses I'd know better than that. But that's putting.

In the beginning, I putted with my feet close together and from a more upright position than most pros. I picked that up from Bob Jones. My weight was evenly balanced. I was a wrist putter. My wrists broke on the backswing and I hit the ball with a slight snap. Jones addressed a putt much like a chip shot and so did I at age twenty. Contact was made on the upswing, with power supplied by the right hand. With that style, from 1935 until World War II, I didn't have a sign of the "yips." On a clean surface, I could make the ball go in three ways—that is, end over end and by applying spin on it from right to left and from left to right. When you can curl them in like that against any break of the green, you have a very fine touch. But it's a young man's touch. It fades fast after ten years or so.

Also mimicking Jones, I used a very light Calamity Jane blade putter, and after a last look at the ball and its relation to the hole, I turned my head slightly to the right, with my left eye mainly fixed on the ball. Since Jones had this habit, it was good enough for me. Later, I met an optometrist who gave me an explanation.

"When I crouch behind a ball," I told him, "I can get a perfect line on a putt. Then, when I get over it, the ball seems aimed to the right of the cup."

"The visual angle can be an illusion," he said. "If you'll cock your head about an inch to the right, bringing your master eye into more play, you'll get the correct line."

I still recommend this head action, because it also helps keep your head down right through the putt.

Before long, however, my whole style had to be discarded. From late 1946 on, I came down with the longest and most terrible case of yips ever seen in the P.G.A. After the British Open, I played Bobby Locke a set of matches on his native South African courses for a guarantee of $10,000. I expected to win most of them. In sixteen matches Locke beat me twelve times. I won only twice and we halved the others. We opened at Locke's home club, Vereeniging, near Johannesburg, and after nine holes I had him 5 down and thought I'd run him right out of Africa; but then he went to work, and after thirty-six holes he had me 8 down and seven holes to play. It got worse. In some of the eighteen-hole matches my ball would be inside his from tee to green on fifteen holes—and Locke would win, 1 up.

Mostly, he did it with a rusty old rattlesnake-headed, hickory-shaft putter and with a style that made no sense at all—until he picked the ball from the hole. By American standards he did everything wrong. But he dropped 30- and 40-footers without thinking twice.

"Cahn y'eemaghin thet, Snead?" he'd say, giving me the needle. "Fantahstic!"

What discouraged me was the way old Droopy Jowls held his putter at the very tip and with his left hand far over the shaft, which was the same grip he used on all shots. The standard reverse overlap grip, with the right little finger on top of the left forefinger, wasn't for Locke. He had a closed stance and hooked his putts instead of straight-lining them. His grip was so light I thought he'd drop the stick. And when he putted, instead of keeping still, he swayed like a Bloomer Girl.

No wristwork at all was used by Locke. He was strictly a pendulum putter. Today I rate him one of the three greatest— for a limited number of years—I've ever seen on a green.

He beat me so often on the greens that I developed a complex I couldn't shake off. At the Bulawayo Club at Shabani in Rhodesia, which borders a jungle, a big gray monkey was leaning against the flagstick when I made my approach shot. "Here, buster, you can do better than me," I said, trying to give the ape my putter.

He ran up a tree and made nasty noises at me while I overshot a 5-footer. Locke had made me so nervous that at the Germiston Country Club I missed 8 putts of less than 2 feet each and lost again.

After that beating, I was glad to leave Africa. Flying home over the Sahara Desert, the Pan American hostess asked how I was shooting and I replied, "Little girl, the only thing that didn't hit me down here was lightning."

About ten minutes later, a lightning bolt knocked the plane sideways and then dropped it like a rock from 22,000 to 15,000 feet in a matter of seconds, all but snapping the necks of everyone aboard—and that's a true story. We were grounded in Dakar for fourteen hours for repairs.

Before I left, Locke asked me, "D'you think I could come to America and make a bean or two?"

"With that putter," I told him, "you could get rich."

I should have kept my mouth shut. Locke's famous U.S. invasion followed, and in five months he took $27,500 in prize money away from the P.G.A. circuit players, me included. The boys were a long time forgiving me for encouraging Locke. The late Clayton Heafner saw Locke putt once and then bet Jimmy Demaret that Locke would beat Demaret and Ben Hogan in every tournament they played. Heafner kept Demaret broke all summer as Locke went from victory to victory.

I didn't like the hook spin Locke gave the ball then and I don't like it now, even though for him it was perfect. He got that left-to-right spin by slightly opening his left hand and closing the face of the blade just a little as it approached and met the ball. It was too tricky for my taste.

But he gave me one valuable clue with his hip sway. I didn't quite appreciate it at the time, but since then I've found that Rule A—*Do not move in putting*—doesn't hold water. Every *great* putter I've known didn't freeze himself over the ball. In fact, they seemed to move just about everything. Bob Jones moved his body and legs with his swing, and so did Johnny Farrell in his prime. Nelson and Hogan had a distinct shoulder sway. They did this because when you remain stationary, you build up tension. You can't be relaxed if you imitate a cigar-store Indian.

Trying to relax was no help to me. My yips became a nightmare. In 1947 in the Masters Tournament (where I tied for twentieth place) and in the All-American Open (tied for sixteenth) I took more putts than all other shots combined. A par golfer can afford 36 putts in a par-72 round. A fifty-fifty balance between putts and shots is fine for him. A subpar pro must shave that greens figure to 30 or less putts if he's to win consistently. In the '47 United States Open a missed 30½-inch putt cost me the play-off match to Lew Worsham. All year I didn't win one individual title, and my earnings fell to $9,703— less than I'd won as a rookie in 1937. In 1948 the yips stayed right with me. While Ben Hogan won $32,000, I won less than $7,000. Two of the lowest points came in California and Florida.

In the St. Petersburg Open, my second shot off the tee fell behind two spreading trees. The tangled limbs left only a tiny opening to the pin. My 5-iron shot bored through that hole 160 yards to stop within 4 feet of the cup.

"Wow!" I heard a fan following me up the fairway tell his friend. "That's why I follow this hillbilly around. Did you ever see a greater recovery than that?"

It gave me a little glow until I heard him say, "Now watch the stupe go up there and blow the putt."

I did. And kept on doing it. At St. Pete I finished forty-second in a tournament I'd won three times before. Some other finishes were these:

> Bing Crosby Invitational—*tied for thirtieth*
> Miami Four-Ball—*defeated first round*
> Tucson Open—*tied for nineteenth*
> Phoenix Open—*tied for fourteenth*
> Jacksonville Invitational—*sixteenth*
> Masters Tournament—*tied for fifteenth*

You don't know grief until you've missed successive putts of twelve, eighteen, and twelve inches, which is what happened to me.

Reaching Los Angeles, I broke down completely. For two rounds of the L. A. Open, my touch mysteriously returned, resulting in 69-69 scores that set a new record for the halfway mark of the event. The yips took me then and tore me apart. The rest of my game was never better, but on the carpet I was like a zombi. Over the ball, I felt like someone else's hands held the putter. All control was gone. No such thing as a straight line to any cup existed. Every green seemed to sprout a hogback or dip. On the fourteenth hole, from 18 inches away, I jabbed the ball 2 feet past, jerked again coming back, and needed 3 to get down.

"You're the most pathetic thing I've ever seen," my old buddy, Porky Oliver, said with tears in his eyes.

It was the worst blowup in the P.G.A. since Wild Bill Mehlborn at Dallas twelve years earlier. Bill got his putter frozen behind the ball, couldn't move it, finally gave it a terrified jerk, and sailed that ball clear onto the fairway. Took him a 30-yard chip shot to get back.

Joe Turnesa suggested I try putting one-handed.

"Everything went black on me one time," said Joe. "In desperation I went to one hand. Won the Long Island Open on those tricky greens at Lakeville right after that."

Neither that nor anything else brought a cure. I tried cross-handed putting, various reverse grips, hitting stiff-armed, hitting with the shoulders, using mallets and gooseneck putters, and I still yipped everything. I was a walking nervous breakdown, and I quit the tour and went home to White Sulphur Springs, licked. Hanging up my clubs, I swore I'd never play like a dog in public again. From now on I'd just teach golf—every part of it except putting.

As the winter dragged on, I got so mad I wanted to cut off my arms. Six years of good putting during which I'd won forty tournaments followed by three years of the yips made no sense. Off by myself on the Old White Course at Greenbrier, I started experimenting all over again.

When Bill Tilden couldn't beat anybody in tennis, he hid out in the Berkshire Mountains and worked the kinks out of his serves and volleys. Before the second Schmeling fight, Joe Louis spent a lot of time alone. Crazy Legs Hirsch did the same when he lost his timing in football. If you sit and listen to the grass grow, sometimes your mind opens to ideas you've been missing.

With me, it was remembering that all the putt artists I'd seen had two things in common. First—they kept their wrists flexible at all times. Second—they used a blade- or Cash-In-type putter without offset and with a center-shafted head that gave

them a straight line parallel to the line of roll. After much testing, I decided on five changes:

1) No more simple breaking of the wrists.
2) No more gooseneck or offset putters.
3) Building comfort into my stance any way I could, even
if it went against the "book."
4) A combined two-hand stroke taking the emphasis off
the right hand and extending my follow-through.
5) A brand-new system (for me) of springing the ball off
the putter face.

Deciding that my wrist action had to go was the hardest, because I'd won more than $125,000 in prize money that way. In
this action my hands hadn't moved very far after the ball when
it was struck. They merely hinged a bit from the original address position, backward and forward. It reduced putting to the
simplest form you can get. However, now I had to admit that
such an action is fine when you're young and nerveless but that
later on gnarls appear and you can't possibly roll your wrists
through the stroke exactly the same way as you rolled them
back. The wrist and hand muscles won't follow the same two-
way path with any consistency. And I saw why. I was thirty-six
years old.

To recover smoothness, I had to introduce more arm movement. I had to "loosen" my stroke. This took many adjustments. Mainly there were these:

Weight Balance: Until now, I'd been slightly back on my
heels, fairly upright, feet close together. Trying Ben Hogan's
"tripod" stance, I liked it. Here my weight, instead of being
evenly spread between the legs, was almost entirely on my left
side, with my right leg acting as a prop. I spread my feet—
Hagen-style—to about the width of my shoulders. I came off my
heels more onto the balls of my feet. My hands were free at
address and backstroke, but my left hand and right forearm

rested against my upper right leg at the conclusion of the stroke. My knees were just slightly flexed. By spreading myself more widely over the ball, I began to feel comfortable.

Hitting Action: Like Hogan, I'd favored the right hand in the past. Unlike Hogan, I'd hit up on the ball off a wrist hinge. Too often I'd left the ball short by "snapping" at it with too brief and punchy a stroke. When I was yipping at my worst, I was spanking or knocking the ball instead of just meeting it, and jerking putts long and short.

So I put both hands to work guiding the putter. Not only that, I blended hands, wrists, and arms, looking for a loosening-up effect, a tension-breaker. With muscles from my elbows down in play, I tried to meet the ball with a "dead" action. By "dead" I mean I practiced to prevent the ball from taking off with a brisk, fast-running start. When you spank it, the ball jumps up and gathers momentum instantly. I wanted it to start off lazy-like and gain speed at an even rate. To get that result, I stopped hitting up. I took the putter straight back in a low line and returned it on the flattest possible arc. It was like making a very delicate shot in billiards—more of a push than a hit—and it took weeks to get any feel of it.

My old style

My new style

Follow-Through: My wrists had stopped soon after contact in my old style. Now I let hands and arms go through a little farther, following the ball along the line to the cup I'd selected. A sense of smoothness followed. Finally, I got the feeling that I was rolling or pushing the ball toward the cup with both hands. My short-putt average went up.

I'd always heard that you never should open or close the clubface during the stroke. Experts claimed that if you let the club turn, you lost your square-to-the-hole angle upon contact. But I think too much attention is paid to that, along with the rule that nothing about the golfer should move during the putt except his hands. In my new style, I relaxed with the stroke and let motion flow through my body and legs. On the backswing, the face opened slightly; on follow-through, with the ball well on its way, the face closed slightly. But this was held to a minimum, because my left hand was well under the shaft and square to the putting line and my right palm also was square to the line, and so the impact was square. It wasn't "perfectly" square, as you'll often be told is an absolute rule of putting. Just approximately square.

As I saw it (and still do), Bob Jones was right in 1938 when he said, "Approximate squareness in striking is all any human can expect to attain. Two much attention to this detail can be very easily overdone. Beyond an approximate square alignment, any added care only causes greater tenseness, which interferes with the fluency of the stroke. And over a sloping green, where touch or pace or range is a factor of importance at least equal to direction, a flowing stroke is a necessity."

As to finding a blade- or Cash-In-type center-shafted putter which I could feel confidence in, that was another problem. I tried thirty or forty sticks and none felt right.

The last and biggest problem, the mental side, remained something I had no answer for. Some of the touring pros had tried hypnotism as a cure for their jumpy nerves, but I was damned if I'd go in for that.

In early 1949 I came out of hiding to enter the Tucson, Arizona, Open. A 275 score good for eighteenth place showed I still had the yips. As I was packing to leave Tucson, I noticed someone had left a strange putter in my locker.

"Who does this belong to?" I asked.

Nobody in the locker room knew, so I took another look. It wasn't new or fancy. It was a stiff-shafted, brass-headed, straight-faced, center-shafted job which "hefted" nicely in my hands. I judged it to weigh about sixteen ounces, or slightly heavier than anything I'd been using. The semimallet setback putter I'd last used made me feel that I was either ahead of or behind the ball. With this one, I felt like I was directly over it.

Still I didn't make any plans to use the stick. At the Greensboro, North Carolina, Open in March, Stan Kertes, the Chicago pro, remarked that it was his putter I'd found.

"You want it back?" I asked.

Kertes said, "No, keep it for now. I'll get it back from you some time or other."

When Stan said that, he did me a better than a $100,000 favor.

At Greensboro, on a hunch, I used the stick. With my new style, I knocked in putts from all sides to tie Lloyd Mangrum for first place and then beat him in a play-off, 69 shots to 71. Confidence in myself still was lacking. So I had to believe it was the putter that made the difference.

The next week, at the Masters Tournament, I was on the practice green when Vic Ghezzi came along. He watched my form and remarked, "That looks very sweet, Sam. Keep it up."

"My jerk is gone," I admitted, "but I still can't lay a good line to the hole with my eye. Any ideas?"

"Here's one that works for me," said Vic. "On putts of 6 feet or less, concentrate on starting the ball on the line you like for the first 3 inches. Sight an imaginary 3-inch line and get the putt started right. I've found that it makes them drop."

Brothers and sisters, did Vic's idea work! In the Masters my opening two rounds of 73-75 left me 8 strokes behind Herman Kaiser, Johnny Palmer, and Byron Nelson. After that I went right back to the practice patch. I holed 18 out of 20 putts from all distances. Now I felt confidence both in myself and in the Kertes putter—which is 90 per cent of putting.

Lester Rice, a friend, was watching me. "But will that stroke hold up on the course?" he wanted to know.

"You're damn right it will," I said, and meant it.

A biting wind almost blew us away the last two days at Augusta, but my 67-67 rounds won the $2,750 pot. My 8 birdies, 7 pars, and 3 bogeys on the final round proved I'd discovered something big. On the eighteenth hole I faced a dipping downhiller of 9 feet, the kind I'd been yipping for three years. Without strain, I stepped up and stroked it in. Altogether I needed only 30 putts that last round to win the Masters for the first time.

"Little dude," I said, kissing my new putter, "how I wish I'd found you sooner."

Actually, about fourteen factors went into my comeback, which had only started. After placing third in the Goodall Round Robin, I faced and eliminated Jackie Burke, Jr., Henry Ransom, and Dave Douglas in my first three matches of the National P.G.A. at the Hermitage Country Club at Richmond, Virginia. Next, against Jimmy Demaret, I plunked two 25-footers, one 30-footer, a 15-footer, and a few 12- and 10-footers to win, 4 and 3.

"The only difference in Snead," said Jimmy, "is that he's gettin' humpbacked from pickin' balls out of the can."

But the difference was sensational. Jim Ferrier left me 2 down with his opening 67 in the semifinals; then I caught him with the putter and other shots to win, 3 and 2.

In the finals, Johnny Palmer led almost all the way and the gallery gave me up for dead a dozen times. I didn't catch Palmer until the twenty-second hole, when I needed a 12-foot sidehill putt across a left-to-right slope for a birdie deuce. It was a question of how much "borrow" I needed to compensate for the curve, or break, of the ball. My method in such cases is to first form a mental image of the path the ball should take. Then I look for a shading or other mark on the grass over which the ball must pass if it takes that path. I aim for that spot and let her go. In this case, a tuft of yellowish turf was my aiming point. When the putt fell, I had Palmer 1 down. He never caught up, although I blew myself to a 6 on the twenty-seventh hole, and I closed him out at the thirty-fourth.

From a scared golfer I became a headliner again. It was nice not to hate myself for a change, too. Some of the sponsors who in 1947-48 maybe were thinking of calling off my endorsement contracts for shoes, balls, hats, and the like were in love with old Sam again. I was the first man ever to win the Masters and Professional Golfers Association titles in one season. Also the oldest gent, at thirty-seven, to take the P.G.A.

"After you're thirty-five," Gene Sarazen had been telling everybody, "you're too old to win big championships."

Well, that's so much horse-droppings. At thirty-nine I won another P.G.A., at forty won the Masters, at forty-three won the Vardon Trophy and another Masters, and at forty-nine (which was just the other day) won the Tournament of Champions. But if I hadn't found my putting game again, none of that would have happened. Ben Hogan might be beating all of us in the 1960s if an incurable case of the yips hadn't caught up with him. He can still do everything as well as any man alive—except drop those 5-footers.

My 1949 hot-putting comeback went on and on. Using only the Kertes putter, I won the Capitol City Open, Reading Open, the Dapper Dan, Western Open, Texas Open, Miami Beach Open, Colonial Invitational, North and South Open, and was named P.G.A. "Golfer of the Year." A few other notes in my ledger book still make juicy reading.

That year I shot twenty-four straight tourney rounds, of which twenty-two were covered in 69 shots or better. In 1950 I set a postwar record by winning nine tournaments, a mark that still stands. From the time I chanced upon the lucky putter,

I was never out of the money in sixty-two straight competitions, worth $87,570 to me before the streak was snapped. I didn't yip a putt again until 1952, when Eddie Thompson, my assistant at The Greenbrier, leaned too hard on the putter and snapped it off at the hosel. Eddie wanted to cut his throat, but I told him, "Never mind. I think I'm cured for a while now." Notice I said "for a while." Nobody ever shakes off the greens freeze permanently.

Educating yourself to sink the short, tough ones never ends. From 1950 on, I worked on the idea of blanking out everything around me. You can force yourself to become deaf to any sound or outside annoyance, like a chess player, if you constantly bear down at it. On the seventy-second hole of one of the Los Angeles Opens, I needed a 15-footer to tie Hogan and force a play-off. About 20,000 fans were going "oooh" and "aahhh" as I studied my lie. For three minutes I quartered the green, looking for both major and minor breaks, estimating the speed needed and inspecting the turf around the cup. Right behind me stood a tree whose limbs hung almost over the fringe of the green. Just as I was set to stroke, a man gave an awful screech and fell out of that tree. He crashed into some vines and bushes, and you could hear him thrashing around while people ran to look, and then he stuck up his head and yelled, "Don't worry! I'm all right!"

A year or two earlier I'd have told him that I wished he'd broken both legs. As it was, I blanked him out of my mind. I won't say the interruption didn't cause me to back off from the putt, then start over. However, only a small corner of my mind paid any attention to the noise and confusion. Ninety-nine per cent of me concentrated on the 15 feet from ball to cup.

This was an amphitheater green with hundreds of excited people perched on top of a hill. When I finally batted that long one in, the 20,000 roared and fifty fans lost their footing and came rolling and tumbling downhill onto the green.

Among those who rolled and tumbled the farthest was Leo

Carrillo, the late famous "Pancho" of television. Leo climbed out from under a lady who was sitting on him, helped her to her feet, and the two of them did a happy war dance around the green.

It was the wildest of Hollywood endings, and still I made the putt that forced a play-off, which I won.

Since then the yips have returned, gone away, come back again. There's no lasting remedy, but I do know this:

Very few players—pro, amateur star, and duffer alike—can make the same putting swing twice in a row. One time your hands are going out, next time you're pulling in, and you're always guessing whether you'll hook or push or stroke the ball straight away. You try, but you can't come through on the same line every time. Among the few exceptions I've seen are some very ordinary players and some out-and-out hackers. They have terrible form, technically, but they get the ball into the hole a high per cent of the time. If I try to imitate anybody in golf, it's these people. You might not believe I'd ever take a 90-shooter for a model, but the fact is that they've found the true secret of putting.

First, they compensate for lack of technique (and show that "correct" form isn't absolutely required) by developing a mechanical handstroke that doesn't waver. It's a fixed habit, based on endless practice. They know the blade is steadily going back and coming through on the line they've picked.

Knowing that, they can stop worrying about length of backswing or pointing the left elbow at the hole or any other factor. They're free to concentrate on how much power to apply. Determining speed of the ball takes real thought. Few of us have the clear head needed for this when crouched over a putt.

Finally, these lucky people have the answer when their putting turns poor. Their stroke and speed are good, which leaves only one possibility: they've picked the wrong line. Correcting that, they begin to rattle the can again.

I'm not in that class, much as I try to be. Few of us ever find a one-piece action that doesn't get to fluttering and changing. Johnny Revolta, for instance, ranks among the dozen best putters in history, and in the Greensboro Open he once broke a 65-footer over two dirty rolls of the green into the cup. On the next hole, with a much easier lie, Revolta used up *6 putts*.

Billy Caspar is the modern equivalent of Revolta—one of the greats. In a New Orleans Open play-off not long ago, Billy needed a 40-footer over a green breaking two ways to beat Ken Venturi. He got it. A few tournaments later, Caspar missed an 8-incher that cost him plenty.

In 1960 the yips returned and I couldn't buy the measliest sort of a putt. I was still in the slump when I went to Israel to dedicate the first golf course in that country. Coming home, I stopped in Rome for an audience with Pope John. Just before seeing the Pope, I got to talking with a monsignor of the Vatican staff.

"I brought along my putter," I said, "on the chance that the Pope would bless it."

The monsignor rolled his eyes. "I know, Mr. Snead," he sympathized. "My putting is absolutely hopeless, too."

It gave me quite a turn. After that remark, I didn't bother the Pope. "My goodness," I told the monsignor, "if you *live* here and can't putt, what chance is there for me?"

About all a Baptist like me can do after that, I guess, is look for the line and pray.

SAM SNEAD'S COMMENT:
THE SECRETS OF SUCCESS ON THE GREENS

One man in hundreds has a natural "touch" or "feel" for the close-up work. Most of us must substitute a mechanical stroke, then try to equalize the "born" putter by closer attention to details. The following summary and example lesson shows how I go about it:

A putt you hit and then forget is all but wasted. You should memorize how every putting surface on your favorite course plays—fast, slow, or medium—and how each varies by geography and in changing weather. A green catching daylong sun naturally will play faster than a shaded green. A saucer, or concave, green will retain more moisture than a windswept plateau or tabletop green—so will need a firmer stroke. Memorize the run of the grain, major breaks, tricky hidden spots. Know at a glance when any green was last mowed.

Begin your putt as soon as your approach shot has left your club. The green may tilt or slant somewhat, a fact you can't detect when you're standing on it. From the fairway get a picture of the whole layout.

At the green, even in a friendly match, stop socializing. Don't talk; put away that pipe or cigarette. You're now faced with the most delicate shot of all. Since 40 to 50 per cent of all strokes are putts, only a sucker wastes his attention. Take an alert, tight-mouthed attitude. Ignore any chatter by your partners.

Walk around, study your putt from every angle. You want to know, first, the distance involved. On long approaches, a quick method is to break down distance into 10-foot divisions. Over 25 feet, think in terms of simply lagging up for a short tap-in.

Next take a good minute to read the contours to determine your putting line. First determine the major, ruling slope of the green. The grain or bent of the grass usually will follow any downhill slope. But also search for swells or drops off the major break. You may find a double break—a roll one way and growth of the grain the other direction. Check this from behind your ball, facing your ball *and* from both sides. Side readings often

turn up contours you've missed. Now go to the area around the cup for a close examination. At this spot, your ball weakens, breaks more radically. If a break exists near the pin, plan to allow for it more strongly than for any other obstacle along the line of roll.

Somewhere in here mark and clean your ball, a little matter of importance many golfers neglect.

Now—until you shoot—forget the line you've picked and the "borrow," if any, you'll need. A poor player concentrates mainly on his line. A good player thinks mainly of speed, or the force of his blow. A putt dead on line is no good if you leave it 6 feet short or run 6 feet over. It's far better to judge speed correctly and stroke it 3 feet off line, which would be an unlikely amount of miss even for a duffer. The line should be obvious after a brief look. Figuring speed takes far more savvy. Check the grass for "hairiness" or fuzz, showing it hasn't been mowed for two or three days. If it's hairy, putt with more force than normally. The sheen of the grass is another easy clue: if it looks shiny, the grain is with you; if not, you're putting against extra resistance. Closely inspect the grass around the cup. If it's lush, it should hold the putt. If it's thin and slick, beware of sliding past the hole. To offset the extra momentum you'll get on a downhill putt, stroke softly, try to start the ball with a slow, lazy run. Loosening the grip a fraction will help.

A downhiller hit much too hard doesn't *have* to overrun the hole. But many players never think of that. Except on short downhillers, leave the flagstick in place: it may stop the ball or even bounce it in.

Once you take your stance, all the information you need should be at hand. Don't hem and haw around—hit it. Indecision and mind-changing at the last minute are fatal. Playing off for the 1947 National Open title, my 30½-incher required about 3 inches of left-to-right break. I decided on that amount of borrow. Then I had a hitch in my thinking. I thought, *No, maybe I'd better not break it so much.* That second guess cost me the Open. I missed by just the amount of borrow I didn't take.

Here are four average putters in action, illustrating some of the finer problems you'll meet:

THE GREEN

A typical medium-size circular green. The rear half is flat, except for a large swell, or ridge, bisecting it. The front half has a 2 per cent drop from midway in the green to the front edge. No other swells or dips here. The pin is planted midway in the front-half slope, 20 feet from the edge nearest the fairway.

THE SITUATION

First player is 5 feet below the cup, putting uphill against the grain and across a left-to-right slope.

THE PLAY

First player strokes, allowing 3 inches of break to the left of and above the cup. He slides by the cup on the uphill side by a good inch. He's made two common errors. The uphill grain he overlooked restricted the amount of break. And the perspective on short putts usually causes golfers to allow for more "borrow" than they need. The lesson: on such putts, cut the amount of "borrow" you seem to need by 50 per cent—in this case, from 3 inches to 1½.

THE SITUATION

Second player is near the back edge, 44 feet away, with a flat-surface run until he reaches the ridge. From there it's downhill 25 feet to the pin, with a small right-to-left break in the last 8 feet.

THE PLAY

Second player lags his 44-footer strongly in order to surmount the ridge and "get up" to the hole. But near the hole his ball slows, falls off left, and drifts 5 feet beyond the target. Due to his concern over crossing the major steep swell, he's neglected to notice the lesser break near the cup. He has no alibi, for a second reason. Obviously the downhill slope beyond the hump will accentuate the left-hand break existing in the final 8 feet. The lesson: any break of the green near the cup is the most important of all considerations.

THE SITUATION

Third player is 7 feet away, hole-high to the right. He's shooting sidehill across a moderate right-to-left slope.

THE PLAY

Third player has correct speed but rims the cup on the lower left side from 7 feet out, the ball almost dropping, then collapsing away. Had he shot to the high outside edge of the sloped cup, he'd have been playing to the "pro side" and would have canned it. But he played to the "weak" or "amateur side"— where downhill pull on the ball was exerted away from the target. Lesson: on sidehill putts, aim to the upside lip every time.

THE SITUATION

Fourth player is 10 feet below the hole, with an easy straight uphill putt against the grain.

THE PLAY

Fourth player putts straight uphill on a perfect line and stops on the lip. Another amateur trick. He should have aimed for, and applied enough force to reach, a point 6 inches *beyond* the cup. Forgetting that the grain and slope were against him, he aimed for the cup. The lesson: when putting uphill, firmly draw a bead three or four ball-turns beyond the tomato can.

7

FROM BUSH TO TREE TO TRAP:

SAND AND HAZARD PLAY

It's a fact about me that I hate to travel. Something is always *after* me when I pack my bags and take off for a competition. There isn't anything that can agitate a man and ruin his digestion that hasn't happened to me in planes, automobiles, and boats, and even after I get to a tournament and am just standing around, hitting balls, I'm not safe.

One time during a tour of South America I was set to blast from a bunker when Jimmy Demaret, my traveling partner, said, "Oh, Sam, look behind you."

I did, and an ostrich was standing there. He was so big you had to look at him three times to take him all in, and he had a beak that was so wide open that it could have lopped off my whole head. He made a noise like a vacuum cleaner at me.

We stood there staring at each other for a while, and he won.

When he made a pass at me, I threw up my hand and the ostrich clamped onto it. I've gone up against panthers and bears in the woods with a gun but never thought I'd have to fight a crazy eight-foot feather duster barehanded. I almost lost three fingers and couldn't hit a good shot for two weeks. A U.S. State Department man who'd helped arrange our "Goodwill Tour"

148

of sixteen South American countries said the ostrich was a golf-course pet and only wanted to eat my straw hat.

Demaret said, "Like hell he did. After Sam got through with that bunker, there wouldn't be any sand left in it, and the ostrich was sore because he'd lose a place to hide his head."

On that same trip, we played in the Argentine Open at Córdoba, Argentina, which is noted for its storms. One minute there was a cool wind blowing and a light rain drizzle and then everything turned black. The hail that came down was the size of Florida tangerines. It tore holes through umbrellas and beat big holes in the greens and knocked a few people cold.

Demaret and I started to run, looking like a couple of bean-ball dodgers in a carnival, and before we reached shelter, both of us had lumps you could hang a hat from. We jumped into a car to escape, and then a river of rain came roaring down the barrancas and up over the running boards and floated us down the road.

"What else can happen to us?" I asked Jimmy.

We found out when we got into some dry clothes and stopped sneezing and reached Buenos Aires, where a big golf show was scheduled at the San Andres Country Club.

On one hole, my long putt rolled right up to the cup and would have dropped, except that the ball bounced a foot backward. The green was perfectly smooth. We inspected the cup and found that someone had planted toothpicks all around it—which was one way of keeping the Norte Americanos from beating the local boys.

On another trip, to Léopoldville in the Belgian Congo, I woke up one morning and like to fainted. I was all covered with blood. It took me a while to realize that some giant mosquitoes had found holes in my bed netting and had chewed on me all night.

"Are those mosquitoes dangerous?" I asked the hotel manager.

"Not if you've had spotted fever, malaria, and dengue fever," he said.

"Hell, I just got here!" I yelled. "Where's a doctor?"

The doctor filled me full of pills and said not to worry—that the kind of bugs that'd bitten me couldn't lay up a man for more than a month. Of course, by then he'd weigh about ninety-eight pounds and would twitch all over and be the color of a chicken's leg. The next day I was gone from Léopoldville.

If it wasn't for the money, I'd have stopped traveling years ago. In Iowa there's a town called Green, with about 2,500 population, but it turned out 3,000 fans for an exhibition appearance I made there in 1959. Those folks couldn't have been nicer. But, upon leaving, I was taken to an old hayfield that was used as an airport. "Over there," they said, "is your chartered plane."

"Over where?" I said. In the weeds you could hardly see the tail sticking up from the one-wing, one-motor kite they were sending me to Chicago in.

The pilot, a young guy, strapped me into the other seat. On the take-off we mushed along without getting airborne, and when we missed two parked planes by inches, I asked him, "What the ——— is wrong?"

"Too much gasload, I guess!" he screeched back.

By that time we'd run out of runway and crashed into a barbed-wire fence. Pieces of propeller and wire flew past my head, and then we cleaned out a couple of advertising signs and more fence and went bouncing and swapping ends into a cornfield, where we piled up in a ditch. With all that gas aboard, I tore off the safety belt and jumped for it. Then I saw where I'd cut my hand across the base of the fingers. The pilot bailed out, too, and started cussing.

"Don't let it throw you," I said to him. "One of these days you'll make it."

Just like with the ostrich, it was a few weeks before my hand healed and I could hit smooth shots again.

In another part of this book I've told how a Constellation airliner taking me to the British Open caught fire and how lightning struck my plane over the Sahara Desert, but I've been jinxed in cars, too—such as the time I was hurrying to reach the Miami Open. The modified racing buggy I was driving had extra horsepower and I was using all of it when I came to a straightaway. Up ahead of me, headed my way, were two cars. I swerved out and shot past them at better than 110 mph, and then I caught a glimpse of the general situation.

The rear car was driven by a Florida state policeman, and he was chasing a speeder.

In a spot like that you can only pour on the power and hope that the cop lets first things come first. However, he dropped the other driver to take out after me, and when he flagged me down, things began to pop.

"Why didn't you stop?" he growled. "Didn't you see I was the law?"

"Yes, sir, I sure did," I said. "But what could I do—stick around and admire your style?"

Before he was through with me, I was lucky to even *stay* in Florida, let alone play in the Miami Open.

I suppose the trip a man remembers most is his honeymoon trip.

In August 1940 I took the big plunge and married Audrey Karns, who is still Mrs. Snead and who was the girl I'd held hands with on the school bus when we attended high school in Hot Springs, Virginia. From the time I was eighteen years old we'd thought about marriage. After we had a quiet family wedding down home, the newspapers tried to snoop out our honeymoon plans, and I said, "Nothing doing. Where we're going is a secret. For once I'm going to have privacy."

The place we'd picked was Niagara Falls, which we figured was so obvious that nobody would look for us there. Also it was near Toronto, where the Royal Canadian Open Championship was scheduled the following week, in which I was entered. Audrey didn't mind that I was mixing business with pleasure— as long as we had some privacy first.

We were nervous, like all newlyweds, when we drove off from Hot Springs, and somewhere in Pennsylvania we missed a few road signs. After we had driven 350 miles the first day and were dog-tired, Audrey said, "Doesn't the scenery look awfully familiar around here?" We asked a man about that and found we'd been all over Pennsylvania and Maryland and back again; in fact, we'd lost forty-five miles.

Instead of a bridal suite in a big-city hotel, we had to settle for a motel in Cumberland, Maryland.

"Don't worry," I promised Audrey, "we'll get there in time."

"What for?" she said, sniffing. "To see the Falls or for you to tee off in the Open?"

Whenever we stopped to ask directions, somebody recognized me, and pretty soon half the people between Hot Springs and Buffalo knew that Mr. and Mrs. Sam Snead were headed for Niagara. You can imagine what happened when we reached Toronto and the tournament. All the pros were waiting for me with the needle out. Jug McSpaden, Craig Wood, Johnny Bulla, Ed Dudley, and the others looked at my pretty bride, grinned, and told the sportswriters, "Oh, boy, what a break for us. For once Snead hasn't a chance. This'll cut 25 yards off his drives."

They kidded me so hard and I was so worn out from wrong-way driving and being "just married" that when I stepped up to my first tee shot, I looked down and saw that I was wearing street shoes. When the gallery saw I'd forgotten to wear spikes, they laughed like fools.

If there'd been any way to leave, I'd have taken it.

While Audrey ran to the hotel to get the spikes, I tried to stall, but the officials said, "Play golf." I slipped on the grass in my stocking feet for three holes until the shoes arrived, and after that I was in and out of traps, couldn't drive, and stabbed my putts. After my first-round score of 72, a news story about me began with:

"Shoeless Sam, the Bashful Bridegroom, the winner of the Canadian Open two years ago, is a 25-1 shot not to repeat, after arriving with a new wife and playing with all the pep of a sleepwalker."

The jokes began to get under my skin and I shot some hard golf the next three days, although I couldn't tell you the details. All I know is that I shaved 9 strokes from par the last thirty-six holes and won the Open with a 281 score.

When they handed me the trophy, there wasn't a wisecrack to be heard. Some of the boys had bet 10-1 I wouldn't have the strength to land in the top ten.

Plenty of other hazards have come my way, including the times I've nearly been killed by lightning on the course. In 1938 at Kansas City, a bolt hit a foursome on the green just ahead of me. It knocked me flat. Two of the people were completely burned alive when I picked myself up. Another was getting first aid nearby, but didn't survive. It was a horrible sight. Horton Smith, who won the Masters Championship in 1934-36, had a 30-foot putt to make on that green. While the corpses were being removed, Smith calmly sank his putt. "What could I do for them?" he said. "I had a shot to make, so I made it."

I'll never be *that* cool around hazards. My brother Pete, who's a fine golfer, once was standing under an umbrella with a girl partner when lightning hit the tee. The girl was killed outright. Pete's metal belt buckle and pants zipper were melted, and the bolt twisted around his ribs, ran down his leg, and scorched off the hair in a zigzag line. Pete was paralyzed from the waist down for a few weeks but recovered.

During a TV match at Miami Springs a few seasons ago, lightning killed a man within 7-iron range of me. There was a streak across the fairway—which was me—and I ran and jumped onto a golf cart driven by Gary Nixon, my business partner. "Get out of here!" I yelled. "That was so close it made my hair stand on end."

Nixon is one of those types who never get excited. I'd lost my hat while running and he stared at my bald head.

"Your *what* is standing on end?" he asked.

"Well, my sideburns, I mean," I said. "Now get the hell out of here!"

Escaping the freak kind of hazards, such as ostriches and planes that won't fly and hailstorms, is one thing, but the single part of golf that one one can avoid is the sort of hazards built into every course. The troubles I've been through while traveling can't compare to the problems you find in sand traps, ditches, and water hazards, behind trees and in the woods and deep rough. In my early days one of my toughest problems was learning bunker play and how to handle other bad lies.

There's a simple reason for that: nobody wants to practice such "headache" shots. When did you last see a golfer hitting balls out of bushes and barrancas when he didn't have to?

Another angle concerns the way we humans are built: we see the traps, but we tell ourselves, "They're not going to get *me*. Let the suckers fall in there."

In the late 1930s, when I was the Great Runner-Up in big tournaments and never a winner, O. B. (Pop) Keeler, a very wise critic, wrote that "Sam doesn't kick away tournaments because he isn't trying. And he doesn't really choke up, the way some people claim. No one can say he isn't a money player with plenty of heart. His basic trouble is his failure to allow for trouble. He lacks imagination. Snead doesn't recognize the traps in front of the brook or the clump of trees in a dog-leg. He doesn't consider the gamble involved when he blithely ignores them. He just steps up and socks the ball, and the next minute he's in a lie where a crowbar wouldn't help him."

Maybe Pop was right, but he couldn't argue that I lacked respect for hazards once I landed in them. Because very early I discovered the answer to what is just about the most important secret of golf, which is:

How to score well when you're playing badly.

If you can do that, you're a golfer. You've mastered the fine art of scrambling. To accomplish it, you must be able to explode, semi-explode, chip and putt from any position in all types of bunkers, and after that to play hanging lies, recoveries from behind obstacles and from within depressions and from heavy rough. You must know the difference between the various textures of sand—such as deep and powdery, newly-spread sand, firm and shallow, wet, silicon-base (coarse), and the dune sand you find at seaside courses. You must be able to weigh the percentages on trying to excavate a fully-buried ball and a "fried egg" ball which is partly buried. There's more than one route out of a fairway or greenside trap and several club possibilities. You should be hep to them all.

I see many veteran players who aren't even aware that from a trap you should use one more club—by number, weight, and striking power—than you would use from the same distance on the fairway. The sand you'll take will deaden the distance of the shot just about one club, sometimes two. The difference depends upon the type sand you're in—heavy, light, fluffy, or hard.

I see others who don't know firm-bottom sand when they see it. They play the explosion from a shallow lie as they would from deep, powdery sand and fly the ball far over the green. With only two or three inches of sand in the trap, they bounce the clubhead off hard ground, then into the ball, with disastrous results.

On the other hand, leaving the ball in the trap after one or two swings is among the biggest errors golfers make. They shy off from taking a real solid, follow-through cut at it. The result is a muffled shot or a pop-up.

Along with that comes failure to get the ball up into the air immediately. One reason is that they "charge" the ball; they try to do something extra to make the ball come up, instead of swinging naturally and letting the loft of the club and the sand itself do the work.

For a play-by-play description of assorted trap trouble, I can give you the 1939 United States Open Championship held at

Spring Mill near Philadelphia. I'll give you this one—and you can keep it. It was the worst experience I've had in my twenty-five tournament years. Spring Mill put the line "to Snead a hole" into the golf book to stay. If I'd murdered someone, I'd have lived it down sooner than the '39 Open.

In the opening two rounds, my 68-71 scores led the field and tied Chick Evans' halfway mark in the Open set at Minikahda back in 1916. A couple of peculiar things happened during these thirty-six holes.

On No. 12 hole, a 480-yard backbreaker, my second shot hooked into a trap guarding the left side of the green. It was a fairly light sand lie, but with a big overhang of shaggy grass above me. The pin was 40 feet away, with little putting surface between the trap exit and cup. I needed quick altitude. Then I needed fast "stop," or backspin. To get both, you take a sand wedge with a wide flange on the bottom and play a cut shot. Here you cut the sand under the ball on the bias, the way a plowshare slices through soil. However, it's not quite the same cut shot you play from deep rough.

Your aim is to come into the ball from the outside in—the same sort of action that produces a slice or fade on a regular shot—and help yourself to a thin cushion of sand under the ball. By bringing the clubhead through on a catercorner angle, you won't bury it in sand and muffle its progress.

In fairway rough, you play the cut shot off the right foot with a very open stance. Your body almost faces the hole, to make certain you get that cutting-across-the-ball action. But in a trap, where you want to take a longer divot to build up that sand cushion, you play the ball more forward, off your left instep.

I guess it almost goes without saying that the clubface never touches the ball in any explosion shot—that you simply are playing a divot of sand out onto the green. Personally, I don't see a golf ball in a trap. I think of it as an extra big grain of sand I want to flip out of there. I aim an inch or two back of the ball and generate plenty of hand speed and fast wrist action at impact with the sand. The biggest "grain" in the trap (the ball) is bound to travel farthest if you don't stop the shot and follow-through until your hands are at least shoulder-high at the finish.

In that No. 12 bunker at Spring Mill, I made sure the face of the wedge was up—or wide open—to get quick loft and altitude. I also slowed down my backswing. Nice lazy timing in a trap pays off, I've found.

And out of the soft sand she popped with the backspin a cut shot gives, and in she rolled for a birdie 3. I've holed longer bunker shots, but none that gave me more of a lift. It made my opening-round 68 possible and did more than that. During the next round, I committed the crime of 4-putting a hole from only 25 feet. Steam started to come out of my ears, but then I thought: *That trap shot yesterday evens up the bad and good breaks—so why worry?*

Going into the final eighteen holes, it looked like I just might win my first National Open. My 212 score tied me with Denny Shute, Clayton Heafner, and Craig Wood, 1 stroke behind Johnny Bulla's first-place 211.

I was loose as a goose, mentally. The night before the final day of play, I did some catsprings and some other calisthenics around the hotel-room floor. My roommate, Gene Sarazen, was already in bed and thought my exercises were tomfoolery.

"This stuff helps me to relax," I told him.

"Yes, and you can sprain your back," said Gene, snapping out the lights and practically ordering me to bed.

I finished my sit-ups in the dark and then slept like a possum in his mother's pouch. I felt another 68 or 69 score coming on when I woke up. Couldn't wait to get out there and win me that $100,000 Open.

With seventy holes played, it looked like I'd make it. Two pars on the finishing holes would give me a 69 for the final round and a seventy-two-hole total of 281. A 281 seemed good enough, as it would tie the all-time Open record. I went for the first par on the par-4 seventy-first, where I hit a beautiful 300-yard drive. My second shot was over the green into thick clover grass. Chipping out short, I missed a 5-foot putt by an inch and took a bogey 5.

Right there is where my most famous "blowup" began.

For some reason, nobody wanted to tell me the facts of the situation I was up against—which wasn't anything to worry about. As matters stood, I needed only a par on the last hole to beat the best score registered so far, Byron Nelson's 284, and win. A bogey would tie Nelson. No one else still playing the course was in shape to beat Nelson.

But I didn't know any of this, and my bogey on the seventy-first had made me nervous. Ed Dudley, my playing partner, and others around me knew what Nelson had done, yet not one of them spoke up. When you're in the dark, your fears close in on you. I felt I had to gamble on a birdie on the par-5, 558-yard closing hole.

People were swarming the fairways and I had a thirty-minute, nerve-racking wait while the marshals cleared the way to build up the decision to play that last hole wide open.

The tee shot was hit squarely, but my right hand turned a bit too quickly and the ball started to hook. I said, "Whoa, ball, whoa"—but it hooked into trampled rough anyway. The lie was in sandy soil. Up ahead were traps, short of the green and around it. Normally you'd use an iron to make sure of getting out and up. It was still 275 yards to the pin, however, and I still had the idea that the only way to win was to gamble.

Taking a custom-made 2-wood, with several degrees more loft than a driver, one of my favorite sticks, I went for the pin instead of playing safely out. Hit badly, the ball had no height. It was a low liner pushed down the fairway, and I said, "Giddyap, giddyap," when I saw it failing near a trap 160 yards away.

It fell into the trap. It was partly buried.

Every expert I've read claims that I played the trap shot before I thought it out. That's not true. With 2 shots used up, I had to reach the green with the next (or believed I did) and the green was still 110 yards away. My bunker lie wasn't too bad.

Half the ball was visible. Above me the collar of the trap had been resodded with squares of soil topped by rough grass. This lip had to be cleared at a height of about 5 feet. A heavy sand wedge would get me up but wouldn't give me the needed distance. I asked the caddie for a shallower-faced club. "Give me the 8-iron," I said.

Even in 1939, when I was only a two-year touring pro, I knew how risky it can be to use a semilofted iron from a semiburied lie. The danger is that you'll catch the ball too clean. If you don't take enough sand, you don't get it up. Weighing that against the need to reach the green in 3, I gambled.

The ball went 4 feet, slammed into the collar, and stuck in a crack left by the resodding. The moans and groans that went up were nothing to my feeling when I caught it too clean and saw it plug in there. In hitting too clean, you don't get under the ball; you hit too high on it and lose the lofted effect of the club. Now I had to chop sod, grass, ball, and all, while standing on sand below the ball.

To cut it out required a sideswiping blow, and she slashed out to the left 40 yards into another bunker. I was sick all over. Still thinking I needed a birdie on No. 72 to win, all my hopes were gone. In landing in that second trap, I'd used up my birdie shot. And now I was shooting 5 from another tough lie in sand.

Just then somebody stepped out of the gallery and said, "Nelson finished at 284. You've got to get down in two more to tie him."

I thought I'd explode at this news. All those gambling shots had been needless. "Why didn't somebody tell me that back on the tee," I snarled, "so I could play it safe?" I was mad enough to plow through that crowd, swinging a club right and left. People will give you nine million miles of advice when you don't need it, but here in the clutch, they had dummied up on me.

If there's anything in this story I'm not ashamed of, it was the 9-iron recovery I made then. I was shaking all over. But I was still thinking. My ball rested 4 or 5 inches below my feet at the bunker's edge. In any situation where you must stand in the trapside grass with the ball below you, the danger is "falling into" the shot and slicing it. Unless you're careful, because your body is tilted forward, you tend to shift weight too soon from your right leg, on the backswing, to the left leg, on the downswing. Which gives you a push or slice. A photo I have of this Spring Mill explosion shows how I avoided that. I bent my knees more than usual, "sitting down" to the ball. My weight was back on my heels to prevent overshifting. I choked down on the club, to make sure I stayed down to the ball throughout the swing. If you rise up even a little bit on a lie like this, you're ruined. The clubface was closed slightly to counteract any slice. And I scraped the ball onto the green, 40 feet from the cup.

To tie Nelson, I needed the putt, and again I'm not ashamed —the 40-footer came close. It lipped the cup and twisted 3 feet away.

After that, I was an awful sight. I didn't give a damn anymore. The collapse was complete when I missed the 3-footer. One more putt gave me an 8—the most talked-about 8 ever taken in golf, I guess. Some women were crying and men were patting me on the back as I walked to the locker room. It was worse in there. There was dead silence. The other pros avoided looking at me, to spare me embarrassment. The sportswriters stayed far away, too. All except one, George Trevor of New York, who walked up with a pencil and notebook in hand and asked, "Sam, what happened on that last hole?"

The boys led Trevor away before I did something I'd regret. When you need only a bogey 6 to tie for the United States Open Championship, and you make an 8, you're ready to take the gas pipe. My score of 286 was good for third place. Craig Wood and Denny Shute came in later with 284s, to tie Nelson, and Byron then won the play-off.

In my heart I know I'd have won, had somebody briefed me on the true situation back at the seventy-second tee.

That night my old pal, Johnny Bulla, took me under tow and, instead of letting me hide out alone in a hotel room, saw to it that I ate dinner in a public place, then took in a show. "The newspapers will cut you to pieces for this," he warned. "So you'd better start facing it right now."

They stuck it in and broke it off. I was called yellow and a bum and a meathead. The Big Eight never has been forgotten. Fans remember it today when they forget my winning 67-67 finish in the 1949 Masters, or the eagle I shot to beat Jim Ferrier in the 1949 P.G.A. semifinals, or my unbroken string of play-off wins over Ben Hogan, or the 70-70-70 I shot in the closing rounds of the 1947 National Open.

To show you how they worked me over, the very next year my first-round Open score was 67 at Canterbury in Cleveland. That was a course record and the lowest first round in Open history up to that time. Walking past the scoreboard, I saw a group of fans, golfers and writers, who waited until I was within earshot.

"Can you see Snead's score?" said one of them, nudging another. "What did he do?"

"He shot a 67," the other guy answered.

"Well, that still gives him a chance to finish somewhere in the money."

Wisecracks like that hurt a man. After Spring Mill, the tension was so great that I felt ready for a nervous breakdown. My weight tailed off to 151 pounds, or thirty below normal, and I played on raw nerves, until a doctor told me, "You can't go on like this without having a complete collapse."

He forced me to take a few weeks of rest after watching me stand up to a practice ball, shaking like a leaf, hardly able to bring down the club.

At Fort Worth, Texas, in the 1941 Open, they pasted a national magazine picture of me—showing my agonized expression on the final green at Spring Mill—in the locker room. Blown-up copies of the photo were stuck up all around the clubhouse. Wherever I went, I saw myself as I'd looked in 1939. What a torture treatment that was.

Then I tore loose some back muscles during the third round at Fort Worth, the pain becoming so bad that on the No. 18

hole I couldn't bend over to line up my putt. I had to putt without lining up the ball and pin, finished with a 77 score and walked inside to hear the smart boys predicting, "Watch Snead blow all the way to an 80 in the final round this afternoon."

Locating Dr. Carl Young of Houston, an old friend, I told him, "Tape me up, Doc, so that I can at least finish this thing. If I withdraw now, they'll be sure I'm yellow and will never believe any injury story."

Young put me on a clubhouse table, tore a big towel into small pieces, pulled out a role of adhesive tape and went to work. He taped me until I could hardly breathe. "You belong in a hospital," the doc said. "One hard swing can ruin those back muscles for good."

But I'm proud to say I finished the Open, carding a 73, and got myself a tie for twelfth place.

Harry Ferguson, the United Press writer, was one who said a kind word. "Those photographs that leered at Snead from every wall had much to do with his decision to go on and take it for eighteen agonizing holes. I think something in him had been so badly wounded that he caught fire; it made him want to show the world he wasn't a 'victim' of an Open neurosis and wasn't a quitter. That was the kind of victory Snead won with his 73 today—and in its way it is almost as important as the first-place finish in the tournament by Craig Wood."

Since the Open is the only major title I've never won, the public believes that my 1939 experience shocked me into a paralysis where this tournament is concerned. But I don't believe the blowup dented my confidence at all. Six times since then I've been in serious contention in the Open. Four times I've been runner-up. Since 1939, I've set two Open scoring records: for the lowest first round and for the lowest two opening rounds. If that's the record of a "choker," then I'm guilty.

I don't believe in hexes or "Open pressure." Once, in 1947, I needed a twisty 18-foot putt on the last hole of the National Open to force a play-off. The Old Hillbilly got that one, and nobody but me was moving the club.

Bunkers can spook you, though. If you ever build up a fear of them, you'll never shake it.

To be able to scramble from trouble, I want to repeat, is the key to winning golf. A lot of what I picked up as a green kid came from watching masters of the sand irons, such as Henry Cotton of England, Ralph Guldahl, Jimmy Demaret, Walter Hagen, Denny Shute, and Johnny Revolta. In June of 1937, as the rookie member of the Ryder Cup team, which challenged the British at Southport, England, I was given a swell chance to study not only Cotton and Alf Padgham, the stars of the opposition, but teammates like Shute, Revolta, and Gene Sarazen. It was Sarazen who invented the sand wedge in 1931, which revolutionized trap play.

As it worked out, it seemed I'd never get to see the stars try for a tough recovery. After winning my Ryder match from Dick Burton of England, I followed the big boys around. Whenever traps were ahead, I hustled down to get a ringside view.

Sarazen was playing Percy Alliss, and on the sixteenth hole he overshot the green. The ball started for a deep bunker but caromed into the lap of a woman sitting on the grass.

"Oh, what'll I do?" she said.

"Get rid of it," said her husband.

So she gave her skirt a fling and tossed the ball onto the green, 20 feet from the cup. The officials didn't see it. It wasn't my business, so I said nothing. Sarazen knew nothing about it. He putted out, winning the hole that decided the match in his favor, 1 up.

Then along came Shute. He overran the green into a drainage ditch. This was a shot I wanted to see. And then another English doll in a big hat scooped up the ball and tossed it into the clear.

"Madam, you simply can't do that," said a bystander.

"Oh, but it was in such a horrible place," she whinnied.

Shute got his par, which enabled him to halve his match with S. L. King and split points.

Our team took home the Ryder Cup by a score of 8-4. With

women like that around, I wondered how England ever had been able to rule the roost all over the world at one time.

On that same trip, my own experiences proved the best teacher. On one hole I was in so much wild country that I didn't once see the flag from the tee until I was ready to putt out. It began when my drive pushed into some 6-foot-high bushes the Scots call gorse. I found the ball stuck in a bush about a foot off the ground. All you can do in such cases is take your sharpest iron and whack toward the fairway. The bush muffled my 9-iron blade and I was lucky to even dislodge the ball. It flew into a pit nearby. This was a real Black Hole of Calcutta, if you ever saw one.

It took a while to climb down into this thing, which could hold a three-story barn and an outhouse, too. Probably it's roofed over today and used for a fallout shelter. We wouldn't allow a horrible thing like that to cross the U.S. borders, but, the way the English figure, if it was good enough for corralling herds of sheep and cows during storms in 1750, it's good enough to play golf out of.

It was a long, narrow trap with a wing at each end, under each of which was a cave. Luckily, my ball was midway in the pit. Shooting straight up the steep side was the short way out and also the riskiest. In extra-steep traps, the smart way out is the long way. You should follow the shallowest part of the terrain to safety, even if it means sacrificing a stroke. When I did this, playing down the length of the pit, my ball disappeared.

"Very neat, sir," said my caddie when he pulled me out. "You're out of Hades and now you're only in Purgatory."

The bunker called Purgatory was almost as deep as the last one. It featured a perpendicular brick wall between me and the green.

"If you strike the bricks," said the caddie, "duck fast, sir. Old Effingham took a rebound recently and had several teeth smashed out."

"What club did old Effy use?" I asked.

"The wedge, sir."

"Well, you just hand me the 9-iron."

In this case, the wedge would do the trick, but it wouldn't get me anywhere except out of the trap. An explosion shot from sand that's properly made won't carry more than 30 yards. I'd used up 3 shots already and still hadn't seen the pin, which was 60 to 70 yards away. The 9-iron is your best tool for getting both extreme elevation and carry. It's good for any distance up to 100 yards. The swing with it from a trap is the same as with the wedge. You play off the left heel, slow down the action for exact timing, and do all the striking with your hands, arms, and shoulders. There's little leg action, other than a slight flexing of the knees. The left heel stays in solid contact with the ground.

I just shut my eyes and cudgeled it with all I had and the last thing I heard was a sound that made me think I'd hit the bricks; instead it was the sizzling of the ball through the rough on top of the wall. Climbing out, I found myself 25 feet from the cup. Two putts gave me a 6 on the par-4 hole—the best scrambling 6 I've ever made.

You must judge your chances carefully in deep traps. On Hades, I'd played safe. On Purgatory, I took a chance, since I didn't dare sacrifice any more safe strokes.

The question of when to use the sand wedge and when to use other clubs of the pitching staff—seven-, eight-, or nine-iron or pitching wedge—was a problem I worked out by trial and error. If you recall, at Spring Mill, in my Big Eight blowup, when I tried lifting a partly-buried ball with an 8-iron, I didn't get out. However, that was a desperation act—and unnecessary, as it turned out. Normally, I'd never attempt such a thing.

When in doubt, I always blast out with the sand wedge. In dry sand, only when the ball sits well up in a very clean lie in a bunker near the green will I consider chipping out. Even then, before I'll take a seven-, eight-, or nine-iron, there must be two other factors in my favor. There must be no bank or obstacle in front of me. And, since the chip won't give me near the "stop," or backspin, of a true explosion, there must be plenty of putting surface between me and the cup. "The chip shot from a bunker," Henry Cotton used to say, "is like the lapidary's stroke of a diamond."

It's real delicate. You must strike the ball cleanly, before taking any sand. If any sand is struck behind the ball, the club-head will hang and smother the shot. To me, the chip from sand is valuable only when the trap is very shallow or the sand is very hard or wet.

In fairway traps, with much distance to be covered and with a flat, clean lie, a long iron or the lofted 4-wood is the proper club. You pick the ball clean before taking sand.

Now and then, I've been inclined to shank the shot out of traps where my stance was abnormal. In the 1950 Los Angeles Open, on a 310-yard hole with the wind behind me, my drive was bunkered in front of the green. The ball was below my feet if I stood on the trap's edge. So it had to be one of those one-foot-in-the-trap-and-one-out shots. Trying to chip from the outside in—the cut shot—in order to get heavy backspin, my downward stroke was more outside than I'd intended. Impact was at the neck of the club. Off to the right she flew, hitting Virginia Bruce, the actress, in the wrist. A real dub's shot.

That's the danger with the cut shot, which is too fine for many golfers to attempt. Your wrist action never must get too loose and you must cut across the ball—but not too sharply. If you come down too much on the outside, like a man chopping a tree, the whole clubface is outside the ball. Then you're bound to shank.

In that same City of Angels Open, one of those pesky uphill bunker lies could have cost me the tournament. I was under the steep front lip of the trap, buried a good inch. Any explosion had to be almost straight up to clear that sharp lip. The first problem was balance. One foot was up on top of the lip, the other buried in sand. Straddled out like that, you want to make sure the hind foot is dug in good and solid. Any little cave-in of sand when you swing ruins everything.

On such uphill explosions, I'd often left myself far short of the pin. And I knew why. Shooting uphill, your clubface is laid open at a steeper angle than normally because of the incline of the sandbank. Actually, since you've already opened the face to get fast loft, you are doubling your angle of projection. The slope of the bank multiplies loft. Hitting uphill, you'll get a higher and shorter ball than you would from a more level lie. Often you'll pop it straight up and barely reach the green.

So it all depended on reminding myself to hit harder than usual and as close to the ball as possible, while still exploding some sand back of the ball.

My wedge bit in about half an inch behind the ball. To counter the shock effect, I applied extra-firm left-arm pressure. Uphill, you also take a whopping amount of sand *ahead* of the ball, so your follow-through must be powerfully strong.

This was no pop-up. The explosion sprayed sand halfway to the cup, 40 feet away, and the ball trickled to 7 feet from the pin. I was proud of that one. I'd damned near dislocated my spine doing it.

With that, I went on and won the tournament.

Wet sand, which scares many people, never has plagued me. I even welcome it. I just swing a bit easier than usual, taking less sand, and allow for the fact that balls kick out farther from wet sand than dry, but, once on the green, won't roll as far. If the wet sand is packed very hard, look out for the club bouncing up and out fast, which can make you skull the ball, That's why a chipping iron comes in handy. The wedge tends to bounce off a hard, wet bottom.

Powdery sand is awful stuff. The ball imbeds itself as it rolls to a rest; then the fluffy texture sucks all the strength from your club. Fine sand has no abrasive quality. It offers so little resistance that you cut too deep under the ball unless you're very cautious. You can't get good "stop" on the ball either. You can only hit hard and allow for a long run on the green.

In Texas one time, I watched Lloyd (The Moustache) Mangrum blasting sensational shots from greenside traps with almost no putting surface between the trap fringe and the hole. He didn't roll one of those shorties past the target.

"What's your gimmick?" I asked.

"You've got to soften the swing," said Lloyd, "and what are the choices? You can take a shorter backswing or a shorter fol-low-through. I like to take a regular backswing and play a normal explosion. On the foreswing, I shorten up. By not coming on through, I don't fly over the hole."

That's one I've used to put money in the bank.

Doc Middlecoff once had the fault of playing mid-trap sand shots like a low pitch, coming out too low and catching the trap collar.

"What's the matter with you?" I said. "When you're in the front bank of a bunker, you get loft real fast. But when you're near the center or rear of the bunker, with plenty of operating room, you hit those clothesliners."

"Yes, and if the ##!*XX! ball doesn't hang up on the edge, it shoots out and runs all the way to Kansas," said Doc.

Later on, I noticed he'd cured the habit. "I just began to build an imaginary mound a couple of feet in front of the ball," he explained. "I tell myself I've got to get over it. And it works."

It was the Doc's good shooting and my own muleheadedness that cost me a chance to win my fourth Masters Championship in 1955. Feeling nice and loose, I was 4 under par going to the thirteenth hole of the final round. Hitting them sweet and far. The thirteenth at the Augusta Masters is 475 yards, par 5, and a good birdie or eagle hole in dry weather. You can pick up a shot here because the contours of the green tend to run your second shot close to the flag. As a "tightener," the Masters committee had stuck a new trap to the left of the green. It was small, with a sort of tongue extending. My second shot fell into this soft tongue, where it buried out of sight.

I was standing there scratching my head when a rules-commit-tee member eased up. "Sam," he said, "you can pick up that ball for purposes of identifying it as yours."

"The hell you can!" I exclaimed. "The rule is that you can't touch any part of any ball in a hazard."

This fellow's intentions were wonderful. However, I'd have suffered a 2-stroke penalty if I'd done more than just brush enough sand off the top to see the pill. As I saw it then, my choice was to dig it out with a wedge onto the fairway, or I could dig harder and try for the green. My first whack toward the green only drove it in deeper. Another whack—same thing. This time I gashed the ball. Any sort of logic would have stopped me there, because I couldn't be sure that I wouldn't go on hitting it forever. But my neck was redder than Tommy Bolt's when he misses a putt. All I could think about was proving that my original decision to reach the green wasn't as stupid as it already looked. I gave it the muscle a third time and had me a hole big enough to bury a cat. When I finally dislodged the ball and got out, I'd used 6 strokes, and then 2 putts gave me an 8 on a hole which I'd birdied at least 50 per cent of the time in the past. When I walked away, with the Masters title lost to Middlecoff, I knew what people were saying:

"There goes Bet-a-Million Snead. When's he going to learn not to gamble everything on one long shot?"

I could tell them about the many times that gambling has won big for me. Here, though, I was all wrong. The most common error in trap strategy is to try for too much. I should have swallowed my pride when I saw that buried ball, admitted I'd lost a stroke through a mistake, and settled for just getting back into play on the fairway. To do that, I could have swallowed a stroke penalty and dropped a new ball. Or I could have simply tried to dislodge the ball without thought of steering it to the green.

When it's medal play, such as the Masters, where total strokes decide the winner, only a sucker takes a chance of multiplying one sorry shot with another.

Staying with it too long in a hazard reminds me of Porky Oliver. All of us in the pro ranks thought the world of Porkchops, who never stopped smiling while cancer was killing him last year. In the Bing Crosby show at Cypress Point, California, his drive over an ocean chasm landed at the base of a 200-foot perpendicular cliff on a sandy beach. Porky hit two provisional balls. These also fell into the chasm. His fourth drive cleared the chasm safely. With the penalties, he was now lying 7, if he chose to play the last shot.

"I can do better than that," said Porky, climbing down the cliff.

Forty minutes later he staggered back up, soaked with water and scratched and his shirt half ripped off.

"How many to clear the cliffs?" Crosby asked. "Five wallops?"

Porky shook his head.

"Ten?"

Porky just glared at old Bingo.

"Don't tell me you took an even dozen?"

"It took me sixteen shots to hole out!" roared Porky. "*And get away from me, you damned crooner!*"

No one blamed Porky for his peeve. His card for the round was 38-50.

A tight spot I've often been in is one where your ball is lying close under a tree or bush, where a normal backswing isn't possible. Since you know you'll lose power, you're tempted to force your hands and wrists into an extra effort. To do that can ruin your direction. Even if your backswing is so restricted that you can't cock your wrists, be satisfied with a shot of medium power. Take the best club for the situation, practice several swings to test the room you've got, then forget distance and concentrate on getting back into good fairway position.

I'm never too quick to call a ball unplayable. A second or third look might show you a way out of a hopeless-looking lie. In the Baltusrol Open, my tee shot on the first hole landed against a fence post. There was no way to get at it two-handed or right-handed.

Turning an 8-iron upside down and swinging it left-handed, I ripped out one of the best recoveries of my life. George Fazio measured it next day as having traveled 145 yards from divot to the spot it stopped. It salvaged a par on the hole.

If a ball's lodged in a tree, it's easy to quit and take the penalty. The least a man should do is shinny up and take a look. During the qualifying for the P.G.A. Championship at St. Paul, my approach wedged into the fork of an oak tree. It cost some skin and a cleaning bill, but by doing a monkey act from a limb, I poked it out with a 2-iron, then chipped up and got my par.

You don't want to wear yourself out fighting a treed ball or wild rough, though. You can't pace yourself through eighteen or thirty-six holes if you're always struggling with trouble. You have to know when to give up gracefully. When Clayton Heafner, the big redhead from North Carolina, first joined the P.G.A. tour, he shot a hole in one and led the Oakland Open by 2 strokes after fifty-four holes. A little later, Clayt drove into "tiger country." Refusing to admit an unplayable ball, he twisted his ankle. Next he skied into a tree on the sixty-sixth hole. Not having had newsreel and newspaper cameras follow him before, Clayt was swollen up with pride and gave them a show. He swarmed up that tree, hung by one leg, couldn't reach the ball, split himself wide open between two limbs, and made one hell of a fantastic recovery. He hit out onto the apron for an easy chip up to 3 inches of the cup.

Clayt was taking bows right and left and as nonchalant as a worn-out man can be when he limped up and tapped that putt. He missed, from 3 inches. It gave Jimmy Demaret the Oakland Open by 1 stroke over Heafner.

"Suffering ———!" yelled Clayt, throwing his putter a block. "I've got a hen back home in Charlotte that can lay an egg further than that!"

When in the woods, hacking and sawing your way out never appealed to me. It spoils your disposition, score, and clubs. Before taking a drop-out penalty, though, I learned to walk away from the ball and study all possible routes of escape. You can hit a golf ball many unusual ways and make it go. In one Ryder Cup match, a hooked drive left me in a seven-foot-deep ditch which was at right angles to the fairway and 25 yards deep in a grove of saplings. Straddling the ditch, I bent down, looked backward between my legs, and saw a small opening. Since I had good balance, it wasn't so hard to pop the ball one-handed between my legs onto the fairway.

As a young player, I had trouble learning how to club myself from still another kind of hazard—deep rough. In Florida, Tommy Armour once remarked to me, "Never use from the rough the same club you'd use from the fairway. Take one club less." As I found out, heavy or moist grass forms a cushion between the clubface and ball, preventing the face from gripping the ball. The ball sails free with little or no backspin. You're liable to get a "flier" which will sail unusual distances. And for sure you'll get more run or roll from the rough than on a clipped surface. I've seen 8-irons carry 170 yards, when 125 should be the maximum. So, often, when the shot seems to call for a 6-iron, I'll use a 7 from rough. In very bad rough, six inches high or more, I'll go to the sand wedge, which can cut through almost anything in the grass or weed division. From the 7-iron up, you get a lofted face. Lofting the ball fast is the No. 1 concern in the rough: you want it to rise up the blades of grass, not travel through them.

When a really strange sort of hazard bites me, I try to think it's fate—what will be, will be—and remember how the really cockeyed happenings even up for you. In the Cleveland Open one year, I was about to collect a few thousand bucks first prize when my approach sailed over the green toward the locker room. The lockers adjoined the green. The ball was sure to bounce back either onto or close to the green.

Just then, a course policeman opened a door; the ball whizzed past his ear and stopped in the last stall of the men's toilet. The 2-stroke penalty cost me the Open by 1 shot.

In the 1954 Palm Beach Round Robin, the 1961 U. S. Open Champ, Gene Littler, was in my foursome. My tee shot was headed over the green into trouble when it conked a spectator on the head, bouncing back only 25 feet from the pin. When the fan recovered, I thanked him for having such a hard knob, but I don't think he appreciated it. His wife gave him hell all the way to the first-aid tent.

Then Littler stepped up and did the same thing. Except that a marshal yelled "Look out!" and the crowd back of the green parted like the Red Sea and Littler's ball rolled all the way to Ashtabula.

Where I lost the Cleveland Open, I won the Palm Beach. It evens out.

What we all need is a cool head amongst hazards like Olin Dutra's. Dutra once had to pass seventeen golfers in the homestretch to win the National Open, and did it. He was one of my opponents in the Tournament at Rochester, New York—the day my 270-yard drive bounced and landed spang in the left pants pocket of the greens-committee chief, Dr. O. S. White. When I got there, Doc White was shaking all over.

"I'm s-s-sorry, S-S-Sneadie," he stuttered, "I s-s-should have m-m-m-moved."

"By God, Doc," I said, "I won't take the penalty. I'm gonna take my sharpest iron and slash that ball right out of your pocket. Now hold real still."

"D-d-don't do that to me!" cried Doc. He was so sure I meant it that his false teeth were clicking and clacking.

On the next shot, my problem was forgotten. Dutra's ball hit a man and split his head open so that the blood poured out. Dutra had a deep tan, but he turned white as a tablecloth. That ball rebounded 50 feet after punching a hole in the fan's skull.

It left Dutra a long, money putt. Don't ask me how he did it, but Dutra sank the putt. Far as I know, the fan lived.

SAM SNEAD'S COMMENT:

PLAYING OUT OF SAND AND HAZARDS

The cardinal rules of trap play (explosion-type) are as follows:

1) Settle your feet firmly, digging in, so that nothing can shift under you during the swing; also, since it's against the rules to ground your club in a trap, this will enable you to test the depth and consistency of the sand.

2) Play the ball off the left heel from a well-open stance and with the clubface laid back as open as possible for quick loft.

3) Let the arms and hands do the work, with little leg action; the swing is straightforward from an upright position, with plenty of wrist snap at impact.

4) Be sure the clubhead goes down and forward and emerges with a full follow-through. If your left palm is facing downward at the finish, you've kept the clubhead open and followed through with good form.

Some particularly tough hazard shots you'll meet and how I play them:

Ball in a footprint: Hit it! Added to the fact that it's an explosion shot, the ball is rimmed around with sand and needs extra excavating. If it's a deep depression, switch from a sand iron to the nine-iron or fairway wedge, both of which have quicker "bite."

Ball bunkered in downhill lie at back of trap: You get these back-slope babies now and then. First, take more sand back of the ball than on the flat: dig in a good two inches behind the ball. Close the clubface a bit to conform to the sand's contour. Play the ball back a bit, off the right heel.

Ball in level lie on shallow, firm sand and with no overhang lip: If these four situations exist, use your putter. Use a flat-arm motion, not a chop, so that the blade is parallel to the sand. If you avoid making contact on either the upswing or downswing, which would loft or mash the ball into sand, and strike squarely in the middle, the putter will take you out nicely. I keep my weight forward.

Ball at front of trap, uphill lie: Keep in mind that you're hitting *up:* therefore, the clubhead will plow through deeper and deeper sand as it moves toward and through the ball. This means (1) you need to hit a bit closer to the ball than on the flat and (2) your follow-through must be especially forceful. My weight remains on the left side and I play the outside-in cut shot, as described before. The clubface stays open and square to the line of flight.

A couple of practice tips I've used:

Ralph Guldahl, a great bunker player, liked to break a sand "slump" by practicing dummy swings in which he aimed to take divots of equal size. He wanted his sand divots to be about six inches long and three-quarters of an inch deep. Then Ralph dropped a ball, took real shots with the same swing.

To improve accuracy at hitting behind the ball, draw a line two inches behind the ball or sink a tee. Now aim for these targets, forgetting the ball.

In the drink—water recoveries:

Maybe you don't need me to tell you that:

1) Water is difficult to compress.

2) Water bends light rays at crazy angles, gives a false picture of the ball's position.

3) The ball may move in water while you're swinging on it.

4) Water and mud in the eye can make you flinch away from future tough recoveries.

My rule is to drop out and take the penalty stroke if no part of the ball shows above water. If the ball isn't entirely submerged, I use the least lofted club that fits the particular situation, hit down and as close to the ball as possible, and follow through as in a sand-blast shot.

8

HAWKS, VULTURES, AND PIGEONS:
GAMBLING GOLF

A SLICKER FROM SOUTH CAROLINA • REVISING THE
HANDICAP DOWN • CORNSTARCH AND RETRIBUTION •
A PLUNGERS' MATCH IN HAVANA • PRIMER FOR "BLIND"
BETTERS • MOBSTERS—AND A THREAT • THE CHAMP—
TITANIC THOMPSON • GOOD AND BAD PIGEONS

After I'd been head professional at The Green-brier for some time, a fellow by the first name of "Cy" turned up at the pro shop. He had a bankroll and the urge of most golfers. Being busy, I turned him over to my assistants.

"This Cy doesn't mind losing his money," the boys told me a week or so later. "He's about a six- or seven-handicapper. We've been giving him two strokes a side and winning without much trouble. Now he insists on playing you."

Cy caught me undressing in the locker room. He was built good and trim, appeared to be about thirty, and mentioned South Carolina as his home. "I hear a healthy bet doesn't scare you," he opened up.

"It scares me," I said, "but I've got the habit. Tried to quit gambling once, but it was about as much use as kicking a hog barefoot."

"Well, since I'm far from being in the pro class," said Cy, "let's square things up. Your staff here knows how I play, so how about giving me five strokes a side? With that handicap, there's no limit to the bet; you name it."

I thought it over. From what we'd seen of him, a no-limit wager at those odds didn't sound awfully risky, but Samuel J. Snead had been burned before. Anyway, it was only his opening maneuver.

"No," I said, testing him. "I'll spot you three shots on the front nine and four coming back. But not five."

"What the hell!" he exclaimed disgustedly. "I wouldn't have a chance."

"Suit yourself; it's raining cats and dogs out there anyway." I began unlacing my spiked shoes.

"Oh, OK," said Cy, sourlike. "If that's the only way I can get to play you."

If I've learned anything, it's that when they switch off arguing handicap strokes with you that fast, you want to look out—there's a hawk in the chickenyard. I'd named my conditions, though, and was stuck with them. Out we went, with a bundle laid on the match.

All at once the Cy we'd been watching was a different man. The shots he began to hit weren't learned in any amateur flight, any more than his handling of bad-weather play. Cy took a wider stance than normal, making sure his feet were dug in. He swung flat-footed off the wet fairways, cut down his body turn on all shots up through the 5-iron, and stroked balls over the sloppy greens like he'd been weaned at St. Andrews.

I was out in 32 strokes and was 1 down! My faking friend had a par 35 on the first nine.

We came to No. 10, an All-American hole at The Greenbrier —235 yards, par 3. Needing something to save the day, I said, "How about a press bet on this one?"

"Two hundred suit you?"

"Fine."

Cy drove a screamer through the rain with a 2-iron, a regular Cary Middlecoff kind of shot 15 feet from the hole.

I turned to Emmett, my caddie. "Boy," I told Emmett, "we've been had, and by an expert."

Luckily, my shot dropped in even closer than his, because the birdie that followed and which won me the press bet was all I salvaged that afternoon. Scrambling like it was the National Open, I just managed to halve the match.

"You're not bad," I remarked at the finish.

Cy just gave me a poker face. His scheme had failed only because I'd been able to come up with a desperation 65 for the round. Cy'd shot a 35-37—72, good enough to win all the bets he'd purposely lost the previous week. He'd done as good a job of disguising his real form as you'll ever see.

Next day on the course a fellow remarked to me, "Never thought you'd fall for that, Sam. This Cy"—and here the man gave "Cy's" real name—"led the Carolina Open not long ago with 68-69 the first two rounds. He travels around and clips the pigeons all over."

I appreciate an artist, but not when it's at my expense. I'll play against a "pigeon," or soft touch, but I won't be one. "Cy" needed a lesson. A few days later I caught him at The Cascades, a course in Virginia which I know well. Before he'd agree to the rematch, "Cy" demanded three shots a side, which I gave him— there being more trees on The Cascades than in the Black Forest of Germany and these trees being especially tough to figure.

"Now that you know me, you'll have to play some real golf today," he warned me chestily.

"I usually try," I said.

He trailed by 4 shots after nine holes, then put together a 3, 3, 3, 3—birdie, par, eagle, birdie—and we reached the final hole all tied up. It was 205 yards long. My drive stopped within spitting distance of the hole. "Cy" was over in the bull pines looking for his ball. I could hear him thrashing around in the jungle, cussing and snarling.

"I hear yooooo-ooo-ooooo!" I caroled to him.

Holing out ten minutes later, he paid off a big wager without showing how much it was hurting him and then said, "I want you to know one thing, Snead. You just taught me how to bet."

I wanted to wring his neck for that crack. As if it had been me who'd rigged the handicapping!

Laying money in golf is a science. Not many understand it, despite the fact that most golfers bet, and how many millions go down the drain needlessly every year I don't know. Somebody who knows the answers should write a guidebook on the golf gamble. I suppose it wouldn't get printed, though, because the subject is off limits and hushed up, even when everybody is betting and good information is hard to find. Mentioning the dodges and devices and downright crooked stuff that goes on is "bad for the game."

I claim you haven't been educated until you know the betting angles.

Hawks like "Cy" can be found at every public or private course, shooting well over their ability until someone is set up for a kill. They're worse than those who lie about their handicaps —which is a number of golfers I'd hate to count.

Early in life I began to go by the basic rule: never gamble with a stranger. Consider him a stranger until you've played around with him at least a dozen times. Even then, bet only when you've compared his game good and hard with your own. Against "Cy," I violated the rule and came close to paying for it through the nose.

A second rule of mine goes: when the other fellow offers to take less shots than you've been giving him, while boosting the wager, back away fast.

With me it happened like this:

A low-80s player had been betting me ten-dollar Nassaus, asking and receiving 14 strokes, or 1 shot on each hole except the par 3s. I scored four straight rounds of between 66 and 68 but won nothing. Each time we broke exactly even. It struck me that this man had handicapped himself perfectly.

Then he proposed, "I feel hot today. You just give me twelve strokes and this time let's make the bet interesting."

The drop from 14 to 12 handicap shots was the bait, the come-on. He was talking in terms of $250 a side.

"You just lost me, mister," I said, walking away.

As was confirmed later, the trap would have been sprung that day. This man's true ability—he'd been careful to conceal it— was par or better. He could have shot a 71 or 72. To avoid defeat, I'd have needed a 58 or 59.

This same bird, it turned out, had spent a year in Hollywood, taking one of the movie stars for $100,000.

Other wrinkles in gambling turned up in my early travels around the States and abroad. Things were in a kind of impoverished condition in 1936, for instance. Only a dozen P.G.A. circuit players earned as much as $3,500, with Horton Smith's $7,900 the top amount won, and a lot of the boys went around with a tin cup in their hands. The game had changed so rapidly that few of them could last long on tour and still feed their families. By that time the shot-placement experts were losing out to the distance hitters. Scores were dropping because pretested steel-shafted clubs had replaced wood and balls were livelier, and also because of a new type of pro who could unwind on the tees at close to 90 per cent of his power and still control his drives. The sluggers were popping up on all sides and they didn't run around with the Prince of Wales or train on hard liquor, the way many stars in the Roaring Twenties had done. They could also putt with most of the Old Masters.

The competition had grown, but the total national P.G.A. purse wasn't much over $100,000, leaving the starving pros no way out but to drive a jalopy or even hitchhike from club to club, making money matches with the members. The danger was that you had to handicap yourself too many strokes. A good amateur could jump up and win your last dime. So the pros took to playing under assumed names. A Texas or California pro could find all the fat pigeons he needed around the rich Long Island layouts—if they didn't know he was a "dew-sweeper." A dew-sweeper could break 70 after sleeping all night in his car, shaving at a gas station, and skipping breakfast.

Florida was one of the best pigeon territories. You could see an amateur hotshot with his chest stuck out everywhere you looked on the Gold Coast. But they could be tricky, too.

Two of them used to hang out just inside the clubhouse door at the Miami-Biltmore with their eye on the newcomers from up north. If a man checking in didn't have a suntan, they'd invite him to share a sandwich and a game of gin. Knowing the pale-faced guy hadn't golfed all winter, they'd suggest a game.

"What's your handicap?" one of the sharps would ask.

"Well, it's ten when I'm playing regularly," the newcomer would say. He was proud of that ten, but before long he wouldn't be.

"Down here," the sharp would say, "mine is a thirteen. Just can't get the hang of this course since I got in from Bimini last week. Been fishing over there—no golf at all. My friend here is a twelve-handicap. So you give me three strokes and him a pair and away we go."

The so-called fishing explained the sharps' dark skin. The "no golf" evened matters. After a few drinks, the pigeon was raring to go, and with that system the sharps—who were star players—averaged $500 to $1,000 per week.

To me, the whole thing smelled, but it wasn't my business.

One day in walked a stranger with no more tan than a librarian and made them the usual big-handicap bet. He took a few cramped swings. You could almost hear his back squeak, he was so rusty.

"Say, what about a few side bets—such as first man on the green, most birdies, and so on?" the sharps suggested.

The stranger hesitated—then bet.

His opening tee shot was a nice lazy 280-yarder down the center. He was a West Coast pro who'd finished high in the Crosby and San Francisco Match-Play events and who knew how to get rid of a suntan.

He'd put cornstarch on his face and hands to whiten them. He took the sharps for everything but their vests.

After that, the sharps never would bet with anybody until

they'd shaken his hand and felt the thickness of his calluses. That's the only sure way to tell anything about a man's honest handicap.

Along with that piece of knowledge, I soon was introduced to big-time gambling in golf. "Hustling" suckers for side money didn't interest me, since tournament winnings kept coming my way. After my 1937 rookie year on tour, I was lucky enough to lead the P.G.A. prize list of 1938 with nearly $20,000 won. Going into the Miami Open of the following winter, I had a string of solid finishes behind me. But I didn't exactly duck when the Mississippi marbles were rolling on the rug or a golf-betting proposition came along. At the St. Paul Open, my shot average of 69.2 per round was good for only third place; at Milwaukee a 67.9 average had brought me a fourth. Only a dozen or so of the seventy-five to one hundred circuit pros were breaking even or better. The talent was bunched so tight that I gave myself only five more years to stay in the money-running.

At Miami my 271 score was good for first place, and next morning I received a summons from L. B. Icely, president of the Wilson Sporting Goods Company. In the golf industry, Mr. Icely was Mr. Big.

At the hotel he looked worried. "Let's go upstairs to Tommy Armour's room," he said. "We have an emergency."

Armour, the former American and British Open champion and a top teacher, knew who I was, but since Hillbilly Snead never had won a major title, there was no telling what he really thought of my game.

Icely explained the situation:

In New York, the well-known sportsman, Tommy Shevlin, and a Cuban sugar king named Thornwald Sanchez had turned a few barroom drinks into an argument—Sanchez claiming that no man alive could beat Rufino Gonzales, the pro at the Havana Country Club, on his home course. Plenty of challengers had tried. Nobody had made the grade.

"Well, I can find a man who can do it," said Shevlin.

"For money or talk?" said Sanchez.

"For $5,000," said Shevlin, "unless you want to cover more."
They shook hands on it.

A while later Shevlin arrived in Havana with his wife and
Sanchez jumped him. "Where's that unbeatable pro you were
bringing?"

Shevlin said, "By golly, I forgot all about the bet."

"Well, you'd better get busy," said Sanchez. "I've spread that
$5,000 you laid me amongst my friends and we're ready to col-
lect. Gonzales is waiting and there's no backing out. You'll have
to forfeit the $5,000 unless you get a man up, and fast."

"Forfeit, hell!" roared Shevlin.

He'd burned up the phone cables to Icely, and now Icely was
asking Armour which U.S. pro he should rush to his friend's
rescue.

Icely had a list of five names: Craig Wood, Byron Nelson,
Jimmy Demaret, Ben Hogan, and Sam Snead.

Armour was in a ticklish spot. He knew that the $5,000 prob-
ably now amounted to ten times that much, the way Shevlin and
his New York crowd and Cuban golf plungers liked to chunk it
in, and a wrong guess wouldn't be popular with a lot of prom-
inent people.

"Sorry to bother you," said Icely, "since we're on opposite
sides of the fence, Tommy. You're with the MacGregor company and I'm Wilson, but there's so much at stake that I need
help with the selection."

"What's wrong with that man right there?" said Armour,
nodding at me.

"This is for high stakes," Icely said. "So think about it hard."

"No thinking necessary," said Armour, paying me quite a
compliment. "Just send this man right here."

That was Monday. Early next morning, over I went, with my
hands already sweating, since I'd never seen a Cuban course and
now faced thirty-six holes of medal play with maybe $100,000
riding on me. In Havana the cockfights and jai alai stopped
drawing; everybody was betting on the match. Fights broke out

at the Havana Country Club and downtown between natives and U.S. tourists. One Cuban was kicked out of the Havana C.C. because he backed me. An "act of treason," the board of governors called it.

Shevlin was on pins and needles. "How much of the bet do you want?" his crowd asked me.

"Betting Sanchez wasn't my idea," I came back. "And I've never laid eyes on this Gonzales. I hadn't figured to get in on it at all."

"Well, you've got $250 of it," they said. "We'll feel better about it that way."

I got their idea: by holding a piece of the action whether I wanted or not, I'd train and practice harder.

It was agreed that Rufino Gonzales and I would play some practice rounds together so that the gamblers could draw comparisons. He was a cool-looking gent, medium build, about 170 pounds, with a flat backswing and very straight off the tee. His putting was amazing. On the slick, sun-cooked greens, the Cuban could putt rings around me. The worst hazard of all was the light. Due to what they called a peculiar refraction effect of the sun, a newcomer had a tendency to see double and misjudge distances. No wonder Gonzales never lost at home.

All the Yankees began to pray for rain.

We got it, at the last minute. Under gray skies, the biggest gallery in Cuban history gathered around the first tee. There were some tough-looking people in the crowd—the kind you wouldn't want around your henhouse after dark.

"Who are they—smugglers?" somebody asked.

"No—Batista's boys," somebody else said. "The dictator, himself, has some pesos down on Gonzales."

Things like that don't help your peace of mind. I could see myself pulling a ball into a palm forest and, if I was leading at the time, not coming out.

After three holes, Gonzales was trailing by 1 stroke, but on No. 4 my ball was all over the carpet for 3 putts. The Cubans cheered and clapped the misses. Rufino squared the match. On the next hole, which I birdied to Rufino's par, the Americans went crazy.

Both sides were glaring blue blazes at each other. I was what you'd call half popular all the time.

Gonzales was dropping long and short putts, never relaxing the pressure, and I remembered that in practice a way had shown itself to equalize him. On the par-5 holes and one long par 4, a power hitter could cut the corner over some trees and save a stroke. The Cuban was 50 yards shorter off the tee than me. On doglegs, he had to take the long way home.

Swinging as hard as I ever have put me on the par-5 greens in 2 shots to his 3 for birdies, and on the par-4 it was the same story. Once I got the hang of the fast greens, that did it. We finished the first eighteen holes with a 71 for Gonzales, a 69 for me.

"Sensational!" said Shevlin. "Another $500 of the bet is yours, and this time it's on the house."

Any time there's an extra money chance, I come out punching, and it didn't slow me down over the final eighteen. It was Rufino who lost his coolness. Luckily, his famous putting ability wasn't there that last round, and he was out in 38 to my 34 before pulling himself together for a fine 33 coming back. His second round of 71 wasn't good enough—I had a 68—and when the last ball dropped, the Cubans were a mighty miserable and angry group. All the way to the clubhouse, jostled by Batista's mugs, the hair stood up on my neck. Havana papers estimated that well over $100,000 was lost, all because Shevlin and Sanchez had gotten into a barroom argument.

"Good luck, pal," I told Gonzales. He had to stay and face his backers, including Batista. I got out by the first plane.

Back in Miami, Mr. Icely, Tommy Armour, and others gave me a whooping reception. "You feel all right, Sam?" they asked.

"No, pooped," I said. "That took too much out of me. Next time the stakes are that high, send Demaret, will you? He likes travel and would make a prettier corpse than me."

But I knew I'd see a lot more of betting and would be performing under the gun many times. One rule I made was never to bet for fun. That's a national habit of American golfers, but with me gambling always had been a dead-serious thing. Porky Oliver said that once I was told a funny story about betting and laughed until you could have heard a pin drop. Well, where's the joke in losing your hard-earned cash? With me, nothing hurts worse.

Unless I like the odds, I never put up a dime. At Meadowbrook on Long Island I once got involved in a high-rolling affair. Bob (Bunny) Bacon, an average player, phoned me in St. Paul, where I'd won the local Open, to say, "I want you to come east and help me give a couple of my dear chums a trimming."

It turned out that Bacon had bet T. Suffron (Tommy) Tailer, one of the country's classiest amateurs, that he could team with a pro of his choosing and lick Tailer and his partner, Dr. Walter Hochschield.

The bet was too full of risks and also too rich for my taste, but I agreed to help Bacon out.

On the first tee, Bacon said to Tailer, "I want to play this match for $7,000."

"Agreed!" snapped Tailer.

So much money made me so jittery that I topped my tee shot and then topped my second shot. Bacon ran over and grabbed me.

"Tell me, Sam," he begged, "that Tailer didn't get to you!" Bacon was only half kidding.

"Hell, no," I said indignantly. "Nobody can fix me."

"Well, don't *you* go getting nervous then and miss any more," pleaded Bacon. "*I'm* the one that's supposed to do the shaking."

I had to *shoot a 32 for the last ten holes* and eagle the seventeenth—that's how good Tailer was—to win Bunny Bacon his $7,000. He handed me $600 for my assistance.

One reason I hadn't wanted in on the bet was lack of information on the other team. Far too many golfers gamble blindly. At any course, you see them taking a stranger's word for his handicap. They remind me of the two players down home who were introduced by an assistant pro. Each claimed to shoot between 90 and 95, and they bet twenty dollars Nassau. Later, one of them rushed into the club, foaming at the mouth, and collared the pro. "Don't ever introduce me to such a phony thief again!"

"What happened?" asked the assistant.

"Why, the lying S.O.B.! I had to shoot a 78 to beat him!"

Another type of losing gambler is the man who doesn't resist pressure well, yet lets his opponents jockey him into "press" bets where the money rides on a few shots. In poker, if he was holding weak cards, he'd fold his hand against a strong challenge. In golf, he does just the opposite.

A third type of bad bet was made by the Cubans in my match with Rufino Gonzales. When a visiting player arrives at your club for a challenge match with your home pro or club champion, never let local pride sway you. Follow the visitor's practice rounds. See exactly how he's adapting to your course and scoring. Also, check up on him; maybe he's been playing much tougher courses where he came from. Or he could be a "ringer" for the advertised opponent.

A fourth bad bet is made by the weekend golfer whose game fluctuates widely. Never knowing what he'll score, the sucker still goes against settled-down players. He might as well throw his money away. He's gambling on producing one of his good rounds. And bucking up against a percentage of from 2-1 to 3-1 —which are the proper odds that you won't score your best golf with cash at stake.

Proving that fact is easy. At Boca Raton, Florida, a low-handicapper told everyone how he hadn't taken a double bogey on any hole in the six weeks he'd been in town.

"Bet you twenty," I said, "you have one today."

The man double-bogeyed twice—because the power of suggestion was there and money was up.

The fifth bad bet—the worst of all—is made by the man who lets gambling affect his form. He'll rake and scrape the ball to the hole any old way, forgetting all he's learned, and not caring, as long as he wins and collects. He's a betting fanatic. There are thousands like him. Here's what happened to one of them—a fellow I once knew:

A mid-70s shooter, this youngster was the most popular man at his club. He had no little ring of friends but played with everyone. Meeting a cross section of the membership helped him a great deal in business. Then he began to gamble—with a certain few members. Soon he'd play with no one else. He was miserable when his betting pals were away on vacation. He turned up his nose at those who didn't bet and became the most unpopular man at the club.

"How'd you do today?" I'd ask him.

"I got out of a bunker on No. 18 and won forty dollars," he'd say.

"Boy, you've got it bad when you give me the money and not the strokes," I'd say.

He confessed that all the fun of golf was gone and that he battled with his wife whenever he lost a heavy bet.

A few who have the fever reform, but not many. This one tried and failed. His game went to pot and he didn't even have a profit to show for it, because under the handicap system you can win only so long before the 'caps get readjusted and your opponents win their money back.

The sixth bad bet hardly needs mentioning: risking more than you can afford and your game merits. In my first two pro years, until I had a sizable bank account, I never risked more than five dollars Nassau.

Smart gamblers who seldom break 90 stick to wagers like "Bingo-Bango-Bungo." The payoff here works three ways: on the first ball to reach the green, on the ball nearest the hole after all balls are on the green, and on the first ball into the cup. All putting is done by rotation, to keep the opportunities fair. Of the three bets, the weak golfer has every bit as good a chance to win two of them as the strong player. Chances are he'll lose the No. 1 bet—first ball on the green. He won't be able to match the drives and long approaches of the better players. But if he lies short of the green after the others are on, he can chip up nearest the hole and collect. Then he has better than a 50-50 edge to sink his putt first.

My first golf boss, Freddie Martin, a par-shooter, once played "Bingo-Bango-Bungo" with two 90-to-100-shooters and lost 85 per cent of the bets to the duffers.

If you can't be happy without something going on the game, and the gambling is on teams, pick your partner carefully. At Palm Beach one year, in the Seminole Pro-Amateur event, Lawson Little was paired with a New York amateur whose name I'm glad to forget. Little and his partner had been purchased in the Calcutta pool by none other than the partner (who could afford it). The pool ran to $100,000—which meant that the winning pair drew down $40,000.

On the par-4 eighteenth hole of the last round, Little and his chum needed only a 5 to win the $40,000. Lawson bunkered his drive, but his partner hit the green in 2 and putted to within 1 foot. This was the best-ball play, with only the lower score of · the team counting, so everything now hinged on the New Yorker.

"We can't miss," Lawson told himself. "He can still take two putts and we win."

The 1-footer stopped an inch short of dropping, which didn't matter. From there the ball could be blown in.

But at the instant the ball stopped rolling, the amateur, who was used to conceding putts on the lip, and having them conceded, reached out to knock it back toward him. "Don't touch it!" screamed Little.

He yelled too late. While the ball was rolling back, his partner tapped it into the cup. The knock-back counted 1 stroke, and for hitting a moving ball the penalty was 2 strokes—for a total of 7.

Forty thousand frogskins went flying down the fairway.

Little took it better than most pros. He didn't kill himself.

There's a certain type of player you should avoid. He's the Bet-a-Million Gates type who can put his house, lot, wife, and dog on the line and thrive on the risk. At the Charleston, South Carolina, Open, to give you a case, some rich members decided to "reform" Leonard Dodson, a pro who they thought was betting too much. The idea was to teach Dodson a lasting lesson.

After fifty-four holes, Dodson was playing like a hacker. He was far back in the pack with a 227 score. My 209 led the field. Close up were Henry Picard at 211 and Harry Cooper at 214.

"We say that you can't beat the scores of any of those three in the final round," the members challenged Dodson.

Dodson said he'd take the bet, $100, three ways, even money, and before it was over, $980 was on the line.

Cool as you please, Leonard shot a 69. Picard had 71, Cooper and me each 76s.

With a big black cigar in his mouth, Dodson was about the meanest operator I ever saw when the chips were on the table. While he never won any major world title, a bet made him all but unbeatable.

Another tip worth mentioning, for anyone who gambles on P.G.A. tournaments: never place a bet on any contestant at bookmaker odds of less than 8-1. Friends of mine who back me frequently accept 3-1 or 4-1 and get stung. No player, from Vardon to Hogan to Palmer, ever was better than 8-1 against a class field. Even then, taking one man against ten or fifteen of equal ability is a risky thing. The few times I've bet on myself in tournaments, each time at good odds, I've lost. Favorites don't really exist in any pro event. That's why the pros don't bet amongst themselves as they once did: we're too closely bunched.

Only rarely will you make a killing. Once, for the Miami Open, Jack Doyle's Broadway book opened with me at 10-1. A few people rushed in before my first-round score of 66, after which the odds dropped to 3-1. When I won, the 10-1 people cleaned up. But that was an exception.

I'd have to say that the London woman who bet fifty quid on me at 100-1 in the 1946 British Open made a smart move, though. Not because I won and paid her approximately $12,000. Simply because of the odds. Of the 225 entrants, less than half qualified. Of these only two dozen or so had a real chance to win.

Bets, high rollers, and ordinary thieves have led me into all kinds of queer spots. Around midnight at the St. Paul Open of 1951, I was sound asleep in the St. Paul Hotel when the phone rang. A high-pitched voice said, "We need to talk to you for a minute."

"What is this?" I said. "Do you know what time it is?"

"The hell with that. Just hang on a minute."

A second voice—deeper than the first—came on the line. "Snead, don't worry about a thing. You'll win this tournament."

"You're out of your mind, whoever you are," I said. "The thing is three-fourths over and I'm eleven shots behind."

"Just don't worry. Relax, shoot your best game, and you'll win. We'll see to that."

The voice hung up.

I'd forgotten it as a crank's call except that Lloyd Mangrum, whose 62 that day had broken the course record and given him the St. Paul lead, had a phone call about the same time.

"Just a little advice, Mangrum," the caller said. "If you don't want to leave town dead, see to it that you don't win tomorrow. If you try to, we'll kill you."

"How you going to do that?" asked Mangrum.

"There's fifty places on the course where a sniper never would be noticed. Don't forget it when you're out there."

It wasn't hard to guess that gamblers had bet on me, as the favorite, and since you can't frisk 15,000 people for guns, it was Mangrum's decision whether to play or not. Naturally, he wouldn't throw the tournament.

Lloyd had been shot up in World War II—at Omaha Beach

and Frankfurt—and he didn't turn a hair. The police threw a ring around him from tee to green, and even with that distraction he scored a 70 to win with his best seventy-two-hole total of the year, 266. The police boxed him in the minute he finished, got him to his hotel, then to the depot and out of town. My 275 was good for an eleventh-place tie, which doesn't make a man friends with mobsters who back him.

There were no cops protecting me. I was packed and out of town almost before Mangrum had the winner's check.

If the mobsters ever move in on pro golf, I'll volunteer to lead a posse that will string them up. Once, in 1957, the gamblers maybe cost me $42,000.

The scene was the $101,000 "world championship of golf" at Tam O'Shanter in Chicago, where after 54 holes my scores of 65-69-72 were good for a one-stroke lead over Mike Souchak, Art Wall, Gene Littler, Dick Mayer, Bob Rosburg, Bill Caspar, Dow Finsterwald, Jerry Barber and others. In the final round, off the first tee, I hit what I thought was a pretty good shot, and it was; my second to the green looked even better, until it kicked over the green into the crowd. A few feet back of the green was a swale backed by an out-of-bounds. When I got there, the ball was past the boundary marker, which meant I had to go back and play another ball—at the cost of two penalty strokes.

Later that day, when it was all over, witnesses came forward to say, "Sam's ball landed in bounds, but was kicked out by a man who ducked before anybody could stop him." There were fifty different descriptions of the man, few of which tallied, and locating him wouldn't have changed matters, anyway.

Then, all around Chicago, word leaked out that a huge pro gambler's bet—said to be $100,000—had been going against me not to win the "world" tournament.

The final winner of the $50,000 first prize: Dick Mayer, with a 279 total for 72 holes. Second: Sam Snead, with 280. But for that out-of-bounds ball, I'd have won the difference between $50,000 first cash and $8,000 second money by one stroke.

As I told Ted Williams one day, after he hit a ball toward the outfield fence and saw it going over for a home run, not a soul in the world could interfere with its flight. In golf, you're wide open to the hawks and the vultures.

Titanic Thompson, now retired from action, was the greatest golf plunger I ever knew—and the shrewdest juggler of odds. Also the best at mixing odd bets with golf.

Ti would lay you $10,000 on one putt. If he missed, he'd give a grin and say, "Double or nothing I can hit a silver dollar with my pistol eight times out of eight from twenty feet." He'd pull a gun from his golf bag and recoup every time, because Ti was as expert with sidearms as he was with a bag of pecans.

Ti ate a lot of pecan nuts. Playing around the course, calculating odds in his head like lightning and making as many as forty or fifty side bets during eighteen holes, he was always glad to share his bag of pecans with his competitors. Finishing up at the two-story clubhouse, he'd stare at the roof and drawl, "Bet I can throw one of these nuts over that building." The proposition was so popular that people lined up to cover him.

While the bets were made, Thompson would casually be eating nuts, which enabled him to palm the one nut he wanted. That one he sailed over the clubhouse—every time. After he'd worked the bet from Pinehurst to Pebble Beach, somebody paid a caddie fifty dollars to bring back Ti's nut.

It was loaded with lead, and the losers began to scream.

"I bet you I could throw *one of these nuts* over the club," said Ti. "The content of the pecan was not specified, so stop squawking."

When I first met Titanic Thompson in the 1930s, he'd just won $12,000 at Galveston by linking fifty side bets and working a betting wrinkle known to big-time hustlers as "fixing a game upwards." Arriving at a club, Ti would show a typical amateur's game, complete with topped shots and slices. At Grassy Sprain

Country Club one time, Leo P. Flynn, ex-manager of Jack Dempsey, backed Thompson against the club pro, George Mc-Lean, whose members put up $20,000. McLean conceded Thompson an 8-stroke handicap. After sixteen holes, Ti was even with McLean, having used up his handicap shots, and it seemed all over but the shouting.

McLean's drive from the seventeenth tee was a beauty, 6 feet from the flag. Ti stepped up and planted one 18 inches from the cup. McLean was still dazed by that one when he missed his putt, which gave Ti the match after he tapped in his ball and halved the final hole in par. The element of surprise and un-expected pressure did McLean in.

"Just how good are you?" I asked Ti one day.

"Play me and find out," he said. "I'll take four strokes a side."

"Oh, no," I told him. "Not until I see your honest swing."

Later on, I learned that Alvin C. Thompson was right around a scratch player when bearing down. Mysterious John Montague —another legend who supposedly broke par using a rake, a shovel, and a driving wood—never was in Ti's class. Thompson could have succeeded on the P.G.A. wheel if he hadn't preferred gambling golf.

He had many secrets. One was timing. "When it's the other man's turn to shoot, especially on or around the greens, then I push him into a big bet," Ti said. "I make it so high that his hair stands up. When he says, 'Isn't that a little stiff?' I sneer and say, 'Oh, hell, then let's make it for a lousy century note.' He can't refuse—and he's got that $100 glued over his eyes while he's shooting.

"Eight times out of ten, because his mind has been divided, he'll tie up and miss."

Another of Ti's methods, worth remembering, was to lay a modest sum on the total match. His opponent teed off with the fixed idea of winning or losing that much.

"Then you compound the felony," Ti said. "After a few holes, you bet that you'll take the next hole. You lose that one, let's say. So you double-or-nothing the bet on the next one. Then you raise the ante again with special side bets when you reach your approach shots and putts. You suggest odds on tough shots, give or take. Every time he lifts his club, your man is involved with figures. The thing gets more complicated than a math equation, until his confusion licks him down the line. With business executives, it's a cinch. They won't admit they can't handle a complex mass of numbers simultaneously."

Thompson was a student of what he called "human capacity under impost"; this had nothing to do with jockeys or horses.

One time he bet a man he couldn't carry an ordinary brick three miles and set it on the bar of a saloon. The man picked up the brick and hoofed it to the bar. When he went to lift his arm, his finger muscles were so constricted that the brick fell out of his hands.

In Tulsa he told the local amateur champion, "In all modesty, I am a great driver. So I'll give you three drives per hole—and you can play the best of them—while I'll take only one drive." Thompson trailed after nine holes. On the back nine, the amateur grew so arm-weary that Ti closed him out on the sixteenth.

When a ranking professional plays an ordinary golfer for money, often he's asked to forfeit so many strokes that he'd need to shoot in the 50s to win. I refuse to be a public charity. If a man is a 14-handicapper, I'll give him 14. But I'll never make it 18, or 2 more a side, as most self-styled "pigeons" demand. They don't want to gamble; they want a lock.

The pro often is accused of hustling someone when he quotes the handicap chart. At Palm Beach one day, a man was losing to me when he got mad. He claimed I'd shortchanged him on strokes. I stopped the game and looked at him.

"What business are you in?" I asked him.

"The cookie business. What the hell's that got to do with it?"

"I'm in the golf business," I told him.

He finished and paid off without any more complaints.

Some pigeons never can be discouraged, and as long as they

can afford it I'll cover their money. A roly-poly Cuban named Tomeu, who had huge cattle holdings around Santiago, appeared at my club one day demanding action. After giving him a stroke a hole and winning, I suggested we forget about it.

"No, hunting season on," Tomeu declared. "I beat you yet."

Next I gave him 2 strokes on all par-5 holes and 1 stroke on all others, then 2 strokes on every hole over 400 yards with 1 stroke on all others. And still Tomeu lost. "C'mon, Tommy, let's quit," I said.

"No, still hunting season," he swore.

Finally, I played him using only a 3-wood on all shots—even for putting. And my score of 78 beat his easily.

I was getting desperate. Tomeu flatly refused to give up, and people were lifting their eyebrows at what it was costing him.

Hiking up in the woods, I cut a swamp-maple limb. Using a hatchet and penknife, I carved the crude sort of clubhead I'd made as a boy. "Tommy," I said, "I'll play you with a stick and a wedge and nothing else and you'll surely beat that."

"What kind of stick?" I showed him the tree limb. "I try it?" he said, looking crafty. Tommy suspected a trick.

"Sure, go ahead."

On the tee, Tommy couldn't get the ball airborne at all with the rough stick. "Game on!" he shouted. "Hunting season getting hot now!"

Much as I wanted to lose, that swamp maple worked as well for me as it had when I was a kid. Using it for tee and fairway shots, chipping and putting with the wedge, I came in with a 76 —beating Tomeu about as badly as ever.

"*Goddam hunting season closed for good!*" he yelled, and went back to Cuba.

You can love a Tomeu for his gameness, but the type of golfer who's always looking for an edge is another matter. His greed knows no bounds.

One day in 1945, while sliding into base in a softball game, I split the radius bone in my right wrist. Being on the shelf for six weeks, it was a good chance to strengthen my left hand. Using my wife's light clubs, I tried a few shots. Driving left-handed was difficult. Short-iron play and putting was easier.

Along came a tourist from up north who didn't recognize me. He walked up to the first tee and gave his name as Bill.

"Mine's Sam," I said.

"I hate to take advantage of a one-armed guy," he said, seeing my arm sling. But at the same time he was reaching for his money.

"How do you play?" I asked.

"Around 90."

"I'm better than that," I said, "so I'll play you even, if that suits you."

As far as he knew, I was just another golfer. But, instead of protesting, he was more than willing to take advantage of my crippled condition by not offering a few strokes. After five holes, Bill was 5 down. On the short No. 6 hole, after landing close to the pin, he gave me one of those now-I've got-you looks.

My drive lit and rolled up for a hole in one.

"God almighty!" he yelled. "Getting shellacked by a one-armed ———!" Bill threw his club almost back to the tee before charging off the course.

Unless he reads this, Bill still doesn't know who provided the competition. It's too bad more Bills don't have such a lesson taught them. If they did, golf would be more fun for a lot more people.

SAM SNEAD'S COMMENT:
GAMBLING GOLF

See to it that your club provides safeguards for true reporting of rounds played by members and that handicaps are dependable. If there's a bad apple in the crowd, don't hesitate to root him out. Scandals have rocked many a club where cheating replaced sportsmanship.

Bet with your head, not your simple pride. Don't give away strokes above your opponent's legitimate handicap just because someone tells you how great you are. Or how sick and ailing they are.

Bet with strangers only when they've become friends.

Be leery of people who generously ask for less strokes than they've been drawing and simultaneously want to increase the bet. Revising the handicap down is a hustler's favorite stunt.

Feel their calluses. If there's a noticeable ridge at the base of the ring and little fingers of the left hand—think twice.

Never bet with a consistent player if your own game is hot and cold.

Avoid suddenly-proposed side bets unless you're steady as a rock under pressure.

Stick to straight Nassau wagers, if you must bet, where eighteen to thirty-six holes tell the story; avoid do-or-die, one-hole bets featuring chips and putts, where the psychological edge is against the taker and with the proposer.

Don't bet with "naturals"—fellows who thrive on the hobby.

Keep your betting simple: Titanic Thompson's trick of piling on enough bets to confuse Einstein is among the best gambling gimmicks ever invented in golf.

Remember this all-important point:

The second you lay a bet on yourself, you increase the odds against staying on your game. Like me, you tell yourself, "Now, I've got to come through"—and that's when the wheels are most likely to leave the tracks.

9

THE ROCKY ROAD TO SHORT PUTTS

YOU CAN'T SHOOT 71 IN BRAZIL • FINESSED AT SHAW-
NEE BY A LIGHTWEIGHT • RIOT AT WESTCHESTER •
BOOMERANG BALLS IN LOS ANGELES • FROM FRINGE
TO CUP—A $100,000 SHOT

Senor Palacios was a stranger to me, but he
had an interesting proposition. Palacios and some of his Brazilian
friends thought it would be a good thing for "international relations" if I'd appear in their national championship of 1956.
Julian Foster, an American in São Paulo, acted as my "agent"
and go-between.

Foster phoned from down there to say, "They're offering a
flat $5,000, plus expenses, as an appearance guarantee. All you
have to do is show up and play four rounds. The $5,000 is a
guarantee exclusive of the tournament money."

"What if I win? What's first money?"

"It's $2,000, but the deal doesn't include that. If you win, the
two grand is subtracted from the $5,000."

"That's kind of an unusual agreement. Do I have to try to
break the course record, too?"

"No, they won't pressure you," said Foster. "Just by taking a
bow in that coconut hat you'll draw a hell of a gate for them,
and *that* they want."

"Anything else I have to do?"

"Shake a few hands, go to a few functions. You'll be in and
out of here in five days."

So I flew down to São Paulo, and the very first night after the
opening round of the Brazilian Open it turned out that Senor

Palacios and his friends felt cheated. We were at dinner when he began to grumble and glower at me. Pretty soon it came out.

"You don't play so good," he said, in front of everybody. "No, you do not play good game at all."

I ate another shrimp and looked at Palacios. There was no use getting sore.

My opening-day score of the seventy-two-hole affair had been 71, leaving me far behind such Latin American stars as Roberto De Vicenzo and Antonio Cerda, who'd shot the grass off the São Paulo Country Club with rounds of from 65 to 67. At that rate, I wouldn't be much of a drawing card.

I'd kept it pretty much to myself, but all that year I'd wondered if after twenty tournament seasons my golf days weren't numbered. A condition called spinal ostosis, which affects the sciatic nerves of the hips and legs, became so painful that at times I couldn't bend to pick the ball from the cup. I slept with my legs elevated (which I still do) and often tossed all night. In U.S. play I couldn't hit a lick in 1956—winning only one P.G.A. event and less than $9,000.

Now I had this Brazilian griping at me. He had the idea I was some sort of phony.

"*Inexperto*," he kept saying. "You don't play so good."

"Look," I said, "I'll play a decent game for you, the best I can do, but it makes no real difference to me whether I shoot 65 or 71. Just keep that in mind. Since I'm not eligible for the prize money, I get paid the same no matter what I do."

The senor chewed on that and frowned, and his friends around the table gave me the chill, and then Julian Foster spoke up. "Where you made your mistake," he told Palacios, "was in not offering Sam a chance at the purse, too."

I glanced at Julian. "If I'm so damned bad, what difference does it make?"

You could almost hear the Brazilian figuring angles—such as my age, wind condition, and score. My opening 71 meant that his money was safe from me, because De Vicenzo and the other local boys knew the course so well that nothing over a 270 total score could win. That left me only 199 more shots, or an impossible average of 66 per round. As long as that was the case, if I could be prodded into some hot golf, my galleries and Palacios' box-office take would increase.

"Hokay," he said at last, "you win, you get the $2,000 too." He smirked when he said it. I've known promoters so crooked they had to screw their socks on, but this was the first one I ever met who privately was betting against his star attraction.

"Repeat that," I said.

"You win, you get the $2,000, too," he said, before witnesses.

One round of play on the São Paulo course had shown me that its hard-baked fairways sent balls bouncing every direction and that the hard, fast greens wouldn't hold normal pitches. I'd have to stay as much in the middle as possible and then make up the lost distance with bull's-eye approaches—low run-up shots and the chip-and-run shot—rather than lob shots with backspin. In South Africa, I'd played on similar courses. Instead of pitching with a lofted 8- or 9-iron, you take a 5 or 6, play the ball off the right foot, and play just short of the green, running the ball up in a series of grass-hugging bounces. To do this, you must exert an extra-strong left-hand pull on the downswing and hit down on the ball with added force. On soft turf, you'd dig in too deeply with this stroke. On hard grass, with a green as fast as concrete ahead of you, it's the only way to approach.

Senor Palacios and Company came out next morning to see me boost their attendance and lose the bonus. I was up earlier than they were—practicing with my short irons.

After easing along under par for nine holes, I came to a par 4 where a 1-iron second shot skidded across the green onto the fringe, 40 open feet from the cup. The 6-iron was the answer. Taking one bounce on the green, the ball dribbled into the hopper for a birdie.

Palacios mopped at his brow and looked uncomfortable.

Next, on No. 11, my approach again slid over the green, across a small mound, 25 feet from the flag. There was no shortage of putting room, so a little 8-iron lifted it over the mound onto the near edge, where it ran up to the cup, teetered around, and fell in for an eagle.

The crowd yelled "Olé!" as if I'd just killed a bull, when all I was killing was Palacios. Two straight holes and no putts. . . .

Coming up to the twelfth green next, my approach landed on a green which wasn't as hard-baked as the others, sucked back, and rolled onto and down a ramp, or little bridge, between fairway and green, until it was 100 feet below the hole.

Palacios was right there, breathing down my neck as I reached into the bag and fingered several clubs.

Now that I knew I could get checkspin and needed fast elevation on this green, out came the 9-iron. My short irons all have powerful shafts, because to get backspin you must take a clean three-quarters of the ball before taking your divot and you want as little armwork and as much clubwork as possible.

Just on the spur of the moment, I stopped and grinned at Senor Palacios. From his ghastly expression he must have felt what was coming.

Up she rose, and on about the third bounce there was a stop action that was beautiful to see and which left just enough legs under the ball to carry it to the rim of the cup. Hats and sun umbrellas of the gallery went flying into the air when it dropped.

Playing three holes in a row without needing a putt staggered me, too, but I had enough left to beat a dozen Brazilians to the ball in the cup, which was a souvenir I wanted myself.

"*Caramba!*" said Palacios. "Why you didn't do this before?"

"I'll give you two thousand guesses," I told him.

My irons didn't cool off. I was getting placement to the greens that had been missing for months by playing the old Scottish-British run-up approach game with the lower-lofted irons. The São Paulo course record was 64. With a birdie on the final hole, I tied it.

Which pulled me out of the ruck and tied me for the tournament lead at 135.

The next day an overflow crowd of jabbering Brazilians turned out, Palacios and his friends sweating the hardest under the sun, when the word got out that I was going for a course record. I had an eagle and a flock of birdies and turned in a new São Paulo club mark of 63.

Now I was out in front of the field by 10 strokes.

On the final day, I just coasted through with a 69 for a total of 267, a Brazilian Open record, and took Palacios' added-money $2,000 by a margin of 11 strokes over the next-nearest finisher. If you called it a runaway, you'd be right.

"*Mucho* thanks," I said when Palacio handed over the cash.

"*Muy dinero*," he said sourly, looking like the fellow who built a snare trap and got hung up in it by the foot.

"It sure is. Three cheers for international relations," I said.

Then I caught the next plane out of Brazil, where they grow good coffee but you can't shoot a 71.

Year in and out, a strong short-iron game—or lack of it—has decided how well I've scored as much as any other factor. The longer anyone plays golf, the more this is true. If you have a physical disability, or you're past the age where your hips turn freely, or have grown a paunch, you'll always have trouble hitting the long wood shots well. And when a man passes the age of forty, the odds are that his putting nerves will slip, not improve. But there's still that big shot-saving area left around the green. The heart of scoring is from 150 yards out from the pin, and the place where most matches are decided is even closer in—from 40 to 50 yards of the hole. It's also the most neglected area in the game.

That should never be, because age, sex, size, or strength doesn't count for much when it comes to the short approaches. I know sixty-year-old women who can chip and pitch and run up with almost a pro's ability.

As a born long hitter who loved to smack them, it took me a while to admit that I could drive like Macdonald Smith and putt like Walter Hagen and still get nowhere without a good part of Paul Runyan in me. I enjoyed the "cute" shots which Runyan played so well, but not to the extent of really honing them fine. In my younger days I was always making bets—such as that I could drive the length of a 4,000-foot airport runway in 4 strokes, or an average of 333 yards per shot. I lost that bet when the long grass prevented the ball from rolling, but by only 105 yards. To win a P.G.A. long-driving contest over Jimmy Hines, Craig Wood, Lawson Little, and Jimmy Thomson when I was twenty-five years old was a thrill, and it set me up to do more slugging. The people paid to see those howitzers—and I collected.

Down in Selma, Alabama, one time, the gallery marshal announced to the crowd that Mr. Snead would make 2 tee shots on the 295-yard eleventh hole. "The first will be his regular drive," he explained. "The second—in response to many requests —will be an attempt to drive the green."

With a little breeze behind me, my first drive stopped in the short grass 15 yards beyond the green.

"Doggone it, marshal," I said, "looks like I'll have to use that second shot to chip back."

The audience laughed and the remark made all the newspapers. Meanwhile, I hadn't won a tournament in a few weeks.

It was a good thing that near the start of my career, around 1938, I took my first plane ride—from Greensboro, North Carolina, to Augusta, Georgia—to meet Bob Jones. I'd never even seen Jones, and the P.G.A. officials thought it was high time. They loaded me into a rattletrap old one-wing, one-motor puddle jumper of an airplane, which looked anything but safe.

We were about to take off when I yelled, "Hold it right here! I'm getting out. I just remembered I promised my folks never to go up in the air."

The P.G.A. boys argued that I couldn't get out. "Jones is waiting for you. You can't stand *him* up."

"Well, I'll walk, if I have to, but I can't go back on my promise," I said, looking at the chicken wire holding the wings up.

"Sam," they said, "if your folks had known Bobby Jones was going to invite you to play with him and this was the only way you could keep the date, they'd never object."

They beat me down and we wobbled along over the hills, the pilot navigating with a gas-station road map. Even the crows had more altitude than we did.

The sportswriters wrote that my hands were shaking when I met the great Jones because I was so "awed." It was that plane ride that caused it. Jones was a regular guy and put me at ease.

We played, and I shot 68 and felt good about it. Jones complimented my long hitting but remarked, "Distance is fine, accuracy is better. Be sure to take an inventory of your whole game, Sam. Do that after every round, with particular attention to how your close shots came off."

Up at Shawnee, Pennsylvania, not long later, a little 128-pound demon proved to me that Jones was right. We met for the P.G.A. championship of 1938, and Paul (Little Poison) Runyan gave away almost fifty pounds and up to 80 yards of distance off the tee and ran me off the course.

On the drives, Runyan would be so far behind I'd lose sight of him at times. On second shots, I'd still be far inside him: and then he'd beat me into the hole.

He did it with the most phenomenal work around the greens ever seen in the P.G.A. I'd have a hole won, as everybody could see, and then he'd sink a shot from behind a bush or chip dead to the cup from a gully or make a pitching-iron recovery from a bunker that I'd have bet 50-1 against.

"This isn't golf," I told him; "it's magic."

"Hard work, Sam, hard work," Runyan said. "Midgets like me can't cut the buck off the tee, so we have to compensate."

An example was the 567-yard seventh hole, par 5. My first 2 shots carried 75 yards further than 3 of his. I was just off the green in 2; Runyan was in behind a mess of trees in 3, 75 yards away. There was no way I could lose the hole. Except that I chipped up, needed 2 putts, and his mashie fourth came through those trees to fall right where he could 1-putt it in. He walked off the green with a par half while I stood there with my mouth open. Runyan had me so bothered that after a while I couldn't have sunk a putt in a bathtub.

Another time, I stymied Runyan, and what did he do but pitch over me with a wedge and into the hole—*on the fly.*

The little man dropped putts of 60 feet from off the green, and when he was through with me he'd gone 64 straight P.G.A. championship tournament holes without once going over par. He beat me 8 and 7—the worst defeat in the history of the event.

Something had to be done, and that was to work overtime with my niblick and mashie (called the No. 9 and No. 5 irons today) and mashie niblick (No. 7 iron) and my sand-blasting clubs. After the P.G.A. show, the action moved to the $5,000 Chicago Open at Olympia Fields. I practiced short irons by the hour. My reward was a first-round 64, which the writers called "the greatest round ever played over a championship layout." I went on to win the fifty-four-hole event by a stroke over Ralph Guldhal. What a form reversal!

One reason for it was that every day I learned something new about myself. A short iron measuring only thirty-six inches and weighing sixteen ounces doesn't feel like much in your hands if you're a strong swinger. You feel that you should dig in and give the club some extra help. Within 120 to 150 yards of the flag I'd often overshot and landed in trouble beyond the green, but then I got to talking to old hands like Denny Shute and Henry Picard.

"Aim those approaches for the middle of the green, not the flag, and soften the shot," they urged me. "You've got a bigger target that way and you leave margin for error."

This wasn't easy to accept, for I saw many of my competitors saving strokes with terrifically accurate iron shots aimed on the flag. But I should have been watching their misses. They missed the green or were bunkered far more often than they stopped within 1-putt distance. What's more, even when a long approach did fly straight on a line to the pin, it didn't gain them much. Usually, they still wound up about as far from the cup as I did by playing to the whole green and stopping somewhere near the middle.

In practice my second shots sometimes stopped in the deep rough. There I picked up another new slant.

You can try to swing for distance from the rough, but usually you won't get it. I'd been more eager to make up for missing the fairway than to make sure I escaped the tall uncut stuff. Using a club without sufficient loft, I'd wind up in worse trouble than before.

Once I began to use a deep 8-iron or wedge to pitch out in a safe direction at the sacrifice of distance, much of my trouble was over.

At the same time, I learned the small but important angles— such as watching the tops of trees for wind signs, checking on the position of all flags and keeping my hands warm and flexible by sticking them in my pockets between shots. When walking from a fairway that was parallel to another, I always glanced over to the hole I'd be playing soon to see where the pin was spotted. It might turn out to be a blind green, from the fairway, where I'd need the information.

That same year of '38, the richest purse of all was the $13,500 Westchester Open at Fenway Country Club in New York. There was one catch: you had to last through a 108-hole marathon. About 20,000 fans mobbed the course, which was a sea of mud from heavy rains.

Down went the gates and fences before a stampede of people, many of whom never had seen a golf tournament but were about to make up for it. Of 20,000 fans, not 2,000 paid to see what the newspapers later called the "One-Eyed Connolly Open."

You couldn't swing a club without almost beheading somebody, but after 107 holes I was hanging onto a 1-stroke lead over
Billy Burke. It was so dark when I reached the finishing hole
that the green was barely visible for my knock-up shot. The
fans in the front lines did a 100-yard dash after it; the ball
bounced off one of them and landed in a muddy depression 40
yards from the green.

"How the hell can I hit out of here?" I asked a policeman. He
was so busy running for his life he didn't have time to discuss
it with me.

Going absolutely berserk, the crowd smashed the cane poles
the cops had tried to herd them with and ran the cops off. I was
left in the middle of the first golf riot I'd seen—at the mercy of a
mob.

They shoved me, grabbed at me, and gave me no room. Taking an 8-iron, swinging in a short arc with a choked-down grip,
I got it out, over their heads, and just onto the green.

Two putts made it a 430-shot total for the 108 holes, which
beat Burke by 2 strokes for the $5,000 first prize. The score was
talked up by the critics for quite a while; I was 2 shots under
even 4s for a lot of holes played under weird conditions. Again,
the short irons had saved me. The greens had been soggy and
trampled, and yet I'd 3-putted only four greens out of 108 and
4-putted only one—all the proof any man would want that your
approaches are second only to putts in importance. My "deadly"
putting could only happen because I'd pitched up so close,
consistently.

As I holed out, the crowd rushed the green to fight for the
ball. Hundreds of people were piled up and the cries were awful.
"Get off, you're breaking my leg!" you'd hear someone yell. "Oh,
my God, my back!" Then there'd be a cracking noise. It was like
fourteen football teams scrimmaging. I don't know how many
they hauled away in ambulances.

They grabbed me, and the next thing I knew they had me on
their shoulders and a man was yelling, "The winnah!" Then I

was walking around on top of people and being hauled this way and that until I thought my spine would break.

"Let me down!" I shouted. They were tearing off my shoes by this time. With no other way out, I gave a jump over their heads and soared over a high hedge behind the green—not knowing that beyond the hedge was a 15-foot drop-off to a lower tee. Upon lighting, I hit on the back of my neck, doing cartwheels all the way to the bottom.

The clubhouse was 75 yards away, and Snead didn't stop until he was behind locked doors.

Over the course of much experimenting, I found that my short and middle irons would be most helpful when used as follows:

When chipping within 25 yards of the cup where the ball must be stopped quickly on the green—the 9-iron.

When the same conditions prevail and a lesser loft and slightly more roll are wanted—the 8-iron.

When chipping within a few unobstructed feet of the putting surface, with a roll-up to the cup wanted (the chip-and-run shot)—the 5- or 6-iron.

When chipping a medium distance, with an extra-long roll intended—the 4- or 5-iron.

When recovering from long, heavy grass or cuppy lies—the 8-iron (my best all-around "trouble" club).

When pitching over obstacles from deep rough, with a quick bite on the green required—the pitching wedge.

When approaching a heavily trapped green from 125 to 135 yards out and where the pin position requires a quick stop of the ball—the 7-iron.

When the ball is semiburied in sand—the 9-iron or fairway (pitching) wedge.

When a long distance is needed from a semiburied trap lie— the 6-iron.

When the ball is otherwise trapped in sand—the sand wedge.

None of these were hard-and-fast rules, since courses and conditions vary so much, but by and large they became my club selections at close quarters. Watching older pros, I saw that they developed a close friendship with a few short irons and did little changing off from these established clubs. Take the 8-iron— a great utility number. In 1952, bidding for my second Masters title, I held a 1-stroke lead on the field at the twelfth hole of the final round—but with Tommy Bolt playing sub-par golf ahead and Ben Hogan going to the whip from behind. At the twelfth, a par 3, I stopped to study the scoreboard there.

Maybe it distracted me—anyway, my 7-iron tee shot was coming down right atop the flag when it was caught in a whirlpool of wind that blows over No. 12 green at the Augusta National and fell into a creek that runs before the green.

I was mad, because it wasn't my fault, and not thinking straight. After dropping a new ball over my shoulder across the creek, I left myself buried in a sandy muck and five inches of grass. I almost dunked that one, too. A semipitch and blast carried only to the side of the far bank, and there it hung in more coarse grass.

That just about took the heart out of me. Dan Topping, Bruce Forbes, and others of my friends said I looked like a guy who'd been in too many play-offs as I stood there sagging. A 6 on the hole seemed so likely that I began calculating in my head what the loss of 3 shots on the field would mean—the championship, without much doubt.

My caddie stepped into view with his hand on the 8-iron. That good old No. 8 lets me down less than any other club. It gives me the best combination of pitch and roll.

"Not yet," I told myself. "It isn't a 6 yet."

Swinging spraddle-legged, I got the ball up out of there—but then turned pale when I saw that a big gob of mud was stuck to it. It went lobbidy-lobbidy-lobbidy across the green, wobbling this way and that, while the gallery groaned. The last wobble was toward the hole instead of away, and in she dropped.

Prettiest bogey 4 I ever saw.

"Well, that did it," I told my caddie. "I think I can really go from now on."

The shot was only one out of 286 I took in the Masters, but it decided everything. From then on I *attacked* the course instead of fearing it and proceeded to play it 3 under par to the finish and win by 4 shots over Jackie Burke, Jr.

Developing a surefire confidence in a few short irons is the best thing for the spirit I know and the surest way not to come up empty, as some otherwise successful pros do, in big events like the Masters. I don't feel so kindly toward the 10-iron and haven't since the Los Angeles Open at Hillcrest in 1942.

Grantland Rice said that Snead at Hillcrest was about the saddest thing he ever saw on the links. He also claimed it was one of my dumbest plays. "Sam can only think in terms of birdies," Rice wrote, "and today that fixation heaped a new disaster on his balding head."

After seventy-one holes of 6-under-par play, I needed a par on the closing seventy-second to tie for first place. A birdie would win. Rice and all others who favored safety notwithstanding, I wasn't interested in par.

Two shots brought me to the bottom of a 70-foot-steep incline leading to a plateau green. The pin stood just over the collar of the green nearest to me. Pitching over the slope to the fat of the green would mean one hell of a lag putt coming back. Par was 5. I wanted down in 4.

My 10-iron shot seemed to have lofted up the ball just right, and I started walking up the hill. Just then I saw a ball rolling back toward me. I thought—*somebody else must have shot.*

Then I saw it was my ball.

It rolled and rolled down where the crowd had trampled the grass and stopped where a policeman had fluffed it all up with his feet. My lie was down in a grassy nest.

So I pitched again, and it hung in the collar and rolled right back down to stop in almost the same place.

The experts claim that at this point I should have pitched high and safely to the middle of the green, but they forget that I'd now used 4 strokes and needed 5 to tie Jimmy Thomson and Ben Hogan.

For a third time I tried to lift the ball just over the collar, and here she came again—rolling back down. A small blanket would have covered the three divots I'd taken. I threw that 10-iron a mile over the crowd.

The agony went on. I holed out in 8 and lost to Ben and Jimmy, 285 to their 282s.

After playing seventy-one holes 6 under par, I'd gone 3 over par on one hole without reaching a trap or encountering any trouble except light rough.

There was no "blowup" in this case, as all the writers said. All three pitches missed landing near the cup by an inch or two. The 10-iron just wasn't my baby that day.

Leo Diegel told me later, "Don't go cutting your throat. These things happen. I ought to know: once I took a 9 on the last hole of the U.S. Open, a lousy little pitch-and-putt hole, and all I wanted was a razor, poison, or a gun. Just keep practicing those cute shots."

Believe me, I did, because, for one thing, I can't putt well enough to make up for weak approaches. One night in Los Angeles, Ben Hogan was in such an aggravated state of mind about his putting that you could hear him in the next room. I wanted to say something to comfort him, but I couldn't.

Ben's wife, Valerie, who traveled everywhere with him, wasn't a talkative woman. But she spoke up in that sweet, quiet way of hers. "Would you like to know how to sink those putts?" she asked.

Ben said, "*You* know how?"

"Yes, I do," said Valerie.

"Then why the —— haven't you told me? How?"

"Just hit them a little closer to the hole."

That's the best golf tip you'll ever read anywhere. All players, both dubs and pros, put too much strain on their putting by not working hard enough on short-iron improvement. And there's more chance for improvement here than anywhere on the course—limited only by your willingness to work at it.

Whenever the short game is mentioned, I think of Bob Hope. At one time Ski-Nose thought that his chip shots all had to be lofted well into the air—which is a shot that looks pretty. He'd use a high-loft 9-iron or wedge when the green was open to him or whenever an obstacle had to be cleared. His chips would land short of the green, hit an uneven spot, and kick sideways.

The shot that educated Hope came in the California State Amateur tournament at Fresno when he faced a tough 20-yard approach over a 10-foot hill. He was set to try a wedge chip over the bank when an old pro friend of his—George Fazio—stepped up. "No, Bob, take a 7-iron, pitch it into that smooth bank, and let it roll on over."

"It sounds screwy," said Hope.

"Try it."

Hope did, his ball bouncing and holding to the turf all the way and dropping in for an eagle.

"Why didn't somebody tell me this?" said Hope. "I always thought you had to fly it up there."

Bing Crosby never had that trouble. We played some Cuban Refugee Fund matches together, and I noticed that Bing would use a 4-iron off the green, hit with little loft, and run his ball up to the hole. He was going by two pro golfer's rules:

1) Floating a shot with heavy backspin takes more ability than you can supply every time you swing. To get reverse spin, you must strike a downward blow which contacts a good three-fourths of the ball before your blade hits the turf. When the hitting edge of the clubface meets the round of the ball above the turf, it squeezes a piece of the ball into the ground—which

is known as "pinching." It isn't beyond most golfers—but things can go wrong.

2) It's simpler to treat the chip as a long putt—lofting on a low line to the green, a crisp little running stroke which lets the ball hug the ground from there on in. Wrist action is at a minimum; in fact, you need none from about four feet before impact to four feet after impact. It's an arm shot with no body pivot at all—as foolproof as any golf shot can get.

Show me the man who uses a club of moderate loft around the green and I'll show you one who'll be closer to the cup than the fellow who uses a deep-faced club with the idea of stopping his shot with reverse spin. The exceptions, of course, are always there. In heavy grass, sand, or loose dirt, for instance, you won't use a 4-iron, but one of the trouble clubs.

Watching women play isn't a hobby of mine, and yet they taught me a lesson about short shots. The girls have unusual "feel" in their hands—I won't argue with that. Louise Suggs, the lady pro champ, beat Dow Finsterwald and me over a par-3 course not long ago. But most women put no smoke into their short irons. They pitch the ball as though they were halfheartedly hitting a full shot. They push at the ball and make a flabby halfmiss of the shot.

One wealthy woman I was teaching screamed at me one day, "I never care if I ever see you again!"

I was keeping the pressure on in trying to make her hit an 8-iron like she meant it.

"Yeah, but it's working, isn't it?" I said.

After getting the idea, my 95-shooter went home and started dusting the girls off regularly in club tournaments. She was saving 10 to 12 shots a round. The next time I saw her, I bet she could beat one of the men players at Boca Raton, Florida. She put some real money in my pocket that day.

Why do women underhit their easy approaches? Maybe it's

because they put too much dependence on their well-known "delicate" touch.

I don't get caught doing that, and haven't for years. I don't choke my iron on the pitches and chips, don't baby them—except at very short range—and follow through without stopping or slowing the tempo of the swing in any way.

From the time in 1938 when Paul Runyan gave me a lesson around the greens in the P.G.A. finals, I worked to eliminate my faults—but also learned to steer clear of golfers with diseases that might be catching.

Once, in Florida, Bing Crosby said to me, "I've been shanking a lot."

"Don't look at me," I said, backing off.

"Don't worry," Bing laughed. "I've solved the problem. It's a matter of distance. I set up the ball outside or off the toe of my iron, and, in reaching for it, I've just about stopped shanking."

"OK, then, I'll play with you. Just don't even mention shanking to me."

Shanks scare me worse than any fault in golf. Mrs. Dodge Sloan was a pupil of mine, and, after watching her awhile, I said, "Well, get up to the ball. You're standing five feet back like the ball was a snake that would bite you."

After moving up, she started shanking. "Now see what you've done!" she said.

She demanded a cure, and that was when I took off at top speed, telling her: "No, ma'am. Nothing doing. You might get me doing it, too."

One of my assistants helped Mrs. Sloan straighten out her shank.

Shanks are so contagious that even watching them is risky, and that includes the pro player. The ball scoots off at almost right angles to the intended direction because the clubface never touches it. Contact happens a half inch or more off the heel of the club. Mainly, the player lets his swing stray so much outside the proper line—usually because of bad weight balance, a restricted pivot, or loose wrist action—that at the moment of contact the whole clubface is outside the ball.

I advise shankers to take a stance with their weight evenly balanced between the balls and heels of their feet, so they have the feeling that they can turn up their toes. I tell them to stop transferring their weight from their heels to their toes on the backswing. This will keep them from coming forward. I tell them to make sure their right hand sits on top of the left at the peak of the backswing.

And then I get far, far away from them.

Of all the "wrong" shots I've made, the one which brought the most criticism came just off the green on the seventy-first hole of the U.S. Open at Medinah Country Club, Chicago, in 1949. The shot can be a valuable lesson to anyone, if you understand that the critics faulted me for the wrong thing. They missed my real mistake.

With two holes left, I needed a pair of pars to tie Cary Middlecoff, who had finished with a 286 score, and force a play-off.

My tee shot on No. 71 dug into the sloping green and backed up 3 feet off the green into the short fringe grass. Should I use a chipping iron or putter? The argument for using a putter in fringe grass is that you're right down over the ball for control, that you eliminate the bounce of a lofted club, and, finally, that you can tilt the putter just a bit and cause the ball to skim over the grass onto the smooth surface. I liked the odds favoring the putter.

It looked like a left-to-right putt to me, and I hit firmly, expecting the fringe grass to check the shot. The gallery groaned when the putt rose into the air over the grass and, with overspin, carried 8 feet past the cup. The return putt was downhill, hit the cup dead center, hopped up, and stopped a half inch away.

There went the National Open and about $100,000. I finished in a second-place tie with Clayton Heafner by 1 stroke.

The sportswriters almost to a man razzed me for not using a chipping iron.

"The Open jinx on Snead ruins his judgment," they wrote.

The real fact was that I failed to examine the lie in the fringe grass closely enough. The ball was in a slight depression. So, on the stroke, it leaped up and over the short grass—robbing me of any braking action. Missing the approach so badly was my fault. But I chose the right club.

In May of 1959 I took a long time examining every lie during the Greenbrier Open at White Sulphur Springs. In eighteen holes I had something like 9 short-iron shots to make. They all came off pretty well, because when I walked up to the scorer's stand at the finish and he asked me what I'd shot, I said, "Fifty-nine."

"You kill me, Sam," he said. "Now what did you shoot?"

"I had a 59," I repeated.

"OK, play jokes," he said. "I can stand here all day if you can."

That scorer almost fell off the stand when they verified my 59—which is said to be the hottest competitive round ever played by anyone. It was posted in the third round of the tournament, and after the final day's play, the Detroit *Times* ran a headline which read:

SNEAD BLOWS TO 63!

But how it all happened, a 59 followed by a 63, is another story. . . .

SAM SNEAD'S COMMENT:
THE SHORT GAME

Graduating into the 80-shooting class or less can be done several ways, all of them time-consuming. The shortcut is to practice 50 to 100 shots before every round from all points of the short-green compass. Begin with a few simple chips just off the green, picking the club with the least loft necessary to drop the ball onto the carpet edge and roll it on up.

The chip shot

Play a dozen pitch shots with a nine-iron or flanged niblick (wedge) over a trap. Take more backswing than you think you need—usually you'll be short and bunkered, because a popping-up ball has little carry. Keep your weight on the left foot throughout with feet close together. Cock the wrists only slightly, minimize body turn, and hit slowly and firmly.

The pitch

Keep moving back, testing and memorizing distances obtained with various short irons swung easily. Practice from deep grass, using a deeply lofted club and grasping the club with extra firmness in the right hand. Practice from downhill lies, with the ball positioned off your right foot, and from uphill lies, off the left foot.

Play a few cut shots from deep rough. Here's how I play the cut shot in order to get the extra height you need.

My stance is well open, the body almost facing the hole—which is to make sure the club cuts across the ball from the outside in. I spot the ball just inside the right foot. Clubface is wide open, and first I hit the ball, then take a divot. From sand, play the ball off the left foot to insure taking a thin cushion of sand behind it.

Give some special attention to the pitching wedge: for a quick stopper on the green, you can't beat this club; it'll bring you more one-putt greens than the 8- or 9-iron within 50 yards of the flag when you don't want the ball to run.

*A full follow-through
with the pitching wedge*

Dick Nixon, when he was Vice-President, couldn't break 100 and was wondering how he'd ever give Ike a game, and then I had a little talk with him. "Play those pitches and chips with a wedge," I advised him, "until you have the feel of it." Nixon soon got down into the 80s, plays a hot game around the greens today.

The next will be tougher, since so few golf clubs think enough of their members' scores to provide them with practice traps. But if you can find a vacant sand trap, sprinkle a dozen balls and remember: on this shot, there's almost no movement of body or knees. You drive the club under and through the ball with full follow-up. Use a chipping iron on balls resting atop sand. Then semibury a few balls and practice explosions with the sand wedge. On the latter shot, never let the blade touch the ball: in deep, dry sand you should strike about two inches back of the ball; hit closer when more distance is needed.

If you have the habit of pitching high and trying to clear every rise of ground on the course, practice what Bob Hope learned: pitching into a bank between you and the green and letting the ball run up and over.

One of the best parts of the game of young Gary Player, who has come along fast in recent years, is his chipping. In our head-to-head matches in 1959-60-61, I was able to win all but one—but not because I could outchip Gary. He knows another secret: to pick an exact landing spot on the green for your little chippy. Player always checks the green carefully before a short approach, making it work for him.

If he is making an 8-iron chip from 30 feet away, he wants to land just on the green—not short of the green, where uneven ground might kick the ball off line—and Player figures on about 15 feet of flight and 15 feet of roll. He picks out a spot on the green, such as a light or dark patch or a cloverleaf, and aims to drop his ball right there.

Like me, he measures the amount of roll you get with every short iron and eliminates guesswork. My normal 6-iron chip, for instance, will roll about twice as far as it flies.

Just as in putting, I take a sober look at the texture of the green near the flagstick. If I see soft turf there, I'll hit a shade harder and play the shot to carry shorter than usual.

Get your wrists into play early in a pitch shot over an obstacle; it will produce greater height and bite to the ball.

Imagine that you're me, three feet off the green with the U. S. Open title and $100,000 at stake and your putter in your hand. You're in short fringe grass. There won't be 20,000 people holding their breath, as they did at Medinah, but if you pretend hard enough, you can get the effect. Study the height, texture, and lean of the border grass. If the grass grows in the opposite direction to the shot, better leave the putter in your bag. Never forget that your ball must travel at two different speeds of roll. You want to roll the ball along the top of the higher grass, so take a smooth sweep and rely on the putter's loft to bring it up slightly. Don't strike the ball on its underside, but in the middle. Most of all—as I didn't at Medinah—look carefully at how the ball lies.

After a 100-ball practice round of approaches, list on paper your two or three ranking weaknesses. At the next practice session concentrate entirely on these.

After six months, if you haven't pared 10 shots per round off your score, you're either a rare bird—or a shanker.

10

"NEEDLES"—AND KNOWING YOURSELF

PSYCHOLOGY AND A REVENUE AGENT • A 30½-INCH
PUTT AT ST. LOUIS • COUNTERING OPPOSITION GIM-
MICKS • GALLERIES AND OFFICIALS CAN NEEDLE YOU •
THE DAY I THREW A MATCH • THE BIGGEST THRILL OF
ALL

Shipwreck Kelly phoned long-distance one
night last September while I was watching a ball game at
Yankee Stadium with Dan Topping, in Dan's box, and said,
"Say, Sam, I have a proposition. How much would you charge
to officiate at the opening of a new peewee golf course in Tea-
neck, New Jersey?"

Kelly and other jokers enjoy ribbing me about my willingness
at the age of fifty to hop anywhere a golf dollar shows its head,
much the same way I did as a youngster when a two-bit tip to a
cabdriver represented a hell of an investment and you could get
me to show up anywhere just by throwing four dollars on the
first tee. Today seven corporations carry my name, with a gross
in good years, at my end, of around $200,000. It's a change I
never thought would happen. In a restaurant nowadays I'll hand
a headwaiter twenty dollars and tell him to stick it in his hollow
tooth, which is more than it cost me to live for two weeks in the
old days. Last year, Lord Rothschild asked me to dedicate the
first golf links in Israel, then I went to Italy and Japan for
exhibitions, then to Las Vegas to win a $10,000 pot in the Tour-
nament of Champions, and after that to Puerto Rico for the
Canada Cup, and then to a lot of other places. My travel bill is

$25,000 a year. I own, or am interested in, golf schools, golf clinics, golf-course-country-club estates, a fishing-tackle business, an oceanarium, par-3 golf courses, and a couple of prizefighters, and sponsors pay me for endorsing golf equipment from top to toe. Usually this means working sixteen hours a day. Most of it, thank the Lord, is spent with a golf club in my hands—which is what keeps the old hillbilly young.

As it stands now, I've lasted through four different waves of golf winners, and have hopes of making it five. The first wave, in the mid-1930s, was led by Henry Picard, Johnny Revolta, Paul Runyan, Craig Wood, Gene Sarazen and the fading-out Walter Hagen. Then came Ben Hogan, Byron Nelson, Lloyd Mangrum, Vic Ghezzi, Jimmy Demaret and others almost as tough. The third wave included Lew Worsham, Chandler Harper, Doc Middlecoff, Tommy Bolt, Jackie Burke, Doug Ford, Jay Hebert and the like. The present-day invasion of what few vets are left brings up Gene Littler, Ken Venturi, Arnold Palmer, Billy Caspar and Gary Player.

After a quarter century of swinging, I'm not afraid to meet any man in the world in a head-to-head match, and that's because I've never let outside business turn me soft and paunchy. My measurements are almost the same as twenty years ago—185 pounds, a thirty-three-inch waist and forty-three-inch chest. Johnny Longden, the jockey, and Archie Moore, the fighter, are the only ones who are my age who're still active. You don't see those boys let hardly a day pass when they aren't on a horse or in the gym.

Time hasn't passed us by because we won't let it: the thrill of winning and living at the top hasn't tailed off a bit.

But I still find my luck hard to believe. Every day or so I play with men who could buy or sell me, but I own about 100 sport jackets, 75 pairs of shoes, 25 sets of clubs, 400 shirts, several houses, a Virginia ranch, and five automobiles. A while back, just for laughs, I ordered a special-made toupee to cover my head when I played trumpet with the Four Populaires band in jam sessions at the lively spots around Hot Springs and White Sulphur. Naturally, when a wigmaker in Greensboro, North Carolina, finished the job, a chartered plane flew down and picked it up. I pal around with some of the most unusual people in the world. I never told the Prince of Wales (the way Walter Hagen did), "Here, Eddie, hold the pin while I putt out."

But I did tell King Farouk of Egypt to suck in his gut and President Ike to stick out his hind end on his drives . . . and they didn't mind a bit.

I'll admit that being Sam Snead is far more fun than anybody deserves . . . even when the Internal Revenue boys give me the treatment, as happened not long ago.

A letter arrived at Sam Snead, Inc., which said: "Dear Mr. Snead: Based on a review of your declared business overhead deductions, you owe the government another $20,000 in income tax. Please send us the money right away."

It wasn't put exactly in those words, but that was the gist, and it gave me a worse case of the yips than when I'm looking down an old snake of a 6-foot putt with first place at stake. The words "revenue agent" naturally make any mountain boy nervous. My business advisers and money handlers are all well-known straight shooters. So the letter was a shock. I punched buttons and asked for George Denton, who handles my stock investments; Barney Barnett of Louisville, my attorney; Gary Nixon, general business manager; and others.

"Do I owe this $20,000?" I asked. "And if so, how come? It'll be a fine thing if people start saying that Sam Snead came up from sticking pigs to a rich man and then cheated Uncle Sam."

After checking everything, the experts said, "No, you don't owe it and we will demand a review of your books."

About a week later, the Internal Revenue sent a man to The Greenbrier Hotel to give my records the X-ray. The minute I saw him, it was 50-1 that I was in trouble. I don't mean he was hatchet-faced or hated golf, but that he wore an inexpensive suit and had scuffed shoes and it was plain he'd had to scratch hard for his own income. He sat down next to my desk in the pro shop and crossed his legs. Looking at his shoe, I had another jolt. There was a big hole showing in the sole of it.

Excusing myself, I told Gary Nixon off to one side, "Oh, man, am I going to have trouble with *this* fellow."

"Well, roll out the red carpet for him," said Gary. "Get on his good side."

Going back, I slapped the Revenuer's back and said, "While you're here at the hotel, I'd like you to be my guest. Ask for anything you want and you've got it."

"Thanks," he said, "but it's against regulations. I pay my own way."

"Well then, at least have dinner with me."

"I accept," he said, "but only if I pick up my own check. Regulations of the Bureau."

All this time his nose was like a bird dog's—it never came out of those books—and then he shot a question that put my nerves even more on edge.

"I see here," he said suspiciously, "that you paid a caddie $250 after a tournament in Palm Beach. Is that an accurate statement?"

"Why, sure, I always tip my caddies $100 to $150," I said, "and if I win, like I did here, I toss in another $100 or so. I've gone $500 and more where the boy did a specially fine job of clubbing me."

The Revenuer got all wide-eyed and clucked his tongue and I went back to Nixon and said, "Holy smoke, with that hole in his shoes and all, I'm afraid he'll show up some place wanting to caddie for me."

"Stay with him," said Nixon. "Find out if he plays golf."

It turned out he was crazy about the game and had always wanted to play with me. When we teed off—the Revenuer insisting on paying his own greens fee and again keeping me from getting friendly—I was hoping he'd be a duffer, so that I could offer a suggestion that would help his game. There was no need to worry. He sliced into the woods on No. 1, No. 2, and No. 3, and on No. 4 he was so deep in the jack pines that he needed an ax to chop his way back. "I don't think this guy is from Internal Revenue at all," I told Nixon, "but from the Forestry Department."

After it ended, I said to the inspector, "I'd like to help that slice of yours, if you'd let me."

He brightened up all over, then looked sad. "No, I couldn't afford your fee. I understand it's thirty dollars a lesson."

"Well, you can forget that," I said. "I just want to help."

"Mr. Snead," he said, "I've had this slice all my life and I'll have to go on living with it. I can't tell you how sad that makes me. I've always hoped to get your advice, but none of us boys in Washington can take advantage of our position."

"Not just one little word for free, even if it straightens you out?" I said. By now the man had me pleading with him not to be so all-fired hard on both of us.

The Revenuer almost had tears in his eyes.

"Not a word," he said, starting off. "I'll see you and the books again in the morning."

By now my friends were holding their sides and betting that I'd pay through the nose to the government, or else go through an expensive appeal, but the fact is that when the inspector filed his report, I didn't owe any $20,000. The case was settled for a small fraction of that amount. I wound up gladder than ever to be an American, even if the workout did take a few months off my life.

One reason I've told this story is that it shows how psychology works. From the moment I saw the hole in the inspector's shoe, he worried me so that I could hardly defend myself. I began building a mental condition that a little thought would have told me wasn't necessary. I assumed he'd be out to get me, when this was anything but true. In golf, this same thing happens— the building up of wrong ideas. When someone plants an idea deliberately, among the professionals it's called "the needles."

Learning to counter "the needles"—deliberate or accidental—was a tough row to hoe for me, but one you can't fail at if you want to win. This holds true whether it's a "friendly" club match or a U. S. Open play-off.

In 1936 I didn't know a thing about how psychology and the needles operate, and it was during a match at the Homestead course that I had my first lesson. In the last round—after shooting a 68 and standing close to the lead of a local Virginia tournament—I was paired with my boss, the club pro. The man was a little jealous of my success so far, though I didn't know it. At the first tee, he looked over and said sympathetically: "Sam, what did you do to your swing? You look ridiculous. I don't know how you ever get the ball in the fairway with your left elbow flipping up like that at the finish."

On the drive, I tried to keep the elbow down and hooked into the woods. Same thing on the recovery shot: I was through the woods, then over the green, into a trap, and wound up with a 7 on the hole. I got self-conscious and went to pieces, taking an 80 for the round to finish third in an event I could have won.

At no time after the first hole did this old pro need to repeat the treatment. He had me needled clear through with that one comment, and not even when the final cards were posted did I realize what he'd done.

Now let's jump ahead eleven years to the United States Open of 1947 at the St. Louis Country Club and one of the great American Open play-offs of all time. The whole facts on what happened there haven't been told until now.

However, I want to make it plain that I hold no grudge against Lew Worsham, the Chin, who was my play-off opponent. He did what he needed to do if he was to win, and if a man can't defend himself against a smart psychologist, he belongs in the clubhouse playing gin and not out there with the big-time cutthroats.

On Saturday afternoon, the final round of the Open, I needed a 20-foot curling downhill putt on the last hole to tie Worsham at 282 strokes and bring on a play-off. Worsham stood with the breathless spectators around the green. They tell me he had fingers crossed on both hands.

The hex didn't work; my putt rolled true as a die and in.

On Sunday, over eighteen holes, we had a slambang match before an overflow gallery, with Worsham outdistancing me (as I've told in Chapter III) when my driver failed, and I was forced to use a brassie. Despite that, when we came up to the sixteenth hole, Chin was 2 shots down. There he holed a great putt from the back of the green and I almost made mine on top of his. Rimming out, I still led by a stroke.

On the seventeenth, trying to bend one around a slight dogleg right, my drive fell in the edge of the rough, but Worsham hit a very bad ducking hook, sailing it over the crowd down to the eighteenth fairway, paralleling the seventeenth. Inspecting the balls, it was found that Chin actually had a better angle to the green than I did. He was able to stop his approach on the green. My 8-iron caught the green's front edge but lacked enough bite and ran over the back into high, coarse grass, which people had trampled down until it was bent and had a terrible nap or grain to it.

I was looking at one of the toughest shots you can meet. The grass grain was against me, which meant that hitting into it would make the rough blades flare up. I could either knock the chip 10 feet or 50 feet through that half-flattened cabbage.

With Worsham already on the green and with me studying the predicament, I became aware of heavy breathing.

"Whoosh-hush . . . whoosh-hush," it went.

Glancing around, I saw Worsham standing not 8 feet from me. He'd just climbed a hill to the green and was panting hard.

"You'd better move back a little, Chin," I said. "Just give me a little more room."

He blinked, as if not realizing that his breathing wasn't helping my concentration, then walked away a bit.

Then I made a chip of from 6 to 7 feet off the carpet, leaving a 6-foot putt. I missed, Worsham took 2 putts, and the match was squared. One reason my chip wasn't better, I'll swear, was that I was upset by Worsham's wheezing, plus the need to remind him of it, and wasn't 100 per cent concentrated on the shot.

We both made pretty good drives on the eighteenth. The Chin's second shot was onto the green's brim, just inches from tall rough, while mine was on the green, 25 feet above the cup. He chipped very fast, the ball hitting the back of the hole, popping up, and halting less than 3 feet below the cup.

My putt looked very slick but died about the same distance as Worsham's and above the cup.

Now we'd both used up 68 shots and the U. S. Open title would depend on what happened next. Life is full of blisters, but I've never felt more pressure than then. The massed crowd was deathly still as we read our putts. I glanced over at Referee Ike Grainger, waiting for him to signify which of us was away. He made no signal.

Worsham's ball was in his hand, his marking coin in his hand. So I assumed I was away and lined up the putt.

Just as I was set to putt, Worsham suddenly stepped in front of me and spoke. "What are you doing?" he said.

"I'm putting out," I said, staring at him.

"Well, maybe not," he said. "Are you sure you're away? I think maybe I am and have first shot."

In any bind like this one, the man who has first putt has an advantage. If he holes out, pressure on the opponent at least doubles.

Worsham then turned and appealed to Referee Ike Grainger, who looked startled, then pulled a tape measure from his pocket.

"I believe it's in the rules," I said, beginning to get hot around the collar, "that once a man's started to putt, he's entitled to finish." Grainger hesitated but didn't answer me. He didn't seem to know the rule I quoted and let Worsham replace his ball and pick up his coin. Then a measurement was taken. I walked off to one side, cocked one foot over the other, leaning on my putter, trying to be calm, but I was burning inside.

The measurement proved I'd been correct. My ball was 30½ inches away to 30 for Worsham.

With a left-to-right break facing me, downhill, and with Worsham coming uphill, mine was the tougher putt. All upset over the interruption, I settled on the speed of the putt but changed my mind at the last instant on both speed and amount of break . . . and, by just the amount of break I didn't allow, the ball missed. I'd tapped it a shade easy, causing it to break out about 2 inches.

Worsham put his right into the middle of the can and was the Open champion. It was the second time I'd been Open runner-up, the bitterest medicine in the world to swallow.

Years of thinking over this incident makes me believe that Chin didn't do it deliberately, yet the needle was there, just the same, on both the seventeenth and eighteenth greens. I'll always believe I'd have won this Open if the two interruptions of my thinking hadn't happened.

Don't ever depend on the rules to protect you: it's dog-eat-dog out there, and I've known few big winners who, consciously or unconsciously, wouldn't rattle the other man any little way they could.

Frankly, I've never gotten over stage fright out there in front of the people, which makes you vulnerable to the smart tricks. Every man's chest has a heart in it, and that thing goes *thump, thump, thump*—and never stops doing it when other folks are standing around, judging you.

After I'd put some age on me, along came a young star who thought he'd upset old Sam and make a headline—and the way he chose to do it was by using the needle.

We were teeing off at Charleston, West Virginia, a course he was more familiar with than I was, and as I placed my ball he spoke up with, "Now watch it, Sam, over to the right. There's woods and a big drop-off there and you can get into real trouble if you hit in there."

This sort of strategy I cut my teeth on—warning a man of something so strongly that it'll prey on his mind to the point of creating an almost magnetic pull when you swing the club. Talk of trouble can draw you straight to trouble.

This youngster needed to be given a lesson for trying such an old gimmick on me. As it happened, he was thirty years old and still a bachelor, the reason being, as everyone said, that he was still tied to his mother's apron strings. And such talk bothered him.

After driving safely to the left, I waited until he stepped up to hit, then remarked, "Billy, when did you say you got married?"

With that he put his ball right into those woods. He lost, 8 and 7.

It was in the Masters Tournament long ago that I discovered how mental images can be planted in the brain—particularly by the golfer himself, which is self-needling. Playing with Jim Turnesa one day, I was intently studying his actions on the tee. Turnesa pushed his drive into timber to the right. The image of everything Turnesa had done was so strong in my mind that I stepped up and my muscles followed the image and I did the same thing, landing almost exactly in the same spot in the jungle as had Jim. After that, I watched my opponents only casual-like.

"Don't ever try to read the other fellow too much," my friend, Victor East, warned me. "But nonhuman hazards are different."

East was playing an English course and came to a hole with a big bush located square in the fairway middle. In trying to steer clear of the bush, he flew into it every time he played the hole. And he lost three tournaments that way. So then he switched completely and *tried* to hit the bush—and never was able to get it in there, or even close.

So you can see that the images work both ways.

Dutch Harrison, the Arkansas Traveler, never went in much for needles, but he had a disguised shot-softening act that threw more opponents into a faint than anything since Walter Hagen's time. Dutch would come to a little par 3 of 150 yards or so, squint his eyes, reach into the bag, and take a 5-iron. Then he'd make what looked like a nice, full swing but actually was a soft shot played right onto the green. The other guy, who had been thinking of an 8-iron, would say, "Oho, Dutch used a 5 and got on, so I'd better lengthen out and use at least a 6-iron." He'd plow right over the green and everything behind it.

Maybe Harrison would have foxed me if a long time earlier I hadn't met up with the canny Scotchman, Willie MacFarlane, who'd beaten Bob Jones in a double play-off for the U. S. Open title back in 1925. We were paired in the Metropolitan Open in New Jersey in 1938. On a 135-yard downhill par-3 hole, I watched like a hawk to see what club he'd use.

MacFarlane took out a stick, a 6-iron, and looked at the ball, shook his head slightly, then replaced it and pulled out a No. 4. He played a deceptive little three-quarter shot plunk into the center of the carpet.

"Gee," I told myself, "I know this isn't a shot calling for either a No. 6 or No. 4—but look what MacFarlane just did."

After a struggle, I used my head, took a No. 8, and landed closer to the cup than MacFarlane.

Walking off the tee, I asked, "Willie, why did you change from a No. 6 to a 4-iron?"

"Loddie," he answered in his thick brogue, "I just wanted to teach you a lesson. I didn't trap you with my little trick, and nobody else will either, I'm thinking. But remember—never pay any attention to what the other man is using. Reason it out for yourself."

"The Mustache"—Lloyd Mangrum—hasn't been the only pro to develop the fidgets on the tee when I'm ready to swing, but I don't mind mentioning his case as an example of how I've had to deal with another form of needling. Mangrum used to have a great habit of standing in the front corner of your vision. As you began your backswing, he'd cross his legs. The movement was just enough to catch your eye and set up a disturbance.

After a few such experiences, I backed off the ball, walked over to Mangrum, and said through my teeth, "You've driven your ball. Now get off the damned tee while I have my chance."

Mangrum didn't cross any more legs on me, but others tried playing on my nerves, and for them I developed just about the best countergimmick I've ever come across.

Any time an opponent was working on me by any means whatever, I'd wait until we came to a green where I'd already holed out and he was standing and sweating over his putt.

Then I'd just turn on my heel and walk off the green. The noise of about 10,000 people following me to the next tee was so much that it cracked the nerves of the best of the "gamesmanship" experts. One lesson was all it ever took.

In mentioning that a crowd will follow me, I don't mean to to seem boastful, only stating the fact that I've always been able to depend on the gallery to help me stick the needler with 10,000 needles.

The practice worked so well, in fact, that I've sometimes found myself needling nice guys like Freddie Haas, Jr., without any intent. At the $100,000 Tam O'Shanter, my approach rolled to 3 inches of the cup. While I tapped it in, people started stampeding to the next tee. And Haas had yet to putt. This wasn't the first time it had happened that day.

"Dammit, Sam!" said Haas. "If you're gonna hole out first all the time, we're just gonna sit here on this green until it's empty."

"Well, Fred, you don't want me to mark a 3-incher, do you?"

"No, but if they think you're leaving, the riot is always on."

Haas was the victim of a crowd reaction I'd started to protect my own self against needlers, so I replied, "From now on, I'll stay with you without moving until we're both down." And I did.

There's no rule that says you have to stick around a green after putting out, but in this case it was only the fair thing to do, and I did it.

Some galleries can needle you as much as your opponent. Let's say you're paired with a local favorite and have taken the early lead: well, then the boys and girls in the audience will be pegging at you all day long. They'll yell, when you're pitching from a buried lie, "You miss this kind easy, Sambo, so be careful!" Anything to make the shot tougher they'll do. My best weapon against this has been to win the gallery's sympathy—or at least their silence—by drawing them right into the match. I'll say to the people packed around the ball, "Looks like I've got to rake and scrape her out, folks" or "I'll look like a dime's worth of dogmeat if I miss this one, but that ain't so unusual." People laugh and then stop gabbing about this and that and settle down to studying the shot with me. Their thought waves are on the same beam as mine; I've got them helping and not hindering me.

Once, in Texas, when a gallery was sticking pins in me, a fan said, "Maybe you can shoot the eyes out of a squirrel in the woods, but you'll never make the green from there."

I was down in a culvert with a drainpipe sticking out 2 feet in front of the ball.

"Say, did I tell you about my cousin?" I said, and everybody listened. "Once he plugged a deer dead with a bullet that first went through his ear, then through his hind foot, and then plumb through his head."

"How'd he ever do that?" someone asked.

"The buck was scratching his ear with his hind foot at the time," I said, giving them a yarn as old as the Blue Ridge Mountains—in fact, so old that it's still good for a laugh. When I made the shot, the people were quiet and maybe even pulling a little for me to make it. Which I didn't—but that was my fault and the drainpipe's.

I play a little game with myself. I keep reminding myself that even though it's a big-money tournament, it's just one more round of golf. Stepping up to a hard recovery, I'll talk to myself and the ball: "C'mon, be a Little Joe from Kokomo" and "Baby needs new shoes." Caddie crap-shooting talk gives me a kick, and I feel a chuckle coming on and then relax.

One time, during the Celebrities Tournament in Washington, D.C., I was given a police escort with sirens blaring all the way to the course and there met such great men as General Omar Bradley and Admiral Chester Nimitz and began to tie up inside for fear of not playing well.

On the course, I got to remembering the time my son, Jackie, who then was about six years old, was waiting in the crowd for me to sink or miss a putt worth $2,000. While I was walking around and crouching and lining it up, he spoke up loudly. "Is Daddy going to win?" he asked his mother.

"If he makes this putt," his mother said.

"Well, I'm hungry! I just wish he'd hurry up."

Compared to Jackie's empty belly, the putt wasn't so important, and recalling the incident loosened me up so that I shot a 65-66—131 for two rounds.

These practices are what I call *knowing yourself*—knowing some tactics that relax you. Everybody can be his own doctor if he knows himself.

Coming back to the needles, I've seen many a few young pros suckered by the mention of a rule that isn't even in the books. Steve Seval, a big boy from upstate New York, once was in a trap, reached for a 7-iron, then decided to blast out with a wedge and changed clubs.

His opponent, an old-timer, drawled, "Sorry, but you can't change clubs while standing in a trap without taking a penalty."

Seval had never heard of such a thing, but, fearing he'd slipped up on his homework with the rules, he went back to the 7. He took a 7 on the hole.

The moral is: know your rules down to the latest changes and beware of other people's information.

In many of the towns I've visited to make exhibitions, the local committee has been counting the days until I got there and they could trot out one of the home heroes who hits golf balls out of shape and who'll put their town on the map by outdriving me. You've got to stomp on these boys from the first shot or they just might do it. In Indiana a few years ago, they brought out a six-foot-six giant with arms like a gorilla and confidence written all over him. But I happened to know that all he could do was slam them; after his drive, he was just another 6-handicapper.

"There's a couple of big-time booking agents here today," I whispered to the giant as we teed up. "You hit some real smokers and then score well and they're liable to take you up to Chicago and sign you for a lot of money. Good luck."

At that thought, he began to shake, and he topped his first drive about 150 yards. I was tempted to take an 8-iron and shoot past him, but instead I hit one out about 350. He tried to match it and went out of bounds. The giant never made a big drive all day.

Psychology is so important that it reminds me of the airline stewardess who overheard some male talk at a banquet not long ago and couldn't help interrupting.

"Oh, you men!" she said. "All you have on your mind is one thing."

After mulling this over for a moment, I said, "You're wrong, miss. A man has three things on his mind. Two of which aren't hardly worth mentioning."

Naturally, I was talking about the fine art of keeping a steady hand on the club when others are out to annoy you and bring on a spell of bogeys.

I don't know how often Jimmy Demaret has turned the tables and won a match on the green by chirping at the other man, "C'mon, friend, go on up there and miss that 6-footer so I can go to work on this 20-footer." Blooey! The magic word is "miss," and on top of that the opponent is irritated over Demaret's cocky belief that he can drop a 20-footer any old time. The combination is all it takes to make the short putt stay out.

Another of the pros, who's now retired, used to hire a man to stand around greens, jingling the change in his pocket, when an opponent was putting. We got rid of him by hiring our own heckler to blow his nose with a terrific *honk!* when it came this man's turn to putt.

But today most of that has changed, we have a fine bunch of boys playing P.G.A. golf, and each man tends pretty much to his own knitting. I don't say that in 1961 we have the tournament-tough greats that we had in the 1930s-1940s; all I say is that there are more top contenders around than ever before and they're strictly businessmen, with college backgrounds, who are out to make it fast. They might not last long, or even care to, but they're the last word in efficiency.

What I'd like to see is a little more color pumped into the sport, more action, a few feuds, and newcomers with the natural ability to play to a gallery, like Porky Oliver, Jimmy Demaret, Babe Didrikson, Wild Bill Mehlhorn, Walter Hagen, Dutch Harrison, and Skip Alexander. I haven't been mixed up in a real old-style feuding match since 1952, and then it took a South African, Bobby Locke, to help make things interesting.

That one began with a tournament official at the Jacksonville, Florida, Open, where my second shot on the tenth hole was in question: it either was or wasn't out-of-bounds. My feeling was that the ball landed inbounds past the stake marking the out-of-bounds, and it was so ruled. But then a Jacksonville sportswriter put the following in the paper:

"If Snead wins this tournament, in which he tied for first place, there'll always be doubt in a lot of people's minds that he deserved it, after the dubious ruling in his favor."

Rather than have that feeling, next morning I conceded a play-off and the money to Doug Ford and drove out of town. The tournament people were unhappy about my leaving, particularly this one badge-wearer, whom I was to meet later. "Our gate was ruined by Snead's withdrawal," he said.

At the Greensboro Open a little later, I was fighting it out with Porky Oliver and Locke as we came up to the seventy-first and next-to-last hole of the tournament. The par-3, 180-yard hole had a creek running alongside and to the right of the green, a parallel water hazard. My drive made a splash about midway in the creek. Normally, under the rules, you'd drop out for a penalty stroke on the side of the creek farthest from the green, but this was impossible, due to the sheer bank at the far side. The Rules Committee was standing there and pointed to the near bank, saying, "Drop it here."

Locke all but jumped out of his baggy pants. Actually, the way the creek bent, I didn't gain more than half an inch by the drop, but Locke claimed it was highway robbery by the Americans and caused a hullabaloo.

Well, he had a right to his say—and he didn't miss any editions of the newspapers.

"I was amazed to see, upon arriving at the green," Locke stated later in print, "Snead dropping his ball on the green side of the creek, *a good 15 or 20 feet closer to the hole.* The lapse simply staggered the crowd. When the round ended, I called for the tournament manager to give a ruling."

As you might guess, the manager turned out to be the party I'd rubbed the wrong way at Jacksonville. What did he do but overrule the Rules Committee, fine me a 2-stroke penalty, and cost me a tournament I'd otherwise have won. My backers blew up at that, and the fur was still flying when I left town.

That's golf: it's either cake or baloney, depending on how you slice it.

Nothing that's happened to me lately, including a fuss with the Professional Golfers Association bigwigs late in 1961 over when and where I should be playing, has caused more excitement, unless it was the Mason Rudolph match of a few seasons ago—a television match that millions of people watched—at Mid Ocean in Bermuda.

This one is my biggest regret in golf. Maybe I played it wrong. It's a sure thing I didn't play it very smart.

Before leaving the clubhouse, I made a mental note to leave my 2-wood in my locker. When we reached the twelfth hole, with rolling cameras covering the action and with the match all square, I reached into the bag for a 3-wood . . . and there sat my 2-wood looking at me. Which meant that I had fifteen on hand, or one over the legal limit. Automatically, on the spot, I'd lost that match.

Under the rules I'd lost every hole played until then and also had ruined an expensive TV production, for which technical crews and producers had flown many miles, by my carelessness. I peeked into the bag again to make sure someone else's club hadn't been put there by mistake . . . but the 2-wood was mine.

Should I destroy the match by announcing my extra club? Or was there another way out of it?

On the twelfth tee, without much time to decide, I thought, "I'll go on, try to make a show out of it anyway and explain later. But I can't win and keep quiet. It's Rudolph's match, by default, and it'll have to come out with him on top."

When we reached the sixteenth hole, still even, and it looked like I might be the winner, I purposely 4-putted so that Rudolph went 1 up. On No. 17 I thought he'd clinch the match. Rudolph wouldn't cooperate: he missed a kick-in putt, forcing me to throw the No. 18 hole to make sure of his victory.

To throw a match is harder than to win one, I found out. When you're geared to giving your best, missing shots deliberately for the first time is a painful thing. By hitting a poor drive on the last hole, then 3-putting—after plenty of dramatic sighting of the putts to make it look good—I wound up losing.

Pro golf is clean. We don't "tank" matches. We've never had a scandal in the P.G.A., which is more than most country clubs can say of the honesty of their members.

But Sam Snead threw that one. I didn't see any other way out if the show was to be saved. Since I was the only loser—of both money and a match to a player I'd had a chance to beat— it seemed like a fair choice.

Afterward, I notified the TV officials of what had happened, expecting they might release the film up to the twelfth hole, then tell the audience the match had been called at that point because of a rules transgression. The producer was flabbergasted and called meetings to decide what he should do.

Then, a short time later, I told the story, off the record, to an Atlanta sportswriter—and the next thing there were headlines: SNEAD ADMITS THROWING TV MATCH.

The story hit right on top of the big television quiz-show payola scandals in New York; for a while, it seemed that televised golf might have been dealt a body blow. People saw only the word "throw," not the rest of it. Some even got "throw" and "fix" mixed up. Ed Carter, Bob Rosburg, and other P.G.A. heads called me to a meeting at Augusta, where I explained my view.

"Actually, I didn't have a match to throw," I reminded them, "since the minute I discovered that extra club, Rudolph was the winner. All I did was play it out and make sure the right man took the money."

Rudolph confused matters still more by making the statement that, "Before I play Snead again, I'll want an affidavit from him that he won't alibi if he's beaten." In short, he meant that he thought my story to be phony. That I invented the illegal club in my bag as an excuse when I saw myself losing.

If anybody took Rudolph seriously, it didn't show up in my fan mail, which ignored his statement. Far more pros than Rudolph know that I don't need alibis. Nevertheless, some people were hurt that I'd do such a thing, for any reason.

No doubt they were right. A far wiser decision would have been to go ahead and try to beat Rudolph, then decline the win with a public explanation. Then I'd have been applauded. But not by the television industry, which has done much to sell golf, when it was stuck with a worthless $50,000 production.

The whole thing gave me such an upset stomach and headache that I went home, swallowed some nerve pills, and climbed under the bedcovers. As the saying goes down home, I took so much medicine that I was sick a long time after I got well.

A hard education in golf is a great thing. Whenever I've been able to pull myself out of a slump, it's been because I didn't forget that breaks always even out, over the long pull, and that the bane of golf—and of life in general—is to remember your mistakes and not your right moves. In clubhouses, you'll see men sitting around complaining and going over their bad shots.

They should think back to their good shots, then try to repeat them.

This is the only way to build that feeling called confidence. You can build it—or tear yourself down. The choice is up to every individual. If you know yourself to be a whiner, you'll never play up to your full ability. It takes guts to be an optimist in golf. He who thinks like a winner will win.

For me, the television scandal was balanced out by the Greenbrier Open of 1959, where I found an answer to a question I'm always asked: "What was the best round of golf you ever shot?" Until then, I'd never been sure. My best might have been the back-to-back scores of 63-63 I posted in the 1950 Texas Open. Or a 64 of years earlier over a tougher course in the Chicago Open. Then there was a round of 60 in the '57 Dallas Open that tied the P.G.A. record. On "rat" courses and shorter links, I've had 61s and 62s.

In the Greenbrier tournament against a field that included Mike Souchak, Doug Sanders, Bob Toski, Porky Oliver, and other good campaigners, my opening rounds of 68-69 weren't good for the lead, and on the third day a sore back had stiffened and I was hoping just to equal par.

Walking to the tee, I met Freddie Martin, the wonderful old-timer who gave me my first good golf job and boost upward back in 1936 at this same course.

"I feel poor," I told Freddie. "Don't look for much from me today."

"That means you'll shoot like Old Weasel-Eye, the Dead Shot," said Freddie. "I know you, Sam. Whenever you're aching and hurting the most, the better you play. A matter of psychology."

"Well, this time you're wrong," I said. "I'm tired, sick, beat-up, and gone stale."

After fourteen holes of that third round, I had the quietest gallery you ever saw. By then I'd used just 46 shots, or a few more than 3 a hole. On the fifteenth hole, par 5, my second shot stopped 35 feet from the glory hole. On the putt the ball seemed to have eyes—ran straight in for an eagle.

With that piece of luck, my birdie putts on No. 16 and No. 18 didn't surprise me, and then everyone was grabbing my hand and the corks began to pop and pandemonium broke loose in The Greenbrier men's grill and locker room. For once, I broke my own rule and drank enough champagne to drown a hog and her whole litter.

My card for the day—which gave me my biggest thrill in golf:

Par Out	434	444	444—35
Snead	333	343	444—31
Par In	344	435	534—35—70
Snead	343	323	433—28—59

I'd always wanted to break 60 in full-tournament play. On this day, which included 9 birdies and an eagle, I finally made it. Old Freddie Martin, who'd predicted years ago that I had a 59 in me and who has been such a friend, through thick and thin, had tears in his eyes.

I went over and handed Freddie the ball I'd used on the round, and for a while we just stood there . . . thinking of a shirttail, hayseed kid who'd been found a long time ago cleaning mud off a ball back of a caddie shack.

The kid has had a hell of a time these past twenty-five years. And he isn't finished yet.

INDEX